The War of 1812

Also by Reginald Horsman

The Causes of the War of 1812 (1962)
Matthew Elliott: British Indian Agent (1964)
Expansion and American Indian Policy (1967)

THE WAR OF 1812

Reginald Horsman

Eyre & Spottiswoode · London

First published 1969
Copyright © 1969 Reginald Horsman
Printed in Great Britain for
Eyre & Spottiswoode (Publishers) Ltd
11, New Fetter Lane, London EC4
by Ebenezer Baylis and Son Limited
The Trinity Press, Worcester, and London

SBN 413 27140 4

TO K. G. HORSMAN

Contents

		page	
	Acknowledgements	page	vi
	Introduction		ix
1	The Origins of the War		1
2	The Invasion of Canada		25
3	Shocks at Sea		52
4	America Tries Again		81
5	Failure		116
6	British Naval Supremacy, 1813–14		138
7	The Attack from Canada		165
8	The Burning of Washington		194
9	The War in the South		215
10	The Peace of Ghent		250
	Bibliographical Note		271
	Index		275

ACKNOWLEDGEMENTS

I would like to thank the John Simon Guggenheim Memorial Foundation for a Fellowship in 1965-66, and the Graduate School of the University of Wisconsin for support which enabled me to complete the work for this book.

Quotations from unpublished Crown-copyright records in the Public Record Office appear by permission of the Controller of H.M. Stationery Office.

Acknowledgements and thanks for permission to reproduce copyright photographs are due to the Mansell Collection for 1a, 1b, 11a, 11b, 12a; the Library of Congress for the endpapers and 5b, 9b, 10a; the British Museum for 2a, 2b, 3a; the National Army Museum for 3b, 4a; the National Maritime Museum for 7, 8b; the Burton Historical Collection of the Detroit Public Library for 4b, 8a; the William L. Clements Library, University of Michigan for 6; the Field Museum of Natural History, Chicago, for 9a; the US Signal Corps, National Archives for 10b; Yale University Art Gallery, Mabel Brady Garvan Collection for 12b.

Illustrations

	The Battle of Plattsburg Bay, 1814	*endpapers*
1a	James Madison	*facing page* 34
1b	Andrew Jackson	34
2a	Admiral Sir John Borlase Warren	35
2b	Admiral Sir Alexander Cockrane	35
3a	Sir George Prevost	50
3b	Major-General Sir Edward Pakenham	50
4a	Major-General Sir Isaac Brock	51
4b	Surrender of Detroit to Sir Isaac Brock, 1812	51
5a	Battle between the *Constitution* and *Guerrière*	82
5b	*Constitution* meets *Guerrière*, 1812	82
6	Massacre of American prisoners at Frenchtown on the River Raisin, 1813	83
7	The capture of the *Chesapeake*, 1813	98
8a	Oliver Hazard Perry	99
8b	Battle on Lake Erie, 1813	99
9a	Tecumseh	194
9b	Battle of the Thames, 1813	194
10a	British woodcut of the Burning of Washington, 1814	195
10b	The Burning of Washington: British troops enter the city	195
11a	Jackson at New Orleans	210
11b	The Battle of New Orleans	210
12a	Pakenham leading the attack on New Orleans	211
12b	Defeat of the British Army: The Battle of New Orleans	211

MAPS

1	The main Theatre of the War of 1812	*page* xii
2	The war on the Canadian Border	23
3	The Chesapeake Bay Region	76
4	New Orleans and the Gulf Theatre of the war	213

Introduction

In late June 1812, as Napoleon's great army crossed the Niemen to invade Russia, a tiny American force was struggling across the Ohio wilderness to begin the invasion of Canada. The United States had declared war against Britain on 18 June, but the British government did not receive the news until late July.

For Britain 1812 was a year of mixed fortune. Since 1810 the country had been enmeshed in a severe economic depression, and by this year there was widespread distress in the manufacturing districts and British trade was stagnant. When Parliament assembled in January the Whig opposition immediately pressed for strong measures to solve Britain's economic problems, and in the arguments gave a dominant position to relations with the United States.

In the years prior to 1812 the governments of Britain and the United States regarded each other with all the distrust of nations tied only thirty years before by colonial bonds. Since 1776, when the Americans had achieved independence, there had been numerous quarrels between the two powers. At first these had mainly been disputes regarding the carrying out of the articles of the treaty of peace, but from the beginning of the Revolutionary and Napoleonic Wars the main source of difficulty had been American neutral trade and the British manner of waging maritime war against France. For a time in the late nineties and at the beginning of the new century there had been reasonably friendly relations, but after the British renewal of the war against France in 1803 Anglo–American relations deteriorated rapidly.

The crux of the problem was that the United States wanted to continue her extensive overseas trade undisturbed by the European conflict, while Britain was determined that neutral trade should not be allowed to aid the French. By a variety of methods British regulations sought to ensure that American trade with French possessions would be made more difficult or impossible, and that the United States should not take advantage of the war to compete with Britain's maritime supremacy. Blockade of the French coast, definitions of contraband, the right of search, restrictions on American trade to French colonies, and the seizing of British deserters on American ships all angered an American people who were jealous of their recently won independence. In practical terms the regulations meant British warships hovering off the American coast, stopping and searching American ships, taking off British deserters and impressing American seamen.

The British government paid little heed to American protests, for the war against France was considered all-important. No neutral was to be allowed to give aid to the enemy, even if British restrictions drove the United States to the brink of war. Britain did not fear American military action. The American regular army consisted of only a few thousand men, and the United States navy had only a handful of ships. Moreover, the British government thought that the American Republic allowed itself to be swayed far too much by popular sentiment to have real strength, and overestimated friendship for Britain within the United States. British leaders gave attention to the Federalist opposition, which hated France and admired Britain. Confident that the United States was too weak to act, and that in any case war was preferable to commercial concession, the British government persisted in its restrictions on American shipping. In an effort to force a change in British policies the American government in the years after 1807 placed a series of restrictions on trade with Britain. It was hoped that economic coercion would avoid the necessity of war, but there seemed little chance of success in Britain until economic depression began to stir the manufacturing districts and provide arguments for the Whig opposition.

In the early months of 1812 the opposition increasingly took up the cry that the solution to the economic difficulties lay in the renewal of friendly commercial relations with the United States. Mass meetings in the manufacturing districts produced a host of petitions to Parliament, and led by Henry Brougham the opposition developed an extensive organization to work for the removal of commercial restrictions regarding the United States. In May witnesses from all

INTRODUCTION

over the country appeared before a committee of the House to tell of their distress and of the importance of the American trade. The renewal of trade with the United States was to be the panacea that would restore Britain's prosperity. In the face of mounting opposition the government was holding firm, but the assassination of the Prime Minister, Spencer Perceval, and the organization of the new government, made possible the repeal of the Orders in Council against neutral trade. In June the Orders were removed amid general rejoicing in the manufacturing districts. Ships were made ready, manufacturers emptied their warehouses, but in late July the news arrived that the United States had declared war.

Throughout the early months of 1812, as the opposition in Britain worked for the restoration of friendly relations with the United States, the American government was moving haltingly towards war, convinced that Britain intended to retain her maritime policies. American leaders did not regard this as coming to the aid of Napoleon in his struggle against Britain. Indeed, some American Congressmen wanted the United States to declare war on France as well as Britain. There were to be no alliances with Britain's enemies in Europe, no combined operations in the manner of the Revolution. This was America's own quarrel with Britain, and by some it was looked upon as a second war for independence. In spite of military weakness, many in the United States talked of the war with confidence. Canada it was hoped would soon fall to a handful of regulars and a host of militia and volunteers. In this way Britain would be forced to make concessions at sea.

When the United States declared war against Britain on 18 June, 1812, she regarded this action as the only way in which the national honour could be maintained and the national interests protected. The Americans had no way of knowing that only two days previously the British government had announced its intention of removing its main restrictions on American commerce. The United States began the war with confidence on land and a feeling of futility at sea. Before the year was out the land operations were a national scandal, but the war at sea had shocked the whole of Britain.

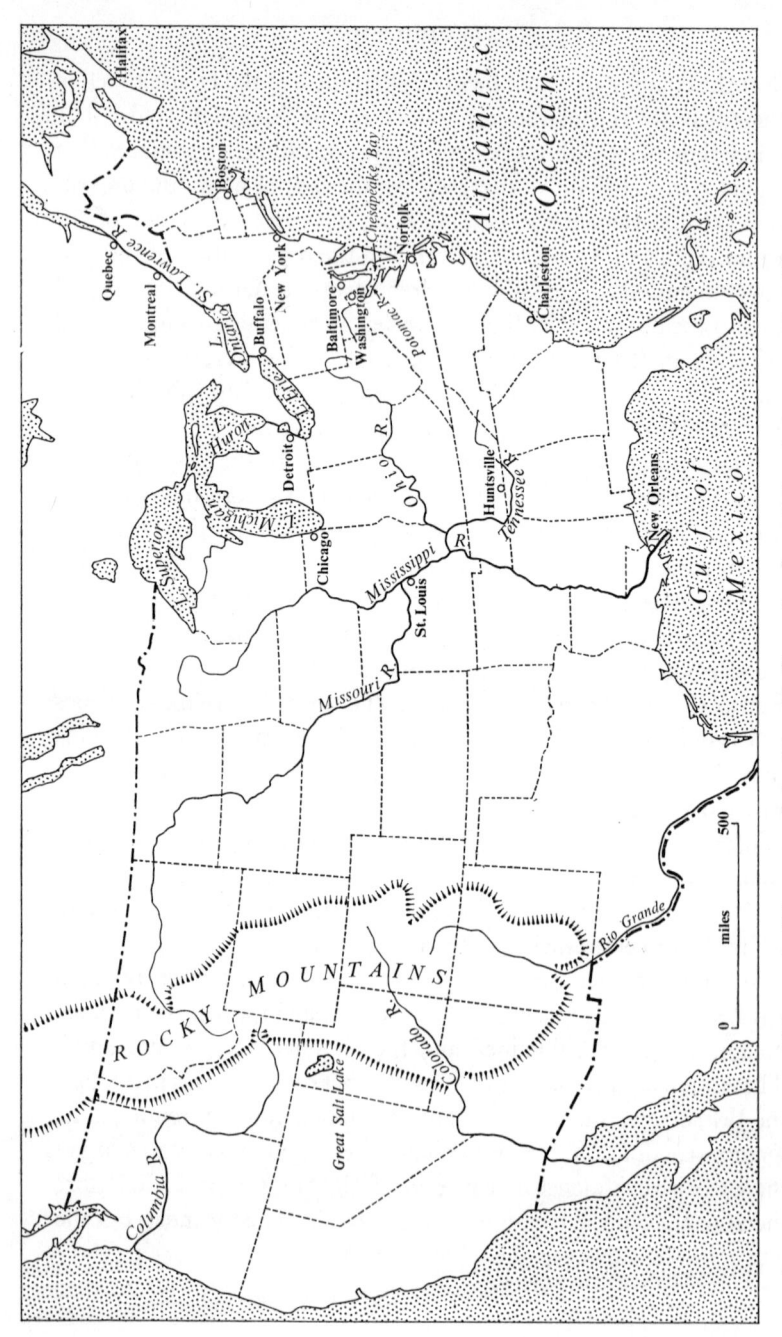

MAP 1 The main Theatres of the War of 1812, showing their relation to each other and to the continent of North America in general

The War of 1812

I

The Origins of the War

The years from the end of the American Revolution in 1783 to the outbreak of the War of 1812 brought a crisis in foreign affairs in both the United States and Britain. For the infant United States the initial problem was one of survival, and the establishment of a form of government that would hold together thirteen disparate states. Within ten years these problems had been complicated by the outbreak of the wars of the French Revolution, in which the United States, as the primary commercial neutral, became inextricably involved. These same wars by 1803 threatened to bring about the invasion and conquest of Britain, and British foreign policy was wholly subordinated to the defeat of France.

It could hardly be expected that the relations of Britain and the United States would be anything but uneasy at the end of a successful colonial revolution. To many in Britain it appeared incredible that the disorganized and disunited ex-colonies across the Atlantic should have won their independence. Many hoped and expected that the 'mob rule' which prevailed in the newly independent country would soon bring about its collapse. Those like Charles James Fox who saw hopes for liberty in the new experiment across the Atlantic were overwhelmed by the Tory squires who saw only anarchy and a rabble who had shattered Britain's first colonial empire.

In America there was a strong dislike and distrust of the British in the years after the Revolution. Many in the United States viewed Britain as a country crushed under the weight of a tyrannic monarchy and a corrupt aristocracy. They intended that the United States would demonstrate to the decadent powers of Europe how a country could live in freedom and in safety. Although the educated in America still read British books, cherished their British heritage, and traded with Britain, they saw themselves as upholding traditions of freedom that Britain had lost. They admired much in Britain, but objected to the manner in which the country was ruled. Only in New England was there a group prepared to take her part. The Revolution did not sever the commercial ties which bound this region to the mother country.

The practical problems of post-Revolutionary Anglo-American relations served to increase the mutual distrust. A substantial cause of future difficulties was the rapid development of commercial rivalry between the two powers. For all America's complaints prior to 1775, her shipping industry had waxed rich within the British imperial system. The innumerable bays and inlets of the long American coast and an abundance of forests gave the Americans ample opportunity to develop a shipbuilding industry. Stimulated by the British Navigation Laws, and helped by a seafaring tradition in their mother country, the Americans were sailing throughout the world in the 1780s. Their ships were fast, well-manned, and skilfully sailed.

At the end of the Revolution a minority, led by Pitt and Shelburne, argued that it was in the best interest of Britain to establish a free and open commercial relationship with the United States. Some hoped that such commercial ties, already extensively formed before the Revolution, would help to cement a political alliance. In spite of the efforts of Pitt and Shelburne, the country was won by the logic of those who argued that as America had declared herself independent she should stand outside the British commercial system. The arguments of those who opposed the United States were strengthened by their conclusion that a waiving of the Navigation Laws would not only produce a loss of trade, but would also weaken the British merchant marine. This in turn would undermine the strength of the regular navy, and lead to a national decline.

At first United States shipping was hurt by its exclusion from normal channels, but it quickly found its way into markets closed under British rule, and became one of Britain's major commercial rivals. This rivalry was apparent well before 1793, but from then on it became more acute because of the outbreak of war in Europe. America's position as the main commercial neutral gave her extensive new trading opportunities, which were much resented by the British shipping interests.

Another basic source of friction in the post-Revolutionary years was the continued British rule in Canada. The vagueness of the details of the 1783 boundary settlement produced difficulty for the next sixty years, but a more important source of dispute was rivalry in the unsettled areas of the American Old Northwest, and the belief of the British officials in Canada that some of the concessions made in that area in 1783 could be rescinded.

In the years after the Revolution American settlers were trekking west over the Appalachian barrier into the Ohio Valley. Between 1783 and 1812 the population of Kentucky increased from 12,000 to over 400,000. In 1783 there were only a handful of settlers beyond the Ohio River in the whole rich area encompassed by the modern states of Ohio, Indiana, Illinois, Michigan, and Wisconsin. These states were then the domain of numerous Indian tribes. At the end of the Revolution the British had agreed that the whole area would be American, and that British troops would withdraw from their line of posts along the southern edge of the Great Lakes. In spite of this agreement the actual withdrawal was delayed for over ten years. At first this was to keep control over the Indians and the fur trade, but by the 1790s many officials in Canada hoped that continued occupation might make possible a readjustment of the boundary. In the early 1790s the agents of the British Indian Department in Canada encouraged the Indian tribes to resist the advance of the American settlers, but it was all to no avail. By 1810 Ohio had a population of over 230,000, and thousands of settlers were pushing on into Indiana and Illinois. The Americans after 1783 resented the British retention of the Northwest posts, and hated the British for their support of the Indians. It kept alive memories of the Revolutionary Anglo-Indian raids along the Wyoming Valley and into Kentucky, and of the slaughter of American pioneers.[1]

Although the commercial rivalry and the tension along the Canadian–American border kept alive hostility and misunderstanding between the two countries, it seemed unlikely to produce an

---

[1] *Historical Statistics of the United States: Colonial Times to 1957* (Washington, 1960), p. 13; Thomas D. Clark, *A History of Kentucky* (New York, 1937), pp. 85–109. The problems of the 1783–1803 period are surveyed in Reginald Horsman, *The Causes of the War of 1812* (Philadelphia, 1962), pp. 13–23.

actual demand for war in the United States. The Americans had no desire to risk all they had gained in eight years of Revolution, and although many British politicians would have been delighted to see the United States collapse, they had no desire to enter upon another long, inglorious war in an effort to bring about that happy event. It took the French Revolution and the wars which followed it to drive Britain and the United States into open hostility.

The wars of the French Revolution and Empire entrapped the United States as surely as the wars of 1914–18 and 1939–45. Since the United States attained her independence in 1783 only on three occasions has Britain engaged in a major European conflict involving large-scale naval warfare. On each occasion the United States has eventually entered the war. The basic problem was one of trade. The United States engaged in extensive overseas commerce. If she wished to continue trading then, unavoidably, her trade would help one or other of the belligerents.

In 1793 the trade of the United States was of greatest immediate help to France. On the outbreak of war between Britain and France, the British navy immediately threatened to sever the commerce between France and her colonies in the West Indies. To evade the British blockade the French threw open the trade between France and her colonies to neutrals, and American vessels flocked to the West Indies to take the place of French vessels. To block this commerce Britain invoked her Rule of 1756 by which a trade closed in time of peace could not be declared open in time of war, and ordered her captains to seize American shipping engaged in this French trade. The eagerness with which they seized these prizes produced a major crisis in Anglo-American relations; a crisis in which many in the United States demanded war. They were able to point out not only that American shipping was being seized, but that also in the Old Northwest American troops and settlers were fighting Indians who were supplied and aided by the British in Canada.

War was avoided in 1793–94 because of American political considerations, and because Britain's policy of maritime regulation was still in its infancy. The movement of the French Revolution from its constitutional to a more extreme phase, the attack on all aspects of the established order, and the use of the guillotine shocked many of the substantial residents in the cities of the eastern seaboard. This feeling was particularly strong in New England, where there were already strong personal and commercial ties to Britain. The Federalist party, which was to govern the United States until 1801, distrusted the French 'jacobins', and spoke of them much as the British spoke of the American 'democrats'. Some of the Federalist leaders were reaching the conclusion that their old enemy Britain was now the bulwark of sound constitutional liberty against the excesses of the French.

In 1794 President Washington sent his Chief Justice John Jay to Britain as a special envoy, and the signing of Jay's Treaty in November of that year helped to restore good relations between the two countries. It was attacked by the American opposition as a sell-out to Britain, as it said nothing about American neutral rights, but it did help to avoid war and Britain at last agreed to withdraw from the Northwest posts. The Federalists did not want war with Britain, and to avoid it were willing to imperil relations with France.[2]

Franco-American relations deteriorated sharply after Jay's Treaty. The French, not unnaturally, viewed America's determination to seek friendly relations with Britain as directed against them, and now acted with far more aggression against American shipping. By 1798 the United States found herself engaged in an undeclared naval war against France. Prospects of continued good relations with Britain now seemed excellent, and in these years Britain helped improve Anglo-American relations by pursuing moderate maritime policies. There was also a relaxation of tension in the Old Northwest. After the American military victory over the Indians at the battle of Fallen Timbers in August 1794, and the signing of Jay's Treaty, Britain for the time being withdrew her support for the Indians on the American frontiers. This improvement in British-American relations reached a peak at the beginning of the nineteenth century when the Peace of

---

[2] The events leading to the agreement with Britain are treated in detail in Samuel F. Bemis, *Jay's Treaty: A Study in Commerce and Diplomacy* (New York, 1923).

Amiens temporarily halted the European wars, and allowed American commerce to sail unmolested throughout the world.[3]

The renewal of the European wars in the spring of 1803 led to a decline in British-American relations that eventually culminated in June 1812 in an American declaration of war against Britain. The basic difficulty was again at sea. The United States objected to a host of British maritime practices, many of which had been carried out in the 1790s, but far less extensively than after this renewal of the war. The reason for a more vigorous British policy was primarily that after 1803 there was a pressing danger of invasion by Napoleon. It seemed that only the Channel and the British fleet stood between the French and the conquest of England. In this crisis there was no regard for the susceptibilities of neutrals; any aid to the French would be resisted. Moreover, the British shipping interest and its supporters were able to point out that the American merchant marine was profiting immensely from the European wars, and that this growth of American shipping was a threat to British commercial supremacy, to British naval power, and to the safety of the country. Restrictions on American commerce would harm France, and at the same time help the British maritime interests in their commercial rivalry with the United States.

Throughout these wars there had been disputes over a variety of matters relating to trade. The United States would have liked to maintain the argument that 'free ships make free goods', and traded anywhere in the world, but the belligerents, particularly Britain, made every effort to contest this point of view. Even the Americans acknowledged that weapons of war would constitute contraband, but the British wanted this list extended to include anything that might aid the French. The British also insisted on the right of stopping and searching ships that might carry illegal goods, although the United States tried to maintain that only an examination of the ship's papers was necessary. General blockades also caused much bitterness. The Americans argued that a blockaded region should be actually invested

---

[3] For the improvement of relations with Britain see Bradford Perkins, *The First Rapprochement: England and the United States, 1795–1805* (Philadelphia, 1955), and for the collapse of the French alliance Alexander DeConde, *Entangling Alliance: Politics and Diplomacy under George Washington* (Durham, N.C., 1958).

by ships directly off the coast, and objected to 'paper blockades' by which Britain declared a whole long coastline under blockade, and then seized ships far out at sea with the argument that they were sailing for the area covered by the blockade order.

Connected with the stopping and searching of American ships was the explosive subject of impressment. Given the conditions below decks in the British navy, sailors often took the first opportunity to desert in American ports. In American merchant vessels they could get better pay and improved conditions. Britain maintained the right to seize these deserters whenever they could be found on board American merchant vessels. American ships were frequently stopped for this purpose, and when British captains needed crewmen, as was frequently the case, they had no hesitation in seizing Americans as well as British deserters; at the outbreak of war in 1812 the British agreed to treat as prisoners of war over 2,500 Americans serving on British ships, and the claims of many more that they were American were denied.[4] The whole subject was complicated by the British doctrine of inalienable allegiance: anyone who had been born a British subject could be seized even if he had emigrated to the United States long before. There were few subjects which could so infuriate American opinion as that of American seamen killed serving on British ships against the French, or flogged for refusing to obey the orders of the ships' captains who had impressed them. With the danger of invasion after 1803, Britain made every possible effort to increase her number of seamen. This produced a much increased rate of impressment, and a corresponding increase in American bitterness.

Between 1803 and 1807 Britain and France attempted to defeat each other by commercial means. The British government decided that French possessions in Europe would be blockaded, and that the only goods reaching Napoleon would be through Britain, and would increase Britain's prosperity and power. The movement towards a stricter policy began in 1805 with the *Essex* decision, by which it was laid down that the Americans would no longer be allowed obvious

---

[4] Admiralty Archives, Adm 98/123, p. 166, Public Record Office, London; *Hansard*, XXIV (1812–13), pp. 601–2.

evasions of the British prohibition of trade between France and her colonies. In the late 1790s Britain had permitted this trade through the so-called 'broken voyage' by which American ships sailed by way of American ports. This was now made far more difficult.

In 1806 and early 1807 the movement towards complete trade restriction was retarded by the Whig ministry of 'All the Talents' which attempted to act towards America as leniently as the war effort against France would allow, but the coming of the Tories to power in March 1807 rapidly brought about strict restrictions on neutral commerce. The comparative moderation of 'Fox's blockade' of May 1806, which enforced a strict blockade only from Ostend to the Seine, and the January 1807 Order in Council which prohibited neutral trade from port to port in the hands of the enemy, ended in the autumn of 1807. The Orders in Council of November stated in essence that neutrals should not trade to French Europe except through British ports and with a British licence.

While Britain established a system to starve France and enhance her own prosperity, Napoleon determined to ruin the British, and destroy the financial backing of the alliance which opposed him. The Berlin Decree of November 1806 declared Britain to be in a state of blockade, and prohibited trade in British goods. Napoleon hoped to carry this into effect not with his navy, which was mostly confined to port, but by closing Continental ports to British goods. His Milan Decree of December 1807 declared that all neutrals who obeyed British trade regulations would be liable to seizure. In theory, this closed the door on American commerce; if American ships ignored British regulations they would be liable to seizure by the British, and if they obeyed them they would be liable to seizure by the French. In practice, trade continued by means of special licences and wholesale evasion.[5]

The American response to the changing maritime situation after 1803 was temporarily affected by the American ambitions in regard to Spanish possessions in North America, but more permanently governed by the underlying beliefs of President Thomas Jefferson

---

[5] Horsman, *Causes of the War of 1812*, pp. 24–43, 63–82, 95–122; Bradford Perkins, *Prologue to War: England and the United States, 1805–1812* (Berkeley, 1961), pp. 1–31, 67–100.

and the administration which took office in 1801. For a time after Jefferson bought the vast Louisiana purchase from France in 1803 he hoped by exerting diplomatic pressure to convince the Spanish and the French that Spanish West Florida, directly east of the Mississippi, had been included in the purchase. This effort failed, but until the end of 1805 the American government moved cautiously in its reaction to British maritime policies because of the involvement with Spain. This attitude changed as the full impact of the *Essex* decision was felt in the United States, and anger against the British grew rapidly.

American governmental reaction to British policies in the years immediately following 1805 was compounded of a mixture of Jeffersonian idealism, previous experience, and military unpreparedness. The American colonists had used economic boycott against the British with good effect before the Revolution, and both Jefferson and his Secretary of State James Madison believed that the United States could change the policies of the European powers by economic means. Jefferson wanted to show Europe that war was not the only solution to conflicts between powers. Yet, over and above any idealistic commitment, the financial policies pursued by the Democratic-Republicans after assuming office in 1801 provided a compelling reason for finding some method other than war to resist the pressures of the European powers. Jefferson, who believed firmly in economy in government and in the supremacy of the civil over the military, made determined efforts to reduce military expenditures. In this endeavour he was enthusiastically supported and advised by his Secretary of the Treasury, Albert Gallatin

As a result of this policy of economy the American regular army, as the United States moved into a period of major crisis in her foreign affairs, had been established at less than 3,500 men. Even more remarkable in this era of maritime problems, Jefferson's administration had been busily engaged since 1801 in reducing the size of the American navy. The war with Tripoli somewhat thwarted this endeavour, but the 74's begun under Adams were discarded, and the navy was starved for funds. Jefferson placed his faith in gunboats which could operate only in coastal waters, and were intended purely for defence. This attack on the navy stemmed not only from the passion for economy, but also from the Republican fear that an increase in the navy would place too much power in the hands of the commercial classes, and threaten the liberty of the nation. Although buffeted by the European conflict the United States was not preparing herself for war.[6]

As an alternative to war, the United States attempted to change the policies of the European belligerents by economic means. The tentative beginning in April 1806 was a non-importation law which forbade the introduction from Britain of a select list of articles which the United States thought she could do without. As a large part of the British export trade was to the United States, it was hoped that this would bring the pressure of the manufacturers to bear on the British government. In the optimism following the death of Pitt in January 1806, and Napoleon's successes on the Continent, the United States decided to suspend the operation of the non-importation law in the hope that it could be used to persuade Britain to sign a general agreement. William Pinkney and James Monroe were appointed as special envoys to secure a treaty by which the British would end impressment, reverse the *Essex* decision, and continue the commercial provisions of Jay's Treaty.

Although Monroe and Pinkney succeeded in signing a treaty in December 1806 which contained some concessions from the short-lived Whig government, the Admiralty absolutely refused to modify its stand on impressment. The British also sent a note to the American commissioners at the close of the negotiations stating that it was expected that the Americans would resist the operations of the recently announced Berlin Decree. Jefferson would not submit this unsatisfactory treaty to the Senate for ratification, and any hope of further concessions ended in March 1807 when the ill-named ministry of 'All the Talents' expired. America's first attempt to change the post-1803 British maritime policies by economic means had failed; the failure was to continue.[7]

The rapid deterioration of events in 1807 made the economic

---

[6] H. H. and Margaret Sprout, *The Rise of American Naval Power, 1776–1918* (Princeton, 1939), pp. 55–60; James R. Jacobs, *The Beginning of the U.S. Army, 1783–1812* (Princeton, 1947), pp. 351–3.

[7] Horsman, *Causes of the War of 1812*, pp. 83–94.

response promised by the non-importation law totally inadequate. If economic coercion were to be an alternative to war it would have to do more than forbid the importation of a select list of British goods. In June the *Chesapeake* incident created the first outbreak of war fever in the United States since 1798. Early in the spring a number of British seamen had deserted from ships in Chesapeake Bay, and some enlisted on the American frigate *Chesapeake*. On 22 June when the American vessel put to sea, she was approached by the British frigate *Leopard*, acting on the orders of the commander in chief of the North American Station, Vice-Admiral George C. Berkeley. The *Leopard* demanded that any deserters should be returned, and when this request was refused first fired across the American's bows, then into her, killing three men. The American vessel struck her colours, and the British took off four suspected deserters. The news of this attack was greeted in America with a popular demand for war against Britain. In Canada the British officials confidently expected invasion, and immediately began to seek the support of the Indian tribes on the frontiers of the United States. The Indians had been neglected since 1795, but now envoys again journeyed south from Fort Malden on the Detroit frontier, and Indians came in to seek advice and supplies from their British friends. The tribes were warned to be ready to take up the hatchet should the Americans declare war.[8]

War was avoided not for any lack of public support, but because Jefferson resolved to continue his policy of avoiding war by economic action. In the summer of 1807 he cooled down the public excitement by announcing he was seeking an explanation from Britain, and when Congress met in the autumn sought more extensive economic retaliation. On 14 December the non-importation law was at last enforced against Britain, and more bad news from Europe in the following days convinced Congress that a radical measure was necessary. In the middle of December word came that Britain had reiterated her stand on impressment and that Napoleon was now strictly enforcing his Berlin Decree of the previous year against American shipping,

---

[8] Impact of *Chesapeake* affair on British Indian policy is discussed in Reginald Horsman, *Matthew Elliott: British Indian Agent* (Detroit, 1964), pp. 157–73.

and there were rumours that Britain was about to impose a much stricter blockade. Even without official news of the November Orders in Council, Jefferson, on 17 December, suggested a total embargo on vessels leaving American ports. This was approved by Congress. The United States was now making the supreme effort at changing the policies of the European belligerents by economic means.

The United States government hoped that the British manufacturers who lost their American markets and raw materials would force the British government to change its policies. In one major respect this calculation was unfortunate, for the French struggle in Portugal and Spain in 1807 and 1808 opened Brazil and the Spanish colonies in South America to British trade. British exports to South America in 1808 practically made up for the loss of exports to the United States. More serious still was Jefferson's misunderstanding of the British government's policy towards the United States. Both Canning, the Foreign Secretary, and Castlereagh, the Secretary for War, thought the Embargo in many ways aided British policy. France would now receive no help from United States shipping, and the British shipping interests would have no reason to fear American competition. Those commercial and manufacturing interests which benefited from the American trade had considerable difficulty in justifying their position of friendship for the United States when the opponents of America were able to enlist patriotism and the safety of Britain on their side.

Although the United States hoped to obtain a relaxation of British restrictions on her commerce by economic pressure, the British government was in fact prepared to engage in war against the United States if peace could be maintained only by yielding to America's concept of neutral rights. Britain did not fear the United States, a country with practically no navy nor army. The main damage the United States could inflict on Britain was commercial, and Britain's commercial regulations were designed to eliminate that danger. Militarily the United States was a nonentity. From 1807 Britain was satisfied with the position of the United States, and wanted if possible to avoid any open conflict. Yet, it was always quite well understood that war was preferable to yielding to American demands.

In the United States the results of the Embargo were disastrous. The commercial interests of New England were appalled that a Virginian President was forcing them to let their ships rot at the wharves, and there was a revival of the fortunes of the Federalist party. The Federalist shippers wanted to take the risk of trading to Europe, and saw no reason why their own government should prevent them. The Federalists condoned British restrictions, and bitterly opposed the Jefferson policies. Jefferson's own supporters also suffered severely under the Embargo. The farmers and plantation owners of the South Atlantic states and the trans-Appalachian West now had no foreign markets for their produce. They had supported Jefferson's alternative to war, but as economic coercion failed they were to demand more positive action.

The failure of the Embargo was a crushing blow to the Democratic-Republicans, for the Federalists had been made more intense in their opposition to Jeffersonian policies, the United States economy and finances had been severely weakened, and her ability to fight a war reduced. The two years following the failure of the Embargo have a curious air of unreality. The United States had used her strongest economic weapon and failed, but as logic demanded a declaration of war against both Britain and France any such declaration seemed completely unrealistic. The United States now persisted in watered-down policies of economic coercion, which seemed of little use even to those who voted for them. Britain, on the contrary, was content with the situation. Her Orders had established the desired system for American commerce, and modifications in the following years were mainly to make British regulations fit a changing European situation, not concessions to the United States. The envoys who were sent to America in 1808 and 1809 – George Henry Rose, David Erskine, and Francis James Jackson – were given instructions permitting no concession. When in the spring of 1809 Erskine made the mistake of going beyond his instructions, and agreed to remove the Orders in return for the United States withdrawing all measures of economic coercion against Britain, he was speedily disavowed by Canning. This dashing of American hopes still further harmed relations between the two countries.

Jefferson had signed the measure removing the Embargo on 1

March, 1809, shortly before he left office. The Embargo was replaced by a non-intercourse act which opened American commerce to all countries with the exception of Britain, France, and their possessions. This meant that an indirect trade could take place between the United States and the belligerents. Not surprisingly after the failure of the Embargo, this measure made no impression on the policies of the European powers. In a desperate attempt to find a substitute the Eleventh Congress, on 1 May, 1810, enacted Macon's Bill No. 2. This act ended commercial restrictions against the belligerents, but also proffered a bribe. If either Britain or France removed their restrictions against the commerce of the United States, and the other would not follow, then the United States would reimpose non-importation against the delinquent power. By this act the United States was offering a friendly neutrality to either of the European powers, and was leaving it to them to decide which European belligerent, if any, she would aid. Napoleon, who had much to gain from the commerce of a neutral America, acted promptly.

In August 1810 the American Minister to France, John Armstrong, was informed that from 1 November France would revoke the Berlin and Milan Decrees if Britain would repeal the Orders in Council or the United States enforce Macon's Bill No. 2. In reality, the French were to continue harassing American commerce long after that date, but at least this French announcement ended one American dilemma; they could direct their enmity against their traditional enemy, Britain. Although war still seemed unrealistic, there no longer seemed much likelihood of a declaration against the foremost land and sea power of the world. Madison announced on 2 November that non-intercourse would be revived against Britain in three months if her Orders were not removed. Britain maintained that France had not in reality removed her decrees, and refused to reconsider her Orders in Council policy. Even if France had removed her decrees, the British attitude would have remained the same; American neutral commerce would not be allowed to help the French war effort.[9]

---

[9] There is a detailed account of the deterioration of relations from 1807 to 1810 in Perkins, *Prologue to War*, pp. 140–252, and Horsman, *Causes of the War of 1812*, pp. 101–88.

From the time of Macon's Bill No. 2 there was a steady growth in the number of Americans who were convinced that only by war would American interests be protected and the national honour maintained. As early as February 1810 young Henry Clay of Kentucky had told the Senate that when peaceful means failed he wanted 'resistance by the *sword*', and he was obtaining increasing support, particularly in the West and South.[10] The Eleventh Congress was dispirited by its failures, but the Twelfth, which was elected in 1810 and took office in November 1811, had a hard core of enthusiasts who were prepared to risk a war.

After fighting a successful Revolution against the British, the Americans had now suffered for years under severe British maritime restrictions. The damage to American trade and the sufferings of American seamen continually provoked the resentment of large sections of the American population. After 1808 American disgust was also increased by the economic depression which affected the agricultural regions of the country. The cotton and tobacco planters of the South Atlantic states, and the farmers of the Mississippi Valley, found that the prices they could obtain for their products declined while their imports continued to be expensive. Many of the difficulties, particularly in the West, were caused by marketing problems, but the farmers had no hesitation in placing the entire blame for their plight on British commercial restrictions.[11]

American resentment was also increased in these years by the renewed British activity among the Indians of the Old Northwest. From the time of the *Chesapeake* affair the British authorities in Canada feared that American anger at British commercial restrictions would lead to war and the invasion of Canada. To aid in its defence they tried to ensure that they would have the support of the Indian tribes. Throughout these years British Indian agents advised and supplied Indians on the American side of the border. The Indians had ample reason to listen to the British, as their lands in

---

[10] *Annals of Congress*, 11th Cong., 1st Sess., p. 579.
[11] George Rogers Taylor, 'Agrarian Discontent in the Mississippi Valley Preceding the War of 1812', *Journal of Political Economy*, XXXIX (1931), pp. 471–505; Margaret Kinard Latimer, 'South Carolina – A Protagonist of the War of 1812', *American Historical Review*, LXI (1955–56), pp. 914–29.

the Old Northwest were under constant pressure from the American settlers. Beginning in 1805 the Shawnee Tecumseh and his brother the Prophet were attempting to organize a general Indian confederacy to resist the American advance, and after 1807 they were aided by the British. Westerners argued that if war became necessary because of repeated British infringements of American neutral rights then the opportunity could be taken to smash the British-Indian alliance. Similarly, some in the Southwest thought that if war came the United States could use the opportunity to exert still more pressure on the Floridas, the possession of Britain's ally Spain.[12]

The crucial issue, however, was at sea, for if Britain would acknowledge the rights of American ships and seamen then there would be no war. If not, there were increasing signs that the United States was willing to fight. American Secretary of the Navy Paul Hamilton made it quite clear to American naval captains in 1810 and 1811 that there should be no abject submission to British pretensions; resentment at British ships hovering off the American coast was reaching breaking-point. In May 1811, after a number of incidents, including the impressing of an American seaman only eighteen miles off New York, the frigate *President* was ordered to sea to protect American shipping. The American navy had bitter memories of the *Chesapeake*, and it was no surprise when, on 16 May the *President* fired on the British sloop *Little Belt*.[13] This sign of an American awakening was welcomed by most Americans. Although the Federalists and large areas of New England still opposed either war or economic retaliation, many in the country now felt that whatever its dangers war was preferable to an ignominious peace.

When Congress met in November 1811 the main question was no longer how could effective economic coercion be achieved but rather how could war be declared. The leadership in the drive for war was provided by Kentuckian Henry Clay and twenty or thirty Demo-

---

[12] Horsman, *Matthew Elliott*, *passim* discusses British backing of the Indians. Julius W. Pratt, *Expansionists of 1812* (New York, 1925), pp. 60–125, argues the importance of the southern desire for the Floridas.

[13] Horsman, *Causes of the War of 1812*, p. 220; Benson J. Lossing, *The Pictorial Field Book of the War of 1812* (New York, 1868), pp. 181–5.

cratic-Republican supporters, most of them from the West and South. The tone of this new Twelfth Congress was immediately apparent, for Henry Clay, whose previous Congressional experience had been in serving out two unexpired Senatorial terms, was elected Speaker of the House. This enabled him to place leading War Hawks on key committees: Peter B. Porter of western New York became chairman of the Foreign Relations Committee, David R. Williams of South Carolina chairman of Military Affairs, and Langdon Cheves from the same state chairman of the Naval Committee. Supporting Porter on the Foreign Relations Committee were John C. Calhoun of South Carolina, Felix Grundy of Tennessee, Joseph Desha of Kentucky, and John A. Harper of New Hampshire.[14]

In his annual message of 5 November, 1811, President James Madison spoke of the failure to achieve redress of grievances by peaceful means, and said that Congress now had to assume the task of 'putting the United States into an armor and an attitude demanded by the crisis'.[15] Later that month Congress was stirred by the news that Governor William Henry Harrison of Indiana had clashed with the Indian confederacy at Tippecanoe on 7 November, but, in spite of this major renewal of Indian warfare, when the Foreign Relations Committee reported to the House on 29 November in answer to that part of the President's message concerning foreign relations its concern was solely maritime affairs. The report stated that the time for peaceful resistance was at an end, and that the United States should claim the right to export her products without losing her ships and men. The committee concluded by recommending specific war preparations.[16]

Although the War Hawks wanted war, even they realized that United States preparations had been woefully inadequate. They also realized that the country was anything but united on this issue. The Federalists thought war against Britain was lunacy, and, as the Federalists were strongest in New England, the support of a vital section of the nation was doubtful. In the debates of 1811–12 the

---

[14] Horsman, *Causes of the War of 1812*, pp. 225–6.
[15] James D. Richardson, *A Compilation of the Messages and Papers of the Presidents, 1789–1897* (10 vols., Washington, 1896–99), I, 494.
[16] *Annals of Congress*, 12th Cong., 1st Sess., pp. 373–7.

War Hawks tried to rekindle a revolutionary fervour. They pointed out that for twenty years Britain had interfered with American commerce and seized American seamen. All peaceful methods of redress had failed, and the United States was in danger of losing the independence she had fought for in the Revolution. This post-Revolutionary generation emphasized the need to defend the liberties won for them by their fathers. 'What are we not to lose by peace?' asked Clay on 31 December, ' – commerce, character, a nation's best treasure, honor!'[17] The War Hawks also talked of the British backing of the Indians, and of the ability of the United States to expand on the North American Continent, but the strongest of their arguments was simply that the United States had failed to change the maritime policies of Britain by peaceful means, and that the time had come to defend ships, seamen, and the national honour by war.[18]

The great delay in declaring war in this session of 1811–12 was primarily because of the lack of means with which to fight, and disagreement even among the War Hawks as to the forces needed and the most effective ways of using them. The strangest feature of these arguments was that the Democratic-Republicans who wanted war were split on the question of whether or not to increase the American navy. Since 1801 the government, in spite of its maritime difficulties, had reduced the navy, placing its faith in harbour defences and in gunboats for the protection of American coastal waters. Although this policy originally stemmed from the desire for economy, and from the Democratic-Republican distrust of maritime interests, it had also been suggested that major ships were not needed to fight a defensive war. When at the end of November 1811 the House Foreign Relations Committee suggested immediate military preparations, it recommended for the navy only the arming of merchantmen and the commissioning of the laid-up ships of war. It seemed likely that only sixteen ships, the largest of them frigates, could be put into commission for the regular American navy.

---

[17] *Ibid.*, p. 599.
[18] Horsman, *Causes of the War of 1812*, pp. 229–32; also Norman K. Risjord, '1812: Conservatives, War Hawks, and the Nation's Honor', *William and Mary Quarterly*, Third Series, vol. XVIII (1961), pp. 196–210.

THE ORIGINS OF THE WAR

In the middle of January 1812 the Naval Committee of the House recommended an appropriation to build twelve ships of the line and twenty-four frigates. This seemed little enough to contend with the British navy, but it immediately caused a split in those arguing for war. Some of the War Hawks, particularly those from the Mississippi Valley, asserted that Britain was so powerful at sea that the building of this force was useless. They feared giving more power to the commercial classes, and argued that Britain could best be brought to recognize American rights by the conquest of Canada, not by ineffectual naval operations. Even though Kentuckian Henry Clay differed from most of the Westerners and spoke for the measure, the bill to increase the navy was defeated by a vote of 62 to 59.[19]

As it was generally agreed, whatever the attitude on the navy, that the invasion of Canada was essential for the coercion of Britain, it was obviously necessary that immediate provision be made for an increase in the army. The House Foreign Relations Committee had recommended an addition of 10,000 regulars, and the raising of 50,000 volunteers. The proposal for regulars was attacked in the Senate as too weak, and after considerable discussion in both houses it was agreed that 25,000 new regulars would be provided, and that the existing army would be filled out to its official strength of 10,000 men. The bill became law on 11 January, but organization and recruitment proceeded exceedingly slowly. It was quite obvious that, if war was declared in this session, the United States would begin its attacks with a very small regular army.[20]

The recommendation for raising 50,000 volunteers, essentially militia, also produced a drawn-out argument. Here there was a constitutional problem: militia, it was argued, could legally be used only for home defence. Even some of the War Hawks espoused the view that the force could not be used outside the country. The argument was bitter, and to avoid the dilemma no decision was taken on this vital matter when the bill became law on 6 February.[21] If the United States declared war and invaded Canada, there was considerable doubt as to whether her main force of troops could be used

---
[19] *Annals of Congress*, 12th Cong., 1st Sess., pp. 803–46, 859–1001.
[20] *Ibid.*, pp. 34–85, 107–10, 596–718, 2229–34.
[21] *Ibid.*, pp. 728–801, 2235–7, 2362.

3

for this purpose. President Madison despaired of action. Of Congress he said, 'with a view to enable the Executive to step at once into Canada they have provided after two months parlay for a regular force requiring twelve to raise it, and after three months for a volunteer force, on terms not likely to raise it at all for that object.'[22] Although Congress was to continue its efforts to improve army organization in the months directly preceding the war, much of the planning was too late.

Another major difficulty that had to be overcome in the drive for war was the traditional Republican dislike of taxation. Since Jefferson had assumed office in 1801 his party had pursued a goal of economy in government and the elimination of the public debt. Albert Gallatin, who served as Secretary of the Treasury under both Jefferson and Madison, originally believed that any war should be financed not by increased taxation but by loans. By 1811 Gallatin perceived that this solution was simply impossible in practice, and that internal taxes would be needed to make up revenue lost by a reduction in income from the customs. Even now, however, loans would presumably cover all extraordinary expenditure. This hope of depending on loans boded ill for American financing of the war, as it seemed likely that there would be considerable difficulty in raising money. The first United States Bank had failed to be rechartered in February, 1811, and there was no longer a powerful central agency for the government to lean on. This difficulty was compounded by the opposition to the war of the New England financial interests, and even in areas in which the war was supported it seemed likely that the British blockade would shatter American prosperity.[23]

In spite of this rather bleak picture, some of the War Hawks still voiced their traditional objections to internal taxation. In the middle of February Ezekiel Bacon, the chairman of the House Ways and Means Committee, recommended doubling the customs duties, placing a direct tax of three million dollars on the states, direct taxes

---

[22] Madison to Jefferson, 7 Feb., 1812, Madison Papers, vol. XLVI, Library of Congress (quoted in Horsman, *Causes of the War of 1812*, p. 240).
[23] Alexander Balinky, *Albert Gallatin* (New Brunswick, N.J., 1958), pp. 167-179.

on certain items such as salt, and the raising of a loan of eleven million dollars. Against opposition these measures were agreed to in March, although the taxes were to be imposed only in the event of actual war; the Republicans still feared that they might get a tax increase and no war.[24]

The long discussions and disagreements among the Democratic-Republicans, and the continued opposition of the Federalists, meant that four months had passed since the President and the House Foreign Relations Committee had indicated that the United States should adopt warlike measures to defend her rights. In March 1812 President Madison tried to accelerate the painfully slow proceedings by disclosing to Congress evidence purporting to show that in 1808 a British agent from Canada, John Henry, had conspired with the New England Federalists with a view to splitting the Union. The evidence was rather doubtful, and many questioned the $50,000 that Madison had paid for the letters, but at least it was becoming quite apparent that the President wanted war. On 1 April he recommended to Congress a sixty-day embargo, a measure which would permit American shipping to make port before an actual declaration of war. The extent of continued American disunity was well shown in the Senate, where the measure was extended from sixty to ninety days, and even then only passed by a vote of 20 to 13. The Hawks, however, were determined to have war, and some even talked wildly of fighting France as well, although here good sense prevailed.[25]

The irony of this situation was that throughout the winter of 1811–12, as the United States painfully strove to organize for war, Britain was engaged in a major argument concerning the wisdom of the Orders in Council policy. Beginning in the summer of 1810 Britain gradually became enmeshed in a severe economic depression, and the Whig opposition argued that prosperity could be restored by the renewal of American trade. The manufacturing districts were particularly hurt by the decline in trade, and from the spring of 1811 petitions were sent to Parliament asking for the repeal of the Orders

---

[24] *Annals of Congress*, 12th Cong., 1st Sess., pp. 1050–56, 1092–1155, 2253.
[25] Horsman, *Causes of the War of 1812*, pp. 242–4; Irving Brant, *James Madison: The President, 1809–1812* (Indianapolis, 1956), pp. 412–20.

in Council and the restoration of friendly commercial relations with the United States. The petitioners were thwarted when Parliament adjourned in July 1811, but when it reassembled in the following January the depression had deepened, and the opposition was ready for an all-out attack on the Orders. The enthusiasm for repeal was increased by the fear that the United States might otherwise go to war, and end all possibility of the renewal of trade.

The leadership in this fight against the Orders was taken by young Henry Brougham, who made it quite clear that he believed Britain's best interest lay in friendship with the United States. Apart from his speeches in Parliament, Brougham and his allies stimulated meetings in the manufacturing districts, and in the spring of 1812 petitions poured in from Yorkshire, Lancashire, Birmingham, the Potteries, and other manufacturing areas. The government was under particular pressure because of extensive rioting in the manufacturing districts: in many places Luddites destroyed the machines which they thought had helped to produce their poverty. By the end of April the opposition had forced the government to appoint a committee to investigate the petitions against the Orders in Council, and in May witnesses from all the manufacturing districts appeared before the committee. Parliament could hardly ignore their extensive evidence. Over one hundred witnesses appeared, and four-fifths of them opposed the Orders, arguing that the American trade was essential to their prosperity. Witness after witness told of widespread unemployment, poverty, and distress. The main support for the government, however, came from the shipping interest, and the government still clung to its policy, convinced that the war against France and British naval power were at stake.

How long the government would have persisted in the face of widespread opposition and threats of revolution was never to be known, for on 11 May the Prime Minister, Spencer Perceval, was shot by a deranged grievance holder. In Leicester and Nottingham the news of the assassination was greeted with outbursts of joy. Not until June did Lord Liverpool begin to form a government, but the enquiry into the Orders continued. On 16 June, in reply to Brougham's motion for the repeal of the Orders, Castlereagh made it clear that the government intended to revoke them. This was done

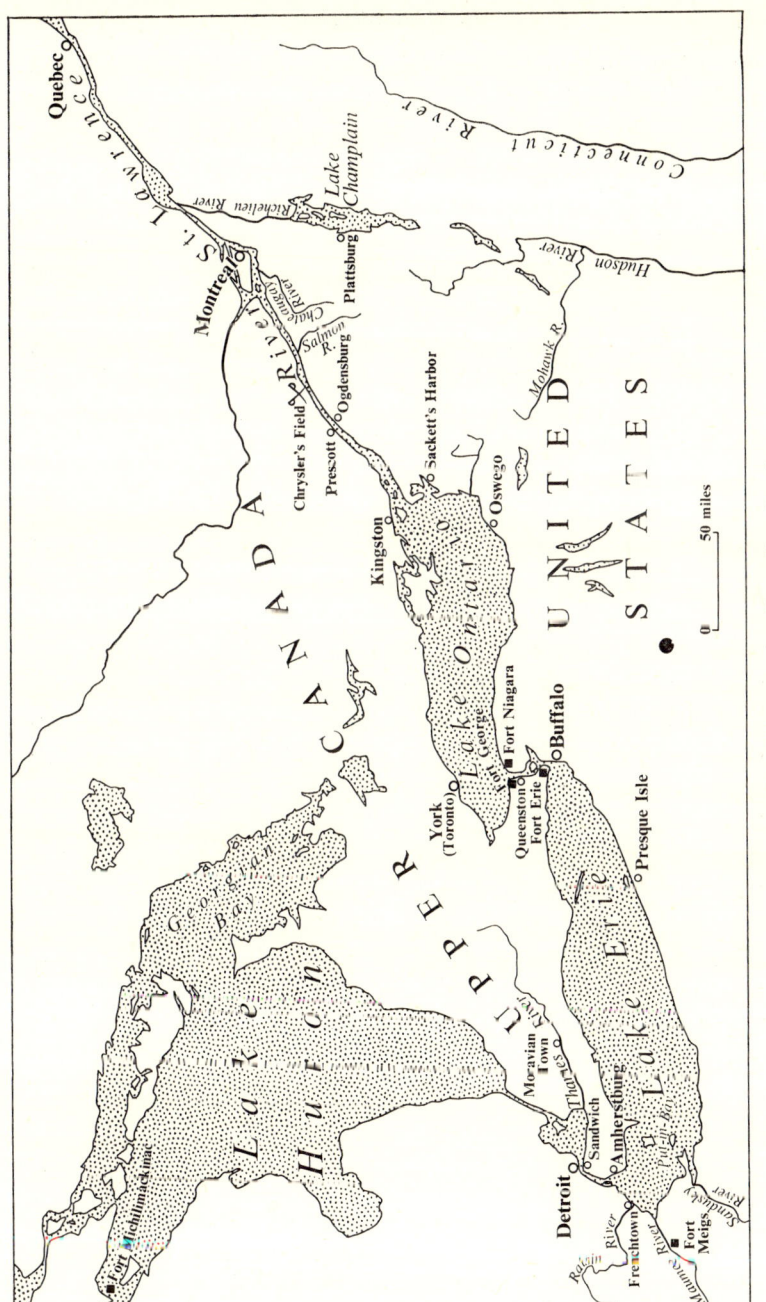

MAP 2 The War on the Canadian Border

on 23 June, and amid general rejoicing the manufacturers prepared to ship their goods to the United States.[26]

It was all too late. On 1 June Madison had asked Congress for a declaration of war against Britain. His war message recited the long list of complaints since 1803 – impressment, harassment off the American coast, blockades, and the recent renewal of Indian warfare. Britain had yielded nothing to negotiation, and Madison argued that war was the only alternative. Congress had debated the reasons for war since the previous November, so little remained to be said. On 4 June the declaration of war passed the House by the ominously divided vote of 79 to 49. The Federalists were solidly opposed to war, and most of this opposition came from the North-Eastern states. The western states – Kentucky, Ohio, and Tennessee – were unanimously for war, and the South Atlantic states favoured it by 37 to 11. In the Senate the issue was even closer. The measure was passed on 17 June by only 19 to 13, and Madison signed it on the following day.[27]

In Britain the government was surprised, the manufacturers shocked; to everyone it seemed a useless war. 'If the Father of evil himself had planned this mischief,' commented the *Examiner*, 'he could not have contrived a rupture more hateful to humanity, or one more destitute of any the most remote advantage to any body, the Imperial Oppressor excepted.'[28] The commercial interests concerned with the American trade thought its loss was disastrous, but the feeling was general in Britain that the United States had made an incredible mistake. Canada was not highly regarded, and it was assumed that the small American navy, and all her merchant vessels, would be swept from the seas, leaving the American coastline open to British attack.

---

[26] Horsman, *Causes of the War of 1812*, pp. 245–58.
[27] *Ibid.*, pp. 260–62. Roger H. Brown, *The Republic in Peril: 1812* (New York, 1964) is a detailed study of Congress and the move for war.
[28] *Examiner* (London), 23 Aug., 1812.

2

The Invasion of Canada

While the American Congress demonstrated to the whole world the deep internal divisions and military weakness of the United States, the British authorities in Canada were preparing to resist the invasion they had long been expecting. In these preparations they could hope for little immediate help from Britain. With Wellington advancing in the Peninsula, and Napoleon about to plunge into Russia, the struggle against revolutionary France was entering its last phase. The British government had not wanted war with the United States, but until it had been too late had been unwilling to make any concessions to avoid it. Now that war had come, Britain intended to divert only a minimum of resources from Europe to the struggle in the New World. The defence of Canada depended upon the British officials and soldiers on the spot and their available resources. The British government in London had in 1812 no intention of mounting any large-scale rescue operation from Europe.[1]

The British North American Colonies included in 1812 four mainland provinces; Lower and Upper Canada, New Brunswick, and Nova Scotia. The Governor-in-Chief of the area was Sir George Prevost, who arrived in Lower Canada in the autumn of 1811. He was a regular soldier, whose Swiss father had also served in the British army, but since 1800 he had undertaken administrative duties as a governor in the West Indies and in Nova Scotia. He was a somewhat pedestrian figure, but the ineptness of the American attack at first helped to obscure his limitations. Although in theory he was responsible for the defence of the whole of Canada, many decisions were in practice taken by the lieutenant-governors in Upper Canada and in Nova Scotia. Major-General Isaac Brock, who commanded in Upper Canada, was an energetic, ambitious officer, far more

---

[1] Liverpool to Prevost, 15 May, 1812, Colonial Office Archives, CO 43/23, pp. 58–60, Public Record Office.

willing to take risks than Prevost, and far better able to inspire those who served under him. He was anxious to win a military reputation, and welcomed the war as providing the opportunity for action he had been seeking for several years.[2] Sir John Sherbrooke, the lieutenant-governor of Nova Scotia, was another regular soldier, but the safety of the maritime provinces depended less upon his efforts than upon the presence of the British navy.

On the face of it there seemed good reason for fearing the results of an American attack. The British regulars in Canada numbered less than 6,000, and were spread very thinly along a great stretch of frontier. The posts were often isolated and lonely, and the men deserted to the United States at every opportunity. Drunkenness, always a problem, became a chronic condition in squalid frontier outposts buried in the depths of a great forest.[3] It had been demonstrated in the Revolution that discipline and order could not always overcome an unfamiliar terrain, distance, and the amateur, ill-trained levies of the United States.

Another problem in Canada was the lack of good, experienced officers. Ambitious soldiers desired to be in the Peninsula, not across the Atlantic, and Wellington wanted the best officers under his command against the French. General Brock spoke of the 41st Regiment, which was serving in Canada, as being 'wretchedly officered', and a Canadian who had served in the war asserted that 'we got the rubbish of every department in the army. Any man whom the Duke deemed unfit for the Peninsula was considered as quite good enough for the Canadian market.'[4]

To supplement the British regulars serving in North America there were the Canadian 'fencibles': regiments recruited in the North

---

[2] Francis Gore, the lieutenant-governor of Upper Canada, had been given a leave of absence to go to England in the autumn of 1811, and Brock assumed civil as well as military authority.

[3] Ferdinand Brock Tupper, *The Life and Correspondence of Major-General Sir Isaac Brock, K.B.* (2nd ed., London, 1847), pp. 33–7; Brock to Liverpool, 23 March, 1812, CO 42/352, p. 7.

[4] Brock to his brother, 18 Sept., 1812, Tupper, *Life and Correspondence of Brock*, p. 316; Dr William Dunlop, *Recollections of the American War, 1812–1814* (Toronto, 1905), p. 63.

American colonies to serve only in that area. These had existed since 1803 in Canada, but were increased in number when the danger of war became imminent. Recruitment, however, was not easy. The Glengarry Light Infantry Fencibles, who had begun to be raised before the war started, in December 1812 still only consisted of 500 rather than the 800 men authorized.[5]

The Canadian militia could hardly be depended upon for the long-term defence of the British possessions. In Lower Canada the French population had no reason to love either the Americans or English, and had no enthusiasm to die fighting for either. In May 1812 Prevost described the 60,000 militia of Lower Canada as 'a mere posse, ill arm'd, and without discipline', and because of the many American immigrants in Upper Canada thought it might not be prudent to arm more than 4,000 of the 11,000 available men. Yet the governor had in April at least managed to secure a new militia act from the Lower Canadian Assembly. This permitted him in the event of war to keep 2,000 bachelors in service for not more than two years, half of whom were to be replaced annually.[6]

Like Prevost, Brock feared the influence of American immigrants in Upper Canada, and at the beginning of 1812 attempted to push through the Upper Canadian legislature a measure requiring militiamen to abjure all foreign powers. The bill was defeated, and this only served to increase Brock's fear of American influence, particularly when he also failed to secure the passage of a bill permitting him to suspend the right of *habeas corpus*. He did, however, obtain a measure which empowered him to form 'flank companies' of militia to train for six days each month: there were to be two flank companies to each battalion.[7] All in all, the Canadian militia promised only limited usefulness, and if it was called out for any length of time agriculture would be disrupted and both residents and regulars cut off from supplies.

---

[5] CO 43/50, p. 108.
[6] Prevost to Liverpool, 18 May, 20 April, 1812, CO 42/146, pp. 197–202, 148–51.
[7] Brock to Prevost, Feb. 1812, Tupper, *Life and Correspondence of Brock*, pp. 153–5; Brock to Liverpool, 23 March, 1812, CO 42/352, pp. 7–11; J. Mackay Hitsman, *The Incredible War of 1812* (Toronto, 1965), pp. 33–7.

On the eve of the War of 1812 the land defences of Canada were hardly such as to inspire confidence. The tenuous system extended nearly 2,000 miles from Halifax, Nova Scotia, on the Atlantic, to Fort St Joseph, east of Michilimackinac in the distant north-west corner of Lake Huron. Halifax itself was the naval base for the British North American squadron. On its land side it was enclosed by a wilderness, and for the rest it could depend on the protection of the British navy. Any serious attack on Nova Scotia, New Brunswick, or into the St Lawrence could only take place in the unlikely event that the United States wrested temporary naval control of the area from the British.

Most of the Canadian population was on the St Lawrence between Quebec and Montreal, and here were the keys to the conquest of Canada. Montreal had no massive fortifications, but it depended for its safety on British control of the St Lawrence and of the approach from the south along the Richelieu River. As in the Revolution, it could be expected that the United States would take advantage of the natural Hudson Valley–Lake Champlain route into Canada. In the event of any attack over 12,000 militia could be mustered for its defence.

Quebec was regarded by Prevost as the heart of his defensive position: to its defence 'every other military operation ought to become subservient'. If Quebec fell then the British would be confined to a precarious enclave on the North American Continent, centred around Halifax. In the months immediately prior to the war Prevost's opinion was that in the event of an American invasion his main hope was a successful defence of Quebec; that post could then be used as a base for any future operations to reconquer the parts of Canada overrun by the Americans.

Prevost was pessimistic regarding his chances of successfully defending Upper Canada. The main post at the western limits of Canadian settlement was Fort Malden at Amherstburg, seventeen miles south of Detroit on the opposite side of the Detroit River. This post seemed particularly vulnerable to American troops from Ohio and Kentucky, and General Brock, in command in Upper Canada, argued that its fall would be made more certain if the British followed Prevost's idea of a defensive war based on Quebec.

Brock feared that unless the British forces in Upper Canada launched an offensive and captured Detroit and Michilimackinac, everything west of Kingston (at the entrance to the St Lawrence from Lake Ontario) was in danger of falling into American hands. There were similar fears, particularly on the part of Prevost, that Forts George, Erie, and Chippawa along the Niagara River were vulnerable to American attack.[8]

Yet, even though the Canadians feared that their forces might be insufficient to repel a determined American attack west of Quebec, there were sufficient reasons, beside possible American ineptness, to throw some doubt on the supposition that the British Provinces lay open to an American invasion. Incredibly, while the American Congress had argued about the precise number of men needed to conquer Canada, they had not obtained naval control of the Great Lakes. Such naval control would have ensured the conquest of Upper Canada. In June 1812 Britain had naval control of both Lake Ontario and Lake Erie, and maintained this during the rest of the year. Naval command of the lakes did not depend on comparative naval strength in the Atlantic, for the rapids on the St Lawrence prevented England sending ships from the ocean into the Lakes. Even Lakes Ontario and Erie had to be considered separately as they were linked only by the Niagara River and the falls. Instead of declaring war and invading Canada after building superior forces on Lakes Erie and Ontario, the United States went to war with no naval force on Lake Erie and an inferior one on Lake Ontario. As a result American forces at Detroit had to be supplied by tenuous trails through a wilderness while British troops at Fort Malden could be supplied by water. To offset this British naval advantage on Lakes Erie and Ontario, the Americans needed to sever the British line of communications by a successful invasion of Canada northwards from Lake Champlain to Montreal. Yet this also required careful preparations, as it involved a long march northwards along a route over which the British confidently expected the Americans to attack.

---

[8] Prevost to Liverpool, 18 May, 1812, CO 42/146, pp. 197-202; Brock to Prevost, 2 Dec., 1811, to Edward Baynes, 12 Feb., 1812, Tupper, *Life and Correspondence of Brock*, pp. 123-9, 147-50.

The Americans had naval control of Lake Champlain, but they had no efficient army ready to march against Montreal.[9]

American preparations for invasion were still hopelessly inadequate at the time of the declaration of war. The long Congressional discussions of the previous winter had failed to produce prompt action for the increase of the American military forces. The 35,000-man regular army provided for in January was still under 7,000 at the beginning of June. Even this force was not poised on the Canadian border, ready to attack as the United States declared war; it was scattered all over the vast area of the United States from Maine to Georgia, and from Michilimackinac to New Orleans. The regulars were daily being reinforced by recruits, but it was quite obvious that the United States would have to place great dependence on short-term volunteers and militia if she were to launch a large-scale attack on Canada. President Madison had been authorized to accept up to 50,000 volunteers if he could find them, and on 10 April he had also been empowered to call into federal service up to 100,000 of the state militia.[10]

The organization of an effective military force was of great difficulty in the United States in the early nineteenth century. Many believed that standing armies were a threat to individual liberties, and Americans weaned on Revolutionary ideals were loath to accept the idea of a harsh military discipline. With an abundance of land, and the absence of any large class of poor, it was difficult to find sufficient recruits. On paper the states could provide a militia of hundreds of thousands of men, but most were reluctant to serve for more than three months at any one time, and there was still considerable doubt as to how many would agree to serve outside the boundaries of the United States.

The opposition of the New England states also gravely hampered the raising of any large force of militia. At the beginning of the war

---

[9] Prevost to Liverpool, 15 July, 1812, CO 42/147, p. 21; Theodore Roosevelt, *The Naval War of 1812* (2 vols., New York, 1882), I, 179–200; Alfred T. Mahan, *Sea Power in its Relations to the War of 1812* (2 vols., Boston, 1905), I, 300–10.

[10] *American State Papers, Military Affairs*, I (Washington, 1832), pp. 319–20 (hereafter cited as *ASP, MA*); *Annals of Congress*, 12th Cong., 1st Sess., 2235–7, 2267–9.

thirty-four Federalist Congressmen issued an address declaring that the war was unnecessary. The New England states would not agree to their state militia being called into federal service, arguing that it was unconstitutional unless their particular state was threatened with invasion. It was quite obvious that only sporadic support, if that, could be expected from New England. Extreme Federalists feared that the Democratic-Republican leadership was impelling the country towards anarchy and destruction, and they were hardened in their opinion in July when a Baltimore mob attacked the newspaper offices of the *Federal Republican*, which had opposed the war, and eventually lynched a group of prominent Federalists who attempted to shelter in the gaol after defending the office.[11] The regular army obtained many of its individual recruits from New England, but the country was unable to use the New England militia for the invasion of Canada. The enthusiasm of the West ensured troops in that region, but unfortunately for the United States it was not possible to inflict a decisive blow against Canada from the Mississippi Valley; enthusiastic troops were needed in the East more than in the West, and American strategy was given a strange imbalance by the lack of uniform support for the war.

American leadership was also lacking in the abilities necessary for conducting a successful offensive war. President James Madison, brilliant as he was, could hardly be regarded as a dynamic war leader, and his Secretary of War, William Eustis, a Revolutionary surgeon, gave little thought to the broad problems of strategy. The commander-in-chief, Henry Dearborn, had been a Major in the Revolution, but English Minister Augustus Foster commented at the time of his appointment that 'his military Reputation does not rank very high'.[12] The United States was also sadly lacking in other officers with any recent military experience, other than that gained in isolated frontier posts and Indian skirmishes. With the coming of

---

[11] James T. Adams, *New England in the Republic, 1776–1850* (Boston, 1927), p. 269; Samuel E. Morison, *The Life and Letters of Harrison Gray Otis. Federalist, 1765–1848* (2 vols., Boston, 1913), II, 48–9, 56–63; *ASP, MA*, I, 323–6.

[12] Leonard D. White,*The Jeffersonians: A Study in Administrative History, 1801–1829* (New York, 1959), p. 217; Foster to Castlereagh, 21 April, 1812, CO 42/148, p. 245.

war much dependence had to be placed on veterans of the Revolution to fill senior military posts. After thirty years of peaceful pursuits many of them were unable to capture the youthful élan that had helped them achieve a reputation in that earlier struggle. As in the Revolution the United States, by trial and error, did eventually find generals who were able to leave civilian life and win a fine military reputation, but this process of natural selection was of no help in the first drive for the conquest of Canada.

Yet, even had the United States possessed a core of brilliant and experienced officers to call upon, it is difficult to see how they could have overcome the problems posed by the inept preparations for the war. There was only a tiny nucleus of regular soldiers, there had been no attempt to win naval control of the Great Lakes, and questions of supply and communications had been left much to chance. At the beginning of 1812 the War Department consisted of the Secretary of War and eight clerks. There was no general staff. Secretary of War Eustis communicated with individual generals, and also acted as Quartermaster General. Only in the spring of 1812 did Congress make a desperate effort to re-establish the vital supply and administrative departments. Separate Quartermaster and Ordnance Departments were created, as well as the post of Commissary General for purchasing. The Quartermaster was supposed to issue and the Commissary General procure, but their functions overlapped. Throughout the war the supply of food to the army was let by public contract to the lowest bidder, but often the food did not arrive or was practically uneatable. The hastily created departments of 1812 could hardly be expected to function smoothly at the outbreak of war, and all in all the Canadians were in less danger than they supposed.[13]

Word of the declaration of war reached Canada with remarkable speed. Trading concerns in Montreal received the news from New York on 24 June, and Canada immediately made preparations to

---

[13] White, *Jeffersonians*, pp. 224–31, 235–7; John A. Huston, *The Sinews of War: Army Logistics, 1775–1953* (Army Historical Series, Washington, 1966), pp. 102–4; Erna Risch, *Quartermaster Support of the Army: A History of the Corps, 1775–1939* (Quartermaster Historian's Office, Washington, 1962), pp. 136–42.

resist the expected invasion.[14] At first the worst fears of the British authorities seemed to be materializing when the embodying of the militia in the villages around Montreal produced a crisis. Some of the men refused to serve, and a mob threatened to march and free those who were already embodied. On their way to seize boats at Lachine the protesters were intercepted by the light company of the 49th Regiment with two field guns, and in an exchange of fire one of the rioters was killed. The rest fled. On the following day order was restored when over four hundred Montreal militia joined with the regular troops to march through the area.[15]

This French-Canadian reaction was exactly what the Americans had hoped for, but it proved to be an isolated rather than a general phenomenon. The militia usually responded when called upon, and there was no general disaffection. Even in Upper Canada, where the British authorities feared that the many settlers of American origin could not be depended upon in time of war, the militia assembled to resist the Americans, although at first Brock called out only the flank companies. For the most part, in spite of the disturbances near Montreal, the British authorities were pleasantly surprised by the first response of the militia.[16]

Instead of advancing rapidly with a powerful force towards Montreal, the United States was obliged by the attitude of New England and the enthusiasm of the West to put particular emphasis on the western phase of American operations. The Americans hoped to attack Canada on a number of fronts – into Upper Canada from Detroit, across the Niagara frontier, and north of Lake Champlain to Montreal. In theory, these efforts should have been co-ordinated to divide British defensive efforts, and should have been supported by American naval forces on the Lakes, but the difficulties of providing a trained army, and the lack of adequate preparations, meant that

---

[14] Prevost to Liverpool, 25 June, 1812, and enclosures, CO 42/147, pp. 1–2; Lady Edgar, ed., *Ten Years of Upper Canada in Peace and War, 1805–1815; being the Ridout Letters* (Toronto, 1890), pp. 129–31.
[15] Prevost to Liverpool, 6 July, 1812, CO 42/147, pp. 15–18; *The Letters of Veritas* (Montreal, 1815), pp. 9–11.
[16] Brock to Prevost, 3 July, 1812, Tupper, *Life and Correspondence of Brock*, pp. 194–5.

the attacks on Canada unfolded in desultory manner from the West.

Along the Detroit frontier the Americans did have the advantage of an army in motion before the war began. In the spring of 1812 William Hull, the governor of Michigan Territory, had been appointed, somewhat against his will, as brigadier-general. Hull had seen distinguished service in the Revolution, but had not risen beyond the rank of lieutenant-colonel. Whatever martial spirit he had once possessed had disappeared in his years of civilian life. His task was to reinforce Detroit with a combination of Ohio militia and regulars, protect the region, and in the event of war invade Canada. Hull took command of his army in Ohio at the end of May. His problems were very great. Although the state had a population of over 250,000, most of these settlers were along the Ohio River and its tributaries. The north-western corner of the state was still in the hands of the Indians. Michigan Territory was practically all Indian country, and Detroit merely the centre for several thousand settlers along the Detroit River. The route from the settled areas of Ohio to Detroit was a track through a heavily wooded wilderness.

Hull finally marched for Detroit from Urbana, Ohio, on 15 June, 1812. Rain fell constantly throughout the next week, and his force of over 2,000, which included the United States Fourth Regiment, struggled slowly through the inundated country, not reaching the Maumee River until 29 June. Hull did not know that war had already been declared, and when he left the Maumee on 1 July to march to Detroit many of his stores, the sick, and some of his papers were put on board a schooner to sail down the Maumee to Lake Erie, into the mouth of the Detroit River, past the British at Fort Malden, and to Detroit. Unfortunately for Hull, the British at Fort Malden had already received news of the war, and seized the schooner. They now knew the strength of Hull's army, and his official orders.[17]

Yet, Hull was still in a position to invade Canada. He had a force of over 2,000 men, while at the end of the first week in July the

---

[17] Hull to Eustis, 18, 24, 26 June, 3 July, 1812, War Department, Secretary of War, Letters Received, Registered Series, National Archives, Washington, DC (hereafter cited as WD, LR, Reg. Series). 'Journal of William K. Beall, July–August 1812', *American Historical Review*, XVII, (July 1912), pp. 784–7.

1a. James Madison

1b. Andrew Jackson

2a. Admiral Sir John Borlase Warren

2b. Admiral Sir Alexander Cockrane

British force at Fort Malden consisted of some 300 regulars, 850 militia, and about 400 Indians.[18] Moreover, the Americans expected many American sympathizers on the Canadian side of the river, and Hull hoped to lure the Canadian militia away from their allegiance. The Americans crossed the Detroit River on 12 July, and the British did not dispute the landing. They intended to make their stand in Fort Malden. Hull took possession of Sandwich, opposite to Detroit, and for a time it seemed that Malden and Upper Canada were his for the taking. He did not, however, move immediately south to attack, but decided to wait until his heavy cannon were mounted on wheels for the march to Malden, and to give time for the Canadian militia to desert the British. To encourage these desertions Hull issued a proclamation on invading Canada in which he promised that the lives and property of the militia would be safe if they remained at home and did not join the British. He also stated that no white man found fighting at the side of the Indians would be taken prisoner.[19]

Hull's chances of success greatly increased in his early days in Canada. The Canadian militia began to leave the British and return to their homes. Within three days about half of them had gone, and the residents of Amherstburg had removed their effects from the village; the British expected an attack almost immediately. When General Isaac Brock, who was at Fort George on the Niagara frontier, received news of the events along the Detroit River he had very little hope that the British would be able to defend Fort Malden. He had reason for his doubts. An American prisoner commented in his diary on 23 July that the fort was 'very weak', and that 'at one leap I could get into the fort'.[20]

As day after day passed with no attack from Hull, the morale of the

---

[18] William Wood, ed., *Select British Documents of the Canadian War of 1812* (3 vols., Toronto, 1920–28), I, 351.
[19] Hull to Eustis, 14, 19, 21, 22 July, 1812. WD, LR, Reg. Series; Alec R. Gilpin, *The War of 1812 in the Old Northwest* (East Lansing, 1958), pp. 73–9; also CO 42/147, p. 35.
[20] Wood, ed., *Select British Documents*, I, 357–9, 369–71; Brock to Prevost, 20 July, 1812, Tupper, *Life and Correspondence of Brock*, pp. 212–14; 'Journal of Beall', *American Historical Review*, XVII, 802.

defenders began to improve. On 26 July Colonel Henry Procter, who had been sent by Brock to assume the command, arrived at the fort. The shortage of militia continued, as the men were now leaving to take part in the harvest, but General Hull had become 'the object of ... jest and ridicule' to the British troops.[21] Procter had brought no reinforcements, but the defenders were daily gaining confidence from Hull's indecision. The few skirmishes that had taken place had never been followed up by any definite move on the part of the Americans. Hull had missed his best chance to attack Fort Malden when its morale was low and the troops there were disheartened by the desertion of many of the militia. He was constantly worried about his precarious supply lines, but if he had attacked and taken the fort the Indians would have fled in confusion. The tenuous trail to Ohio would have only been threatened by such Indians as cared to keep in the field without British support. Victory at Fort Malden would have at least temporarily offset the British naval control of Lake Erie, and given new heart to the American war effort.

Not until 7 August were the guns of the American army mounted and ready to proceed to the attack on Fort Malden, and by that time Hull's diffidence had begun to change to panic. His fears were based on the vulnerability of his supply lines, the lack of any naval support, the failure of the Americans on the Niagara front to help him by attacking, and perhaps most of all by the news of the fall of Michilimackinac.

Michilimackinac had long been the key to the fur trade west of Lake Michigan. The British had given it up to the Americans in 1796, but Canadian fur interests had continued to have strong influence in the settlement, and the British had merely moved their military post a short distance to the east to St Joseph's Island. In this distant region the Americans again suffered, as they had at Detroit, from the strange circumstance that although they had declared war, it was the British along the Canadian frontier who learned of it first. At St Joseph's Captain Charles Roberts was informed of the declaration of war on 8 July, and immediately

---

[21] Wood, ed., *Select British Documents*, I, 414–15; 'Journal of Beall', *American Historical Review*, XVII, 802–3.

decided to attack Michilimackinac. He had less than 50 regulars, but he recruited about 180 French-Canadians and over 300 Indians. He approached Mackinac Island without alarming the Americans, hauled a small gun to a height commanding the fort, and on 17 July the garrison, not knowing that war had been declared, were summoned to surrender. As the total American force amounted to 57 men, and the fort was commanded by the British gun, the Americans capitulated. The number of men involved was small, but Michilimackinac dominated the western country, and the Indians west of Lake Michigan now had ample reason to join the British.[22]

On the Detroit frontier Hull shivered when he heard of the fall of Michilimackinac. He wrote to Secretary of War Eustis that he feared many Indians would now travel south to join the British; his view later in the month, when he was attempting to excuse his failures, was that 'the Northern hive of Indians . . . were swarming down in every direction'. This was not true, but Hull's nerve began to break at the beginning of August. Even though his guns were almost ready, he suggested to Eustis on 4 August that with the new threat from the Indians, and the constant threat to his supply lines, he might have to retreat.[23]

Hull's supply lines were indeed in danger in the early days of August. Emboldened by Hull's failure to attack, the British and Indians at Fort Malden were harassing the rough trail which ran through the woods along the opposite side of the Detroit River. Hull determined to clear this route, and obtain safe passage for a supply train that was coming to him from Ohio. On 4 August some 200 men under Major Thomas Van Horne were sent to meet the supplies and provide an escort. At Brownstown, south of Detroit, they were ambushed by an Indian force under the famous Shawnee Tecumseh. Van Horne's force was turned back with seventeen killed, and Hull's letters to the War Department fell into British hands. This time he told them of his fears that his position was untenable, and that he

---

[22] Roberts to Adjutant General, 17 July, 1812, and enclosure, CO 42/147, pp. 108-11; P. Hanks to Hull, 4 Aug., 1812, WD, LR, Reg. Series (in the 'D' letters).

[23] Hull to Eustis, 4 Aug., 1812, CO 42/147, pp. 153-5; Hull to Eustis, 26 Aug., 1812, WD, LR, Reg. Series.

would soon be assailed by hordes of Indians from west of Lake Michigan. The news from Michilimackinac and the failure of Van Horne were too much for Hull to bear. When he heard on 7 August that British reinforcements were on their way from the Niagara River, he decided to withdraw across the Detroit River to the supposed safety of Fort Detroit; its wooden walls were to be the coffin, not the sanctuary, of his north-western army.[24]

While Hull vacillated, General Brock had been organizing the defence of the Niagara frontier, and attending to his other duties as civil leader of the Province. In the last week in July he had left the Niagara frontier for York to attend the meeting of the Upper Canadian legislature. He was infuriated by its proceedings. As a soldier he thought that in the presence of invasion, the legislature should hand over much of its power to the military. He wanted a suspension of *habeas corpus* and partial martial law. When the legislature hesitated to do what he wanted, he obtained the agreement of the council that the assembly should be prorogued and martial law declared. Brock later argued that the Assembly had tried more 'to avoid by their proceedings incurring the indignation of the Enemy, than the honest fulfilment of their duty.'[25]

Although Brock feared American influence in the Province, and bewailed the desertion among the western militia, he received 500 volunteers when he asked for militia to go with him to relieve Fort Malden. As he feared weakening other areas, Brock eventually moved with a smaller force, but with naval control of Lake Erie he was able to go by boat via Long Point to the Detroit River. He finally arrived at Amherstburg on the night of 13 August with some 250 militia and about 40 regulars of the 41st Regiment.[26]

As Brock travelled west, Hull was in despair, and his doubts and

---

[24] Hull to Eustis, 7 Aug., 1812, John Brannan, *Official Letters of the Military and Naval Officers of the United States during the War with Great Britain in the Years 1812, 13, 14 & 15* (Washington, 1823), p. 36.

[25] Brock to Liverpool, 29 Aug., 1812, CO 42/352, p. 105; also CO 42/147, pp. 141–2.

[26] Prevost to Bathurst, 26 Aug., 1812, CO 42/147, pp. 159–64; Brock to Prevost, 29 July, 1812, Tupper, *Life and Correspondence of Brock*, pp. 225–6; also CO 42/352, pp. 105–6.

fears were sapping the morale of his men. On 8 August, after recrossing the Detroit River, he had again attempted to open his supply route to Ohio; this time with 600 men under the command of Lieutenant-Colonel James Miller. The use of such a large proportion of his total force clearly demonstrated the anxiety with which Hull viewed the position along his line of communications. Once again the British and their Indian allies were waiting in ambush, this time at Monguagon about fourteen miles south of Detroit. The British force consisted of about 150 regulars and militia under Captain Adam Muir, and some 250 Indians under Tecumseh. On this occasion the Americans were initially more successful than on their earlier attempt to open the supply line; the British and Indians were driven off, losing about 100 killed and wounded, most of them Indians. The Americans had over 80 casualties. Even this partial victory led to nothing constructive, for Miller encamped instead of driving on to open communications and join the supply column, and Hull recalled him to Detroit.[27] Hull had now made two unsuccessful attempts to link up with his supply column at the River Raisin, and his fears of complete encirclement were growing daily. With Brock's arrival on 13 August, the British forces were ready to increase the pressure on Hull.

Brock quickly decided that instead of precariously clinging to Fort Malden, he would attack Hull in Fort Detroit. He was greatly helped in this decision by the captured American letters in which Hull told of his fears, and by his knowledge that the American army had lost confidence in their general. Procter had already begun to construct batteries across the river from Detroit, and these were ready to open fire by 15 August. By this time Hull had still further weakened his position, for on the 14th he had detached 350 of his best men to meet his supply train which was now coming from the River Raisin by an indirect route through the woods.

On 15 August Brock summoned Hull to surrender. Playing on Hull's fears, he stated that should he be obliged to take Detroit by storm he could not guarantee restraining the Indians who would

---

[27] Hull to Eustis, 13 Aug., 1812, Brannan, *Official Letters*, pp. 36–8; Procter to Brock, 11 Aug., 1812, Wood, ed., *Select British Documents*, I, 456–7.

attack with him. Hull refused to surrender, but his nagging fears increased. On the evening of the 15th the British batteries opened up across the Detroit River, and were answered by the American guns. Brock was now ready to attack, and was able to take with him over 300 regulars, 400 militia, and 600 Indians. The Indians, led by British Indian agent Matthew Elliott, crossed the river on the night of 15–16 August, and on the following morning, just after daylight, they were followed by Brock's force.

Brock had hoped that he could draw Hull out to a battle in the open, but knowing that Hull had detached several hundred men he was afraid that they might return and attack him in the rear. Accordingly, he immediately advanced to attack the fort. This was a dangerous manœuvre, as the British troops had to advance across open ground in to the face of American guns; and the American gunners were confident. Yet, as the Indians began to flank the American position, and Brock's troops steadily moved forward, Hull surrendered. Hull's decision had become increasingly likely in the first weeks of August. His vacillation had shattered the confidence of his own troops in their leadership. By the beginning of August American officers were even talking of arresting their General, and taking over the defence of Detroit. When Hull saw the British advancing, his main fear seems to have been that if they stormed the fort the Indians would massacre the many women and children sheltering there. Later he justified himself by arguing that he had only one day's supply of powder, and a few days' provisions, but this was denied both by the British who captured the fort, and by Hull's own officers.[28]

By the time of the attack Hull had allowed himself to be outnumbered; he probably only had a thousand effectives to meet the advancing British and Indian force, but he had the fortifications of Detroit to shelter behind, and the Indians, who formed an essential part of the British army, were notoriously reluctant to throw

---

[28] Brock to Prevost, 17 Aug., 1812, and enclosure, CO 42/147, pp. 175–82; Tupper, *Life and Correspondence of Brock*, pp. 284–6, 304–5; Wood, ed., *Select British Documents*, I, 474, 497; Edgar, ed., *Ten Years of Upper Canada*, p. 246; Hull to Eustis, 26 Aug., 1812, WD, LR, Reg. Series; Brannan, *Official Letters* pp. 38–9, 40–42, 56–60.

themselves into attack against entrenched positions. The battle was in the balance, and the Americans might well have won, but Hull surrendered without a fight. The Americans yielded their whole army in the region, including the 350 detached men and the supply column at the River Raisin. It seemed that Hull could hardly find enough to surrender. His campaign had cost the United States some 2,000 men, and shattered American morale. Hull was courtmartialled, sentenced to death, and eventually reprieved by the President on account of his services in the Revolution.

Hull undoubtedly deserved much of the blame for the complete fiasco of this western attack on Canada, but in truth only a dynamic general could have overcome the difficulties sown by the inept American governmental preparations. Before the campaign had even started Hull had pointed out the need of an American naval force on Lake Erie, but he had been obliged to advance at the end of a tenuous, exposed supply line, while the British could receive supplies and reinforcements by water. Hull at first had numerical superiority and enthusiastic men, and faced a demoralized Canadian militia, but he missed his chance. Brock, who at first thought Fort Malden would fall, made no such mistake. When he saw the weaknesses and fears of his enemy he struck quickly, and took complete control of the Detroit frontier, ensuring that still more Indians would flock to his colours.

American gloom was complete when news arrived that not only had Detroit and Michilimackinac been lost, but that also on the day before the fall of Detroit the tiny American garrison at Fort Dearborn (on the site of Chicago) had been overwhelmed by the Indians while attempting to retreat southwards along Lake Michigan. Some died, along with their families, at the first Indian onslaught, others were tortured to death after the battle, and the lucky ones were taken prisoner and eventually freed.[29] By the middle of August 1812 the western segment of the easy march into Canada was in ruins, and if that was all the enthusiastic west could accomplish chances of a successful attack further east looked bleak.

---

[29] Louise P. Kellogg, *The British Régime in Wisconsin and the Northwest* (Madison, 1935), pp. 285–7.

By the time the news of the surrender of Detroit reached Lower Canada, the Canadians had realized that the Americans did not pose a threat of sudden, swift invasion. In one sense this created difficulties, for militia who had been assembled to meet an immediate threat of invasion were reluctant to remain away from their families and farms when nothing appeared to be happening, and having served one abortive period were less likely to respond enthusiastically if dire necessity forced them to be called again. Also, the British authorities were encountering difficulty owing to the great shortage of specie to pay for military needs. In the middle of July Prevost turned to Army Bills to meet the need for a circulating medium; he simply did not have the hard cash to pay his military costs.[30]

In spite of Hull's invasion of Upper Canada, Prevost was loath in the early months of the war to assume anything but a quiet defensive attitude. He felt that with the great dissension in the New England states, it would be prudent to avoid any measures that would serve to unite American opinion. Prevost also believed that the strength of his army did not justify risking any offensive operations, and knew quite well that the British government viewed his role as essentially defensive. This well suited Prevost's own temperament. He was unwilling to take risks to ensure safety, and his feelings in this regard hardened considerably at the beginning of August when he heard of the repeal of the Orders in Council, and of Britain's hopes that the United States would now end the war. Because of this news Prevost asked Major-General Henry Dearborn if he would agree to an armistice until the attitude of the United States government was known. Dearborn, who showed the same reluctance as Prevost to commit himself to positive military action, replied that he did not have the authority to sign an armistice, but that he would order the officers on the eastern fronts of the war to confine themselves to defensive operations, and that he would '*advise*' Hull to suspend any attacks.[31] Hull hardly needed advice in this regard, and

---

[30] Prevost to Liverpool, 18, 30 July, 3 Aug., to Bathurst, 24 Sept., 1812, and enclosures, CO 42/147, pp. 23–6, 41, 43–4, 47–53, 57, 197.

[31] Prevost to Brock, 10 July, 1812, Tupper *Life and Correspondence of Brock*, pp. 200–201; Prevost to Liverpool, 15 July, 5 Aug., to Bathurst, 17 Aug., 1812, and enclosures, CO 42/147, pp. 19–22, 80–82, 84–7, 117–19, 121–7.

THE INVASION OF CANADA 43

only by a liberal interpretation could the marching he had undertaken be called offensive. As part of the agreement reached by Dearborn and Prevost's envoy, Colonel Edward Baynes, it was decided that convoys of reinforcements and stores could continue to go west without molestation. Prevost could thus strengthen Canadian defences without fear of interference from the Americans. Moreover, Colonel Baynes was received so courteously in Dearborn's camp when he went to present the proposal for an armistice that he was able to report to Prevost on American military strength and prospects.[32]

In Upper Canada Brock knew that after the failure at Fort Malden the next threat was likely to come along the Niagara frontier, and immediately visited it. The inability of the United States to coordinate its attacks meant that the British could use their best general to defend the two main Upper Canadian fronts. Madison had informed Dearborn that the United States was not calling off the war, and that he should resume his operations. After notifying Prevost, Dearborn did so early in September, but still, over two months after the war had begun, the American forces on the Niagara and Lake Champlain fronts were not organized for offensive warfare. Brock arrived at Fort George on the Niagara frontier just before hostilities were formally renewed there on 8 September. He had been anxious since his victory at Detroit to move on to the offensive, but was restrained by strict instructions from Prevost.[33] Neither Prevost, nor the British government in London, thought in terms of offensive operations on the Canadian frontier. Prevost's instructions were to make the best use of the resources he had, and any reinforcements that could be spared, to defend Canada. He was essentially fighting a holding action, hopefully until the United States should abandon the war.

The United States operations on the Niagara frontier were nominally under the command of General Dearborn, who was responsible for directing the invasion of Canada. Dearborn, however,

---

[32] CO 42/147, pp. 121-4.
[33] Henry Adams, *History of the United States during the Administrations of Jefferson and Madison* (9 vols., New York, 1889-91), VI, 340-44; Brock to Prevost, 7 Sept., 1812, Wood, ed., *Select British Documents*, I, 586-7.

issued no strict timetable for an offensive. Even if he had done so, it seems hardly possible it could have been adhered to, for it took the whole summer to assemble enough American troops to launch an attack. The commander on the Niagara front, Stephen Van Renssalaer, was a political appointment by the governor of New York; as New York militia would form the majority of the troops on this battlefront, a New York politician would lead them. The commander leaned heavily on the advice of the more experienced Colonel Solomon Van Renssalaer, his cousin.

By the end of September, with the arrival of over 1,600 regulars under Brigadier-General Alexander Smyth, Van Renssalaer theoretically had some 6,000 men under his command. Yet the militia, although impatient for action so they could go home, were ill-trained for the amphibious operation necessary on the Niagara frontier, and the regulars did not wish to trust their fortunes to the orders of a militia commander. Smyth, an Irishman who had settled in Virginia, showed a marked reluctance to place the national interests before the usual resentment of regulars against militia officers. In the first week of October he ignored Van Renssalaer's request that they should meet to discuss the manner in which the regulars would combine with the militia in an attack across the river.[34]

In spite of this dissension, it seemed for a time that events might be going the way of the Americans. Lieutenant Jesse D. Elliott of the United States navy had been sent to Lake Erie to organize a naval force to dispute British supremacy on the lake. On 8 October, showing some of the initiative of his uncle Matthew who had led the British Indians at the capture of Detroit, he commanded a small force of a hundred or so American sailors and soldiers in an attack on two small British brigs which had come from Amherstburg and anchored under the protection of Fort Erie. Elliott's small force rowed across the Niagara River in two boats on the night of 8-9 October. In an audacious stroke, typical of American naval action throughout this War of 1812, Elliott quickly seized the two British brigs. The wind was not strong enough to take the two vessels into the lake, and the Americans were obliged to run down the river under

---

[34] Adams, *History*, VI, 341-6.

heavy fire from the British forts. The *Caledonia* was safely beached under the protection of one of the American batteries at Black Rock, but the *Detroit* could not be extricated, and after a spirited struggle was destroyed. For the Americans it had been a great morale booster, of the type which the British expected their own navy to perform.[35]

Elliott's successful sortie seemed a good omen, and in any case it was obvious that Van Renssalaer would soon have to attack the British positions. His force was now much superior to the British, who had less than 2,000 men even including the Indians, and the American militia were demanding action. Van Renssalaer had sent a spy to the British side of the river, and it appeared that even without the active co-operation of General Smyth he could launch an attack with the New York militia and the regulars who were with them. Van Renssalaer's force was gathered around the village of Lewiston, directly opposite to Queenston Heights. The British had most of their troops at Fort George, near the mouth of the Niagara River, and at Forts Erie and Chippawa above the falls. The main difficulty with crossing at Queenston was that, though the river was only some 250 yards wide, the current was swift.

Van Renssalaer determined to cross the Niagara, capture the heights, and from there win command of the whole region. The problem with his plan was that there seemed no real chance of surprise. He would have to cross a swift river with inexperienced troops, probably in the face of stiff resistance. His difficulties became fully apparent early on the morning of 11 October when the attack was supposed to be launched. The boats did not arrive when the troops needed them, and Van Renssalaer was obliged to call off the attack for that day after his troops had spent most of the night preparing for action.

At dawn on the 13th the Americans tried again. Van Renssalaer wanted to send two columns, each of 300 men, across the river to make the first assault, after which the boats would return and ferry

---

[35] Elliott to Paul Hamilton, 9 Oct., 1812, Secretary of the Navy, Officers Letters, 1812, vol. 3, p. 93, National Archives (hereafter cited as SN, OL.); Brock to Prevost, 11 Oct., 1812, Tupper, *Life and Correspondence of Brock*, pp. 324–6.

reinforcements to the first assault columns. Even without Smyth's co-operation, Van Renssalaer had enough regulars to form one of the columns. On this occasion the boats were ready in the early morning and the troops embarked, but the Americans were soon spotted by the British. The militia column under Colonel Solomon Van Renssalaer landed first under heavy fire, and the commander quickly suffered several wounds. The column of regulars was delayed by difficulty with the boats, but when they also landed the small British force was soon in difficulties. Additional American reinforcements were brought across, and British Indians who came up from Chippawa were driven off.

On the British side General Brock had spent the night at Fort George. Hearing the firing he quickly rode to Queenston. Soon after he arrived, disturbed by the early American gains, he led an attack on foot in an effort to regain possession of the heights, was shot in the chest, and killed. The British were driven off, and another attempt at taking the heights by Lieutenant-Colonel John MacDonell, Brock's aide, also failed. MacDonell later died of his wounds. The Americans were successfully defending their first positions on the British side of the river, but their compatriots on the American bank were throwing the whole attack into confusion. Many of the militia now refused to cross, in spite of the exhortations of the officers, and the flow of reinforcements to the Americans practically ceased.

The American position now suddenly became precarious, for Major-General Roger Sheaffe, an American-born British regular, hurried from Fort George with reinforcements, joined up with the Indians, and attacked the hastily established American positions. Sheaffe had over 1,000 men (including the Indians), and the Americans broke. Their chances of escaping back across the river disappeared when it was discovered that many of the boatmen had fled in panic and the boats had dispersed. The cost was heavy; over 900 Americans (nearly half of them regulars) were taken prisoner, and over 300 killed and wounded. The British lost 14 killed, 77 wounded, and 28 missing. In spite of the death of General Brock, it was a major American defeat, and after the loss of Detroit was a crushing blow. Those American troops who had fought bravely had been sacrificed by inept preparations, quarrelling officers, inadequate

THE INVASION OF CANADA 47

training, and chaotic organization. The British under Brock and Sheaffe had acted promptly, and as at Detroit had discovered that because of American disorganization they did not have to contend with the marked superiority in numbers that had been expected at the beginning of the war. American General Smyth later commented about operations along the Niagara that it was 'a caution against relying on crowds, who go to the banks of Niagara, to look at a battle as on a theatrical exhibition; who, if they are disappointed at the sights, break their muskets; or, if they are without rations for a day, desert.'[36]

Even yet the Americans hoped to salvage something from this disastrous campaign on the Niagara frontier. Van Renssalaer could do little else but resign, and Brigadier-General Smyth was given the command. After arranging an armistice with Sheaffe, which could be terminated on twenty-four hours' notice, he made preparations for another invasion of Canada. Dearborn insisted that such an invasion should consist of a main assault force of at least 3,000 men. It was late November before Smyth considered himself ready to act, and by then conditions on the British side could have been a help to him. The Canadian militia had been under arms throughout the summer and fall, their farms and families were being neglected, and their own condition was made far worse by the failure of the British to transport the supply of clothing and blankets that had been bought for them in Lower Canada.[37]

The armistice terminated at Smyth's request on 20 November, and by the 27th he had between 4,000 and 5,000 effectives under his command. Smyth's regulars were supplemented by volunteers from New York, Pennsylvania, and Maryland. On the night of 27 November two advance parties were sent across the Niagara River; one to destroy batteries opposite Black Rock, the other to destroy a

---

[36] Van Renssalaer to Dearborn, 14 Oct., 1812, WD, LR, Reg. Series; Sheaffe to Prevost, 13 Oct., 1812, CO 42/147, pp. 225-31, also CO 42/148, pp. 17, 19; Edgar, ed., *Ten Years of Upper Canada*, pp. 150-60; Brannan, *Official Letters*, pp. 103-4 (Smyth comment).

[37] Van Renssalaer to Dearborn, 20 Oct., 1812, WD, LR, Reg. Series; Dearborn to Smyth, 21 Oct., 1812, *ASP*, *MA*, I, 493-4; Sheaffe to Bathurst, 20 Oct., 31 Dec., 1812, CO 42/352, pp. 160-62, 176-8; Adams, *History*, VI, 353-7.

bridge on the road to Chippawa. The object was to prepare for a major invasion, this time above the falls where the current was not as strong. The advance parties had only limited success, capturing the British batteries for a time, but their efforts were outstanding compared to the actions of the main army on the following day. In theory, there were supposed to be enough boats to embark the 3,000 men considered necessary for the attack, but the staff work and organization were incredibly bad. This was the first time that the troops had actually been embarked in the boats, and there was great confusion. Some boats were only half-filled, and by afternoon many of the troops were still on shore. No one knew just how many had actually been embarked; Smyth argued that not many more than 1,200 were in the boats, while Peter B. Porter of the New York militia thought that there were over 2,000. After moving the boats up river a little way to Black Rock, Smyth decided that he did not have enough men to launch the attack, and ordered the men to disembark.

Smyth still thought that the attack should take place as soon as possible, and 29 November was a day of preparation. Originally it was intended that the new embarkation would take place on the following morning, but some of the officers objected to an attack in daylight with the British fully alerted. Accordingly, the attack was again postponed – until before dawn on the morning of 1 December. Once again it proved impossible to execute the plan; two hours after daylight there were still only 1,500 men in the boats. After consulting with his officers Smyth called off the invasion. Yet again the men disembarked, firing their muskets in disgust and mixing in utter confusion with those who had been waiting so long to get into the boats.[38]

It would be difficult to imagine a worse military operation than that carried out by the Americans on the Niagara frontier. The government did not provide the trained men, the general officers did not produce a viable plan, the junior officers were unable to execute

---

[38] Smyth to Dearborn, 4, 14 Dec., 1812, WD, LR, Reg. Series; Brannan, *Official Letters*, pp. 105–9; Sheaffe to Prevost, 30 Nov., 1812, Bisshopp to Sheaffe, 1 Dec., 1812, CO 42/148, pp. 101–2, 105–9.

such orders as they were given, and many of the men disobeyed orders and milled around as a disorganized rabble. The transportation of several thousand men across the swift flowing Niagara River in an assault on the British who had expected an attack all summer called for a sophisticated military operation. As at Detroit the results were less tragic than ludicrous. In the first phase of the Queenston battle, the American regulars and militia had shown they could fight effectively when given the chance, but they needed leadership and training. The British defence had been carried out by a core of professional soldiers, aided by the Canadian militia. These militia had been a questionable factor at the beginning of the war, but had been stiffened in their morale by the very ineptness of the American attacks.

In spite of the failures at Detroit and Niagara, the whole situation could still change decisively in favour of the Americans if General Dearborn could carry out a successful attack northwards against Montreal. It was obvious to both sides that this was where the main blow should fall, and that a victorious American drive against Montreal would negate all the British victories further to the west. Yet, once again, totally inadequate preparations sadly handicapped the Americans. Ideally, the main attack should have been launched shortly after the declaration of war, but there were no troops to make it. The British, therefore, had the whole summer to strengthen their defences south of Montreal. The key line was that from Laprairie on the St Lawrence to Chambly on the Richelieu River. During the summer strong defence works were built on the Isle aux Noix in the Richelieu, effectively commanding the river. Also, a force of 150 Indians was stationed in advance of the Canadian line of defence to warn of any American movements. The British commander in this region was Major-General Francis, Baron de Rottenburg, a very experienced soldier on the Continent before he joined the British army, although his officers were more impressed by his 'fair, beautiful, lively, discreet, witty, affable' young wife. By the fall De Rottenburg had some 2,500 regulars and 3,000 embodied militia under his command in the defence of Montreal. As the weather deteriorated in October, he moved them into winter quarters, but they were still within easy distance of the line of defence south of Montreal.[39]

While the British prepared to meet an attack, General Dearborn was laboriously collecting an army at Greenbush, near Albany. In the autumn he moved north to Plattsburg on Lake Champlain, and prepared, with no great optimism, to push forward into Canada. This movement eventually took place very late in the season, in the middle of November. The American troops, some 6,000 strong, were ill-prepared and ill-equipped. They marched north through mud and water, sleeping in the open with no tents and few blankets. The British quickly learned of the American advance, militia flocked into Montreal from all quarters, and nearly 2,000 regulars and militia were sent forward.

The Americans marched to the village of Champlain near the Canadian border, and advance parties fought some skirmishes in Lower Canada. Many of Dearborn's militia, however, refused to go into Canada, and the General soon decided to retreat. His advance north can hardly be regarded as a serious attempt at the invasion of Canada. There were not enough troops, it was an exceedingly poor time of the year for effective campaigning, and even Prevost did not look upon the advance as a serious threat. It seems that Dearborn was more interested in showing his volunteers and public opinion some sort of advance than in undertaking a serious attack. As it was, the whole episode further damaged American morale. The army retreated to Plattsburg, and existed in miserable conditions before dispersing. An army surgeon spoke of them lying in the soaking woods, seized with dysentery, fevers, pleurisy, pneumonia and other ailments, 'which made the very woods ring with coughing and groaning.'[40]

From the Detroit River to Lake Champlain it was a tale of poor

---

[39] Prevost to Bathurst, 22 Sept., 17 Oct., 1812, CO 42/147, pp. 193–6, 215–19; Prevost to Duke of York, 7 Oct., 1812, War Office Archives, WO 1/96, p. 49; Tupper, *Life and Letters of Brock*, p. 84 (De Rottenburg's wife).

[40] Dearborn to Eustis, 24 Nov., 1812, WD, LR, Reg. Series; Prevost to Bathurst, 21, 28 Nov., 1812, CO 42/148, pp. 52–5, 60–62; Jesse S. Myer, *Life and Letters of Dr William Beaumont* (St Louis, 1912), p. 50 (comment of army surgeon).

3a. Sir George Prevost: a caricature of the Governor-in-chief of the British North American Colonies

3b. Major-General Sir Edward Pakenham, British commander at New Orleans

4a. Major-General Sir Isaac Brock, Canadian hero of Detroit and Queenston Heights

4b. Surrender of Detroit to Sir Isaac Brock, 1812

supplies, inept leadership, untrained soldiers, and a deficient overall strategy. The American government had simply not prepared for the war it was fighting. It had hoped confidently to capture Canada, but had done little to make this possible. The British on their part could be nothing but pleasantly surprised. The regular officers were not the best that Britain could muster, and many of the troops would have liked nothing better than the opportunity to desert to the United States. But against an ineffective American attack, they fought well, like the professionals they were. The Canadian militia had served far more effectively than the British authorities had expected. The American leaders had infuriated and disgusted their own militia, and had thrown away that burst of enthusiasm with which many in the Mississippi Valley greeted the war. From the British and Canadian point of view the land war of 1812 had been far more successful than expected. For the Americans it was a bitter disappointment; their operations had a ludicrous, comic-opera quality. Only at sea was their national pride assuaged, and here it was the British who suffered major shocks.

3
Shocks at Sea

Before the War of 1812 few in either Britain or the United States thought in terms of any serious, well-fought war at sea between the two countries. Britain had the greatest navy in the world. When in the winter of 1811–12 the American Congress publicly began to discuss what increase in the naval force might be needed to fight a war at sea, the British newspapers treated it as a joke, commenting that the Americans were unable to decide whether to defeat the British navy with a few extra frigates, or perhaps one or two ships of the line. Many in the United States also thought that it was futile to think of any real war at sea, and the official lists of the United States navy only served to increase this feeling of futility. At the beginning of the war the American navy consisted of sixteen vessels, and some of these were not ready for action. The largest ships in the navy (seven of them) were frigates, and the best of these were rated 44's. Against this the British had in commission in this period not only over one hundred frigates, but also well over a hundred ships of the line, of which none were rated less than 74's. On the face of it any contest would be futile.[1]

Yet the apparent farcical nature of such a contest was not borne out in practice. For one thing Britain's navy was committed in oceans all over the world. The war that mattered to the British was in Europe. Britain's resources were already stretched thin to meet

---

[1] For American strength at beginning of war see Roosevelt, *Naval War of 1812*, I, 76–104. In 1812 fighting ships were classified in general in three groups: ships of the line, frigates, and a variety of smaller vessels. The ships were rated in terms of guns carried, but often they carried more guns than their official rate. By this time ships of the line were rated as at least 74's, frigates generally ranged from 32's to 44's, and sloops and brigs were usually rated at the most as 22's. In the accounts of naval warfare in this book the official rate is given in parenthesis after the name of the ship.

the many naval commitments. Only a portion of the navy could be sent to the North American station. In the first period of the war the British were also suffering from over-confidence; the United States was not treated seriously as an adversary. This attitude soon changed. It was quickly discovered that the British navy would have its hands full in dealing with the innumerable privateers that sailed from American ports to attack the exposed British shipping lines. The American merchant marine had prospered since the Revolution, reaping great benefits from the opportunities offered by the war in Europe. Prior to 1812 American vessels had been seen in ports all over the world, and hundreds of merchant vessels became privateers after the outbreak of hostilities. Suddenly the British were to find that a large section of their navy had to be employed in protecting British commerce in the West Indies, and off the Canadian coast, or even in the Irish Sea and the Channel.

What came as a particularly harsh shock to the British public was the quality of American ships and seamen. The United States had a long tradition of shipbuilding, and it was quickly discovered that many of the privateers could simply outsail the more heavily armoured British vessels. To the very end of the war American privateers were able to risk sailing around the very coasts of Britain. Many were captured, but others escaped with a variety of British prizes.

Although the regular American navy was so small, it also provided considerable surprises for the British Admiralty and public in the first year of the war. The three largest American frigates – the *United States*, the *Constitution*, and the *President* – were quickly discovered to be the finest frigates afloat. They were rated 44's, but like all vessels in the period actually carried more guns than they were rated. In reality, they were more powerful than any British frigate. At first, as had been the case in so many engagements with the French over the previous twenty years, British captains expected to overcome any slight deficiency in force and win single ship engagements. The British public had grown accustomed to this, but was soon to be shaken out of its complacency. The navy was soon losing single ship engagements with American vessels of slightly larger or even equal force. The Admiralty attempted to explain this away by saying that

American frigates were actually line-of-battle ships in all but name, but the truth was that, though they were more powerful, the discrepancy in force was no more than British vessels had grown accustomed to overcoming in combats with the French. In the long run the Admiralty were obliged to issue secret orders that British frigates should not risk single ship engagements with American frigates, but should merely keep them under observation until a ship of the line could be summoned.[2]

Apart from the vessels themselves, another great problem that faced the British was the question of manning their navy. The Admiralty faced a constant shortage of experienced seamen, and was often obliged to fill up the crews with inexperienced landsmen. An incessant complaint of captains on the North American station was that they were below full complement, and that many of the men they had were practically useless as seamen. In time of war the hard core of experienced British seamen had to be spread thinly over the many new ships that were brought into commission. The problem was complicated by the incredible hardship and brutality of life in the British men-of-war. Desertion was commonplace, and the favourite place to which to desert was the United States. Conditions on American ships were better, and in the years before the war any British ship visiting an American port was in danger of losing a large part of her crew. An American naval prisoner in Dartmoor wrote in his journal that a fact worth the attention of any British politician was that '*an American, in England, pines to get home; while an Englishman and an Irishman longs to become an American citizen.*'[3] Perhaps the most significant backing for the American claim that their country was the home of liberty and opportunity for the oppressed of Europe was the manner in which the correspondence of both the British army and navy had to concern itself so much with the dangers of British soldiers and sailors deserting to the United States.

An additional problem on British ships in 1812 were the many

---

[2] Adm 2/1375, pp. 365–73; 2/1377, pp. 14–16.
[3] Benjamin Waterhouse, *A Journal of a Young Man of Massachusetts* (Boston, 1816; reprinted as Extra No. 18 of the *Magazine of History*, New York, 1911), p. 60.

Americans who had been impressed into the British service from American merchantmen in the years before the war, and who now refused to fight against their own country. The 2,500 Americans who were released from the British navy into British prisons because they refused to fight against the United States caused an additional shortage of seamen.[4] On their part the British protested bitterly that there were so many British seamen in the American navy. Naturalization did not affect the doctrine of inalienable allegiance; the sovereign had the right to the allegiance of his subjects – 'it began with their birth, and can only terminate with their existence.'[5] In theory, anyone born in Britain, even if he had emigrated to the United States years before, was liable to trial and a sentence of death if found fighting for the Americans. In practice, because of the fear of retaliation, such action was not strictly enforced. There were examples, however, and in July 1813 a British subject captured on board an American privateer was hanged. The Admiral in command of the North American station was ordered to have this brought to the attention of all British crews. 'We must on no account shrink from the duty of putting to death every British subject caught fighting against his country,' *The Times* was inspired to write. 'The Americans cannot, by any verbal process whatever, rob England of her right to the services of English-born subjects. They cannot naturalize against nature.'[6]

Yet it was clear that the Americans had no reason to depend on British deserters to man their ships. The regular American navy had so few vessels that the complements were always more than large enough, and even experienced seamen were turned away. British captains complained that the American navy was able to reject men who would have been considered able seamen in the British navy, even though able seamen often formed only a quarter of a British crew. A British captain sent out to American waters as late as the spring of 1814 commented privately that 'I cannot help feeling some

---

[4] Adm 98/123, p. 166; also *Hansard*, XXIV (1812–13), pp. 601–2 (statement of Castlereagh).

[5] 'Declaration of His Royal Highness the Prince Regent Relative to the Cause and Origin of the war with America', 9 Jan., 1813, *Hansard*, XXIV, 375.

[6] *Times*, 2 Aug., 1813, also 31 July; Adm 1/504, p. 257.

anxiety as an officer where I am liable to meet with an enemy so superior in size of ship, weight of metal, and number and quality of men.'[7] The American navy in the War of 1812 shocked British opinion, and in the long run necessitated the use of an exceedingly large British force on the North American station. Even the rabidly anti-American *Times* was obliged to comment ruefully by the summer of 1813 that 'we have now been kindly weaned of any too presumptuous confidence which we might place in the valour of our seamen. It was nevertheless a blessed, and a useful delusion too.'[8]

When the United States declared war on Britain, the British did not have a vast force off the American coast. The main vessels were the *Africa* (64), *Acasta* (40), *Guerrière* (38), *Belvidera* (36), *Shannon* (36), *Aeolus* (32), *Southampton* (32), and *Minerva* (32). The commander-in-chief of the North American station was Vice-Admiral Sir Herbert Sawyer, one of the less important figures in the British navy of the period. His squadron was based on Halifax, Nova Scotia. In May the Admiralty warned him, as well as those in command at Newfoundland, Jamaica, and the Leeward Islands, that war was a possibility, and that if he received official notification of it from Canada or the British Minister in the United States he could begin hostilities against American ships.[9]

Unlike American forces on the Canadian border, the American navy took the opportunity to act before the news of war reached the British. The main American naval force was concentrated in New York harbour in June 1812 under the command of Commodore John Rodgers. As soon as he heard of the declaration of war, on 21 June, he sailed in the *President* (44), in company with the *United States* (44), *Congress* (38), *Hornet* (18), and *Argus* (16). His object was a British convoy which he had heard was homeward-bound from

---

[7] Captain David Milne to George Home, 26 April, 1814, *Report on the Manuscripts of Colonel David Milne Home of Wedderburn Castle, N.B.* (H.M.C., London, 1902), p. 162.

[8] *Times*, 16 June, 1813.

[9] Adm 2/1374, pp. 357-63; Roosevelt, *Naval War of 1812*, I, 106. The British Minister in Washington, Augustus J. Foster, had given Admiral Sawyer information on the strength and situation of American frigates just before the war began, Adm 1/502, pp. 143-4.

Jamaica. Two days later the American squadron was diverted from its main task when it chased and failed to catch the British frigate *Belvidera* (36). The *Belvidera* had not heard of the war, but fled before the guns of the American squadron. She suffered some casualties, but escaped when the lead American ship made the mistake of yawing to deliver broadsides rather than sailing ahead to come up alongside the British vessel.

Rodgers had more disappointments. His ships missed the British convoy, although they chased it within less than a day's sail of the English Channel. The squadron put back into Boston late in August after making only seven captures, but by diverting British efforts Rodgers had allowed American privateers to take many prizes. The *Essex* (32), which had left New York on 3 July, had more success. She captured a British troop transport which was sailing to Quebec with over 150 men of the first battalion of the Royal Scots on board, the British ship *Alert* (16), and ten other prizes.

As soon as Admiral Sawyer heard of the declaration of war he sent a British squadron to cruise off New York, after first appearing off American ports to the north. The squadron consisted of the *Africa* (64), and four frigates. Like American Commodore Rodgers, the British commander, Captain Philip Bowes Vere Broke, had a major disappointment. The Squadron captured the brig *Nautilus* (14) in the middle of July, but the frigate *Constitution* (44) escaped after a three-day chase.[10]

In the first months of the war the British still generally believed that the United States would stop fighting when she learned of the repeal of the Orders in Council. At first Admiral Sawyer tried to ensure that nothing was done which would encourage the Americans to continue hostilities, and the British did not carry out a formal, extensive blockade of the American coast. Although many American ships were seized, the British were prepared to issue licences for the export of goods from the United States in American and neutral vessels. One of the main purposes of this concession was to maintain

---

[10] For these first skirmishes of the war see Adm 1/502, pp. 144–53; WO 1/96, p. 47; Rodgers to Hamilton, 1 Sept., 1812, D. Porter to Hamilton, 3 Sept., 1812, Secretary of the Navy, Captains' Letters, 1812, vol. 3, pp. 2, 12, National Archives. Hereafter cited as SN, CL.

the flow of provisions to the British troops in the Peninsula. As in previous years contracts for this had been signed, and licences were issued to allow these contracts to be carried out. The British Consul in Boston, Andrew Allen, found that New England merchants were quite prepared to continue supplying the British. It was emphasized in instructions from Britain and Admiral Sawyer that if possible the southern states, who favoured the war, should be made to feel its sternest effects, while the north-eastern states should be encouraged in their friendship for Britain.

The New England merchants, in spite of the American government's efforts to prevent trading with the enemy, had no hesitation in sending provisions to the British both in American and neutral vessels, not only to the Peninsula, but also through neutral ports to the British West Indies, and to Newfoundland, New Brunswick, Nova Scotia, and the rest of Canada. At times in the war it would have been exceedingly difficult to supply British troops in Canada without the provisions from New England. To some extent this trade was reciprocated, as in the first summer of the war the British government, anxious not to ruin the export trade of its manufacturers, allowed them to export some £5,000,000 worth of manufactured goods to the United States.[11]

In the summer of 1812 the Admiralty and its captains became increasingly disturbed that so many of the ships they stopped were sailing under licences, and there were signs that the British were beginning to treat the war at sea as a more serious struggle. In August Sir Herbert Sawyer was superseded in command of the North American station by Admiral Sir John Borlase Warren. Warren had rather a strange background for a naval officer. At one time he had intended to enter the church, and had been at Emmanuel before joining the navy. Helped by influential friends, he had advanced rapidly, and in order to co-ordinate the American war effort his new command included not only the traditional North American station but also the West Indian command based on Bermuda.

---

[11] *Hansard*, XXIV, pp. 576–7; Adm 1/502, pp. 140, 195, 207, 209, 221–3, 312; 2/163, pp. 9, 47; CO 43/49, pp. 233–4.

The need for a more rigorous prosecution of the naval war against the United States was becoming obvious as the summer wore on. As soon as the war began American privateers sailed to attack British commerce. Off Canada they took advantage of the lack of British naval protection in the Bay of Fundy, and threatened all ships sailing to New Brunswick and Quebec. A great variety of ships became privateers; those captured by the British in that region during the first summer of the war ranged from a vessel of 172 men and 16 guns to one of 8 men and 1 gun. When in late September Admiral Warren arrived at Halifax, he sent the *Africa* (64) and the *San Domingo* (74) to cruise off the Gulf of St Lawrence and the Newfoundland Banks to protect commerce. By the beginning of November 1812 American privateers had captured 150 merchant vessels in the area supposedly protected by the Halifax station.[12]

In the same month the Governor of Barbados wrote of the seas in his area being 'infested' with American privateers, fully manned and superior to British naval vessels in sailing qualities. The Admiralty soon began to feel the impact of this situation, for by January 1813 the influential association of West India merchants at Liverpool was complaining of the lack of protection. That they had good reason was borne out by young British soldier Charles Napier, later the conqueror of Sind. 'Two pacquets are due, and we fear they have been taken,' he wrote from Bermuda in January 1813, 'for the Yankees swarm here: and when a frigate goes out to drive them off, by Jove they take her! Yankees fight well, and are gentlemen in their mode of warfare.... These Yankees, though so much abused are really fine fellows.' Little wonder that Warren in the same month was requesting reinforcements to help cope with American privateers.[13]

Privateers provided a massive increase to American naval strength. During the whole war over 500 privateers were commissioned, and

---

[12] Adm 1/502, pp. 249, 303-4, 337; Tupper, *Life and Correspondence of Brock*, p. 215.
[13] Gov. Beckwith to Warren, 22 Nov., 1812, Adm 1/503, pp. 51-2; Adm 2/1376, pp. 1-6 (answer to complaints of West India merchants); Lieutenant-General Sir W. Napier, K.C.B., *The Life and Opinions of General Sir Charles Napier* (4 vols., London, 1857), I, 194.

they took over 1,300 British vessels of all types, although several hundred of these were eventually freed. In this profitable enterprise the New Englanders showed less reluctance than in the war on land. Of 500 privateers, some 200 sailed from New England ports. The British also engaged in privateering, with vessels from English ports and from the Canadian Atlantic Provinces, but after the early months of the war American merchant vessels were often blockaded in their own ports, and prizes became quite rare. British privateers also had to contend with the many ships of the regular navy.[14]

The activities of the American privateers produced great pressure on the Admiralty from British merchants, but the British public in general was most affected by the clashes between the British and United States navies in the first six months of the war. There had never been any doubt in Britain that the United States navy would be completely crushed should it ever dare to show a sail outside of port. In the first summer of the war, while American troops on the Canadian border were shattering American morale, the American sailors were rebuilding it.

Early in August the *Constitution* (44), under the command of Captain Isaac Hull, sailed from Boston, just a few weeks after narrowly escaping from the British squadron. Hull was an experienced officer, who had served both in the quasi-war against France in the late 1790s and in the Mediterranean during the American war against Tripoli. After sailing off the Gulf of St Lawrence, Hull turned south, and on 19 August at 2.00 p.m. in lat. 41°30′N. and long. 55°48′W. a sail was sighted in the distance. Hull had found the British frigate *Guerrière* (38), under the command of Captain James R. Dacres, who had previously issued a general challenge to any American frigate of equal force that wanted to fight. Hull made full sail in pursuit of the still unknown vessel. By 3.00 p.m. Dacres made out his pursuer as a man of war, prepared for action, and waited for the American ship. Hull's ship was undoubtedly more powerful, but in this first major engagement of the

---

[14] Edgar Stanton Maclay, *A History of American Privateers* (New York, 1924), pp. 225–8, 506–7; William S. MacNutt, *The Atlantic Provinces: The Emergence of Colonial Society, 1712–1857* (Toronto, 1965), p. 151; Gomer Williams, *History of the Liverpool Privateers* (London, 1897), pp. 431–52.

war the British still believed that the discrepancy in force could be overcome. The *Constitution*, rated 44, actually mounted 55 guns, while the *Guerrière*, rated 38, mounted 49; in weight of metal the broadside from the *Constitution* was over 700 lbs. while that from the *Guerrière* was just over 550. Like so many of the British ships in this period, the *Guerrière* was undermanned; its crew of some 280 men included ten Americans who were allowed to go below rather than fight against their own countrymen. The *Constitution* carried over 460 men.

The American ship bore down as swiftly as possible on the opposing frigate in an effort to bring her to close action, but was thwarted when the *Guerrière* fired a broadside, wore, and delivered another broadside on the opposite tack. These broadsides were ineffective, missing the American ship. After inconclusive manœvring for nearly an hour, Hull brought the *Constitution* to within fifty or sixty yards of the British vessel, and poured in a heavy fire. In fifteen minutes the *Guerrière's* mizzenmast fell over her starboard quarter, and her hull, rigging, and sails were badly cut up. Hull now placed his ship on the larboard bow of the *Guerrière*, where the British could only bring a few of their bow guns to bear. From this position he raked the British vessel, and inflicted heavy damage. For a time the two ships lay tangled together, but once they separated the ruin of the *Guerrière* was practically complete when her fore and mainmasts went over the side, leaving the ship an unmanageable wreck. The British cleared away as much of the debris as they could and prepared to continue the action, but the *Guerrière* was rolling in a trough of the sea, her main deck guns dipping under the water, and she was in no condition to put up any resistance. At 7.00 p.m. she struck her colours. The action had lasted over two hours; the *Guerrière* lost 15 killed and 63 wounded (some later to die), and the *Constitution* 7 killed and 7 wounded.[15]

On both sides it had been a bravely fought action. Hull reflected his delight in his report that 'from the smallest boy on the Ship to

---

[15] Dacres to Sawyer, 7 Sept., 1812, Adm 1/502, pp. 270–72; see also Adm 1/502, pp. 301–2; Hull to Hamilton, 30 Aug., 18 Sept., 1812, SN, CL, 1812, vol. 2, p. 219, vol. 3, p. 59; Roosevelt, *Naval War of 1812*, I, 123–35; Mahan, *Sea Power in its Relations to the War of 1812*, I, 330–35.

the oldest seamen not a look of fear was seen. They all went into action, giving three cheers, and requesting to be laid close alongside the Enemy.' On the British side the inquiries into the disaster laid much stress on the early loss of the masts, which was ascribed to their defective state, and also on the superior force of the Americans. Yet, it was also apparent that the gunnery on the American ship had been particularly efficient, and that the general fighting qualities of the American frigate had been a profound shock to the British. *The Times* reported Captain Hull's victory on the same day that it contained the news that his uncle, William Hull, had surrendered Detroit. There was no doubt that the sea battle made the biggest impact, and *The Times* commented that 'the loss of the *Guerrière* spread a degree of gloom through the town, which it was painful to observe.' In the following weeks the newspaper kept returning to the same theme, asserting that at one time some captains would have gone down with their colours flying rather than submit to the Americans, and admitting that, next to the British, the American sailors were the best in the world, and that their frigates were 'larger, finer, better built' than any the British possessed.[16]

The British hope that this American victory in a single ship action would prove to be an isolated mischance proved false in the following months. The tiny American navy was not swept from the seas by British power, and showed not only a willingness to engage but also the ability to win. The first American victory in the autumn was a comparatively minor affair, but served to demonstrate that the victory of the *Constitution* had been no fluke of faulty masts. In the middle of October the American sloop *Wasp* (18), Captain Jacob Jones, sailed south-east from the Delaware to intercept vessels trading with the West Indies. On the night of 17 October she sighted several sails, and chasing them on the 18th discovered a convoy of six vessels escorted by a brig. The brig was the *Frolic* (18), Captain Thomas Whinyates. She was about the same strength as the *Wasp*, but had a crew of about 110 as against over 130 on the American vessel, and on the 18th had suffered damage in a gale; she had lost her main yard arm and topsails, and had sprung the main topmast.

---

[16] SN, CL, 1812, vol. 2, p. 219; *Times*, 7 Oct., 1812, also *ibid.*, 10, 21, 29 Oct., 1812.

In the same gale, the *Wasp* had lost her jib-boom and two men.

On the morning of the 18th, as the seamen on the *Frolic* were repairing the damage, they sighted the American vessel chasing after the convoy. While the merchant vessels sailed on under full sail, the *Frolic* dropped astern and hoisted Spanish colours, in the hope of decoying the sloop under her guns. The American vessel ignored the ruse, and in mid-morning the battle began. The *Frolic*'s gaff and head braces were quickly shot away, and with no sail on the mainmast the brig became unmanageable. The *Wasp* manœuvred into position to rake the British vessel, while the *Frolic* could not bring her guns to bear. After suffering extensive damage the British ship tangled with the *Wasp*, her bowsprit between the American's main and mizen rigging. The *Wasp* had lost her maintopmast and most of the rigging, but the *Frolic* had suffered far more extensively. With the vessels tangled, the Americans boarded the *Frolic*, and took it without real resistance from the shattered British crew. British losses were 17 killed and 23 wounded, the Americans 5 killed and 5 wounded. The whole action had taken some fifty minutes. It had been fought in very heavy seas, but as in the *Constitution–Guerrière* action the American gunnery had been extremely accurate. It was small consolation to the British that later in the day the British ship of the line *Poictiers* captured the *Wasp*, unable to escape because of her damage, and recaptured the *Frolic*.[17]

Within a week the two navies met again, this time in a frigate action. On 8 October Commodore John Rodgers demonstrated the confidence of the small American navy when he left Boston on another cruise with the *President* (44), *United States* (44), *Congress* (38), and *Argus* (16). The *President* and *Congress* cruised in company, taking only a few prizes before returning to Boston at the end of the year. The *Argus*, cruising separately, had more success, taking a number of prizes, while the *United States* had most success of all.[18]

---

[17] Whinyates to Warren, 23 Oct., 1812, Beresford to Warren, 18 Oct., 1812, Adm 1/502, pp. 339–42; Jones to Hamilton, 24 Nov., 1812, Secretary of Navy, Masters Commandant Letters, 1812, p. 118 (hereafter cited as SN, MCL); Roosevelt, *Naval War of 1812*, I, 140, gives higher casualty figures for the British.

[18] Roosevelt, *Naval War of 1812*, I, 43–4.

This frigate was under the command of Captain Stephen Decatur, one of the heroes of the war with Tripoli. Sailing east on 25 October, in lat. 29N. and 29°30′W. he sighted a British frigate; it was the *Macedonian* (38), under the command of Captain John Surman Carden.

The *Macedonian* was a fairly new ship, and Captain Carden, although he did not like his crew, called her 'a fine frigate' when he assumed command in April 1811. The crew disliked Carden as much as he disliked them. One sailor who served on her, and later joined the Americans, called him a 'heartless, unfeeling lover of whip discipline'. In September he had left Spithead to escort an East Indiaman, and had finally left her on 22 October and began his cruise. Carden had a crew of under 300 on his ship against the 478 on the *United States*. He later argued that his frigate was perhaps 'the worst Man'd Ship in the British Navy', but he was of course anxious to excuse his own failures in the action.[19] As in the fight between the *Constitution* and the *Guerrière*, the American ship outweighed the British in broadside in the proportions of about 7 to 5.

At first, after the two ships came in sight of each other, the *Macedonian* had the advantage of being to windward, but Captain Carden failed to take advantage by closing rapidly to engage the American frigate; the court martial, damagingly for Carden's reputation, later pointed this out in its verdict which acquitted him for loss of his vessel. The early part of the action was fought at long distance, and the American gunnery was more accurate than that of the British, undoubtedly partly as a result of the presence of far more trained and experienced seamen. The *Macedonian* suffered very heavy damage, losing her mizen top mast, which fell forward into the main top. Carden then belatedly tried to close with the intention of boarding, but his damage and losses increased so rapidly that he was forced to surrender. One of the British crew commented that 'so terrible had been the work of destruction round us, it was termed the

---

[19] Carden's comments are in John Surman Carden, *A Curtail'd Memoir of Incidents and Occurrences in the Life of John Surman Carden, Vice Admiral in the British Navy*, ed. by C. T. Atkinson (Oxford, 1912), pp. 250, 269. The comments of the seaman are in Samuel Leech, *Thirty Years from Home or A Voice from the Main Deck* (Boston, 1843), p. 87.

slaughter-house'. British losses were 36 killed and 64 wounded, over a third of the crew, while the Americans had only 7 killed and 5 wounded.[20]

The American ship was more powerful, but its crushing victory was also due to the superiority of its gunnery, its crew, and even of its captain. One of the advantages of having so few ships in the American navy was that they could be commanded by seamen of the very highest quality. It is unlikely that the crew of the *Macedonian* was as bad as Captain Carden said it was, but the member of that crew who later joined the Americans asserted that many in the British crew were there against their will, while the Americans were volunteers: 'They understood what they fought for; they were better used in the service.'[21]

The final blow of 1812 came on 29 December off the coast of Brazil when the *Constitution* (44) met the *Java* (38). After Captain Isaac Hull had resigned the command of the *Constitution* it was given to Captain William Bainbridge, who sailed from Boston late in October. On the 29th he sighted the *Java*, and began a two-hour action at 2.00 p.m. Once again the American frigate was larger, although in this case its superiority in weight of broadside was in proportion of about 6 to 5 rather than the 7 to 5 of the two earlier frigate actions. There was also considerably less discrepancy in the complements of the two ships, as the *Java* was carrying over a hundred seamen to join British ships of war in the East Indies. Her complement was well over 400; not much under the *Constitution*'s crew of 475.

At the beginning of the action Bainbridge had to fight at a longer range than he wanted, but managed to close after about forty minutes. As she came up the *Constitution* inflicted very heavy damage on the British ship, and rapidly took command of the engagement at very close range. The British captain was mortally wounded, and after two hours' fighting the position of the *Java* was hopeless. She

---

[20] Details of the action are in Carden, *Curtail'd Memoir*, pp. 260–69, 303–5, 310–12; Leech, *Thirty Years*, pp. 126–50 ('slaughter-house' comment is on p. 132); Decatur to Hamilton, 30 Oct., 1812, SN, CL, 1812, vol. 3, p. 154. Three of those killed on the British ship were Americans.

[21] Leech, *Thirty Years*, p. 150.

had lost all of her masts, and had to strike her colours. She had suffered well over 100 casualties against 34 on the *Constitution*. The *Java* was so badly damaged that Captain Bainbridge destroyed her. The American ship was much cut in her sails and rigging, but her damage was not serious.[22]

The results of this first year of the war at sea had been a profound shock to the British. In the first six months of the war the regular American navy lost only three small vessels while cruising extensively, and all three lost ships had been taken by force so superior that no defence could be made: the *Wasp* (18) was taken by a 74 after its successful engagement with the *Frolic*, the *Nautilus* (14) fell in with a whole British squadron, and the *Vixen* (14) was taken by the *Southampton* (32). In the last case both vessels were wrecked on the rocks soon after the capture.[23]

On their part the British had lost three frigates – the *Guerrière*, the *Macedonian*, and the *Java* – in action with American frigates. The American frigates involved were acknowledged to be superior in force, but this was little consolation to a navy quite accustomed to overcoming odds. Moreover, the *Frolic* had been lost in an engagement with a ship of equal size before being recaptured, and the *Alert* (16) had been taken by the American frigate *Essex* (32). *The Times* in March 1813 noted that Lloyd's list contained notice of upwards of 500 British vessels captured in seven months by the Americans: '*Five hundred merchantmen, and three frigates!* Can these statements be true; and can the English people hear them unmoved?' Anyone who had predicted this a year before, the argument continued, would have been called a madman or a traitor. When an account was printed of a bloody battle with a French frigate, it was argued that the French were encouraged to bravery by the triumphs of the American navy – the French no longer had to go into battle convinced they were going to lose.[24]

---

[22] Bainbridge to Jones, 3 Jan., 1813, and journal extract, SN, CL, 1813, vol. I, pp. 5, 8½; Mahan, *Sea Power in its Relations to the War of 1812*, II, 1–7.

[23] James Lucas Yeo to Warren, 22 Nov., 1812, Warren to Croker, 2 Jan., 1813, Adm 1/503, pp. 57, 59; Roosevelt, *Naval War of 1812*, I, 116, 173.

[24] *Times*, 20, 24 March, 1813; Porter to Hamilton, 3 Sept., 1812, SN, CL, 1812, vol. 3, p. 12.

The navy obviously could not ignore the events of 1812, and soon after Admiral Warren assumed the command of the North American station he began to press for reinforcements, arguing that the difficulties of blockading the American coast, chasing privateers, watching for the American navy, and escorting convoys imposed too great a strain on his resources. In the winter of 1812–13 he increased his pressure for assistance from Britain. At the end of December he argued that the American frigates, because of their armament, large efficient crews, superiority in sailing, and large numbers of rifle and musket men had a great advantage over any single British frigate. As the United States was now confident at sea because of her maritime victories, and also might receive aid from ships escaping from France, Warren thought his force would be considerably helped by six or seven good sailing ships of the line, cut down as razees, and each carrying a complement of 360 men. In addition, he thought more men should be added to the complements of the British frigates on the North American station. All this was necessary, argued Warren, because there were swarms of privateers, and disorder and pillage existed in 'a very alarming degree'. Warren's task had become so complicated during the winter that he also became anxious to divest himself of responsibility for the West Indies, and argued that the commanders there should act independently of his control.[25]

The British Admiralty could do little else but respond to some of the requests of their new North American Commander-in-Chief, but while they supplied him with reinforcements they showed little sympathy with his difficulties. In a secret dispatch sent by Secretary of the Admiralty John Wilson Croker in the middle of November 1812 he commented dryly that it appeared that the national navy of the United States consisted of five frigates, three sloops, and six brigs. To contend with this, wrote Croker, Warren had been given three ships of the line, twenty-one frigates, twenty-nine sloops, and fifteen smaller vessels. The Admiralty was in process of sending him an additional three ships of the line, ten frigates, and four sloops, and he was authorized to buy some smaller vessels in Canada.[26]

---

[25] Warren to Croker, 5 Oct., 29 Dec., 1812, 25 Jan., 26 Feb., 1813, Adm 1/502, p. 306; 1/503, pp. 49–50, 110, 119.
[26] Croker to Warren, 18 Nov., 1812, Adm 2/1375, pp. 252–9.

It became obvious as the winter progressed that in spite of reinforcements Admiral Warren was unable to take control of the seas around America, and by January 1813 the Admiralty informed Warren that he would be given still more reinforcements; to accomplish this ships would be withdrawn from other services. Disappointment was again expressed that Warren, with his already large force, had been unable to intercept and capture American ships when they attempted to leave port. 'It is of the highest importance to the character and interests of the country,' wrote Croker, 'that the Naval force of the Enemy should be quickly and completely disposed of.' To accomplish this Warren would be sent more ships, including four more ships of the line. His number of frigates was to be established at thirty and sloops at fifty. To avoid any reoccurrence of the public shock at the loss of British frigates, Warren was told that 'it is highly desirable that ships should not, by being detached singly, be exposed to the risk of meeting a superior force of the Enemy'.[27]

In spite of reinforcements Warren continued to argue that he had insufficient ships to meet all his responsibilities. In February this produced a sharp reaction from the Admiralty. Again a detailed comparison was made between the paltry American navy and the huge British force, and on this occasion he was told that rather than receiving any more ships the British strength on the North American station might have to be reduced. Warren was rebuked for 'the facility and safety with which the American navy has hitherto found it possible to put to sea'. Presumably, the Admiralty commented sarcastically, Warren was exaggerating when he talked of '*swarms*' of American privateers, as they could not conceive he had left the principal American ports so unguarded that such numbers could escape.[28]

The Admiralty and Croker were being somewhat unfair to Warren. An effective blockade of the entire American coast would have needed far more ships than Britain could provide. In spite of the Admiralty's assertion that Warren had enough ships to close the American ports, it was quite obvious that the numerous bays and

---

[27] *Ibid.*, 9 Jan., 1813, pp. 365–73.
[28] *Ibid.*, 10 Feb., 1813, Adm 2/1376, pp. 73–87.

inlets on the east coast of America allowed American privateers to evade practically any blockade. Even the major ports could not be sealed for the entire year. The severe winter weather off the northern coasts meant that from November to March ships were likely to be driven out of position and many opportunities for escape presented. In less exasperated moments even the Admiralty was prepared to admit that Boston could not be blockaded with certainty during the winter months.[29]

In spite of all the difficulties, the navy began to tighten a noose around the American coastline from the beginning of 1813. Late in November the Admiralty had ordered Warren to institute a strict blockade on the Chesapeake and Delaware Bays. This blockade was formally proclaimed by Warren on 6 February, and it became more general in the spring when the Admiralty ordered him to institute a strict blockade of New York, Charleston, Port Royal, Savannah, and the Mississippi. It had also been emphasized in instructions to Warren that he was to impose a *de facto* blockade of all ports from which American privateers or naval vessels were likely to harass British trade. Any neutrals that attempted to enter or leave such a blockaded port before they heard of the blockade could be warned off or returned into port, rather than seized. In the spring and summer of 1813 it became far more difficult for American ships to leave port, although it was still impossible to watch all the river mouths and coves of this long coast.[30]

Along with the tightening blockade came an increasing care by the British that they should not engage in any single-ship engagements that they might lose. This had been indicated in Admiralty instructions since the end of 1812, and the orders became more specific in the spring of 1813. Warren was told that whenever possible he was to keep a ship of the line with each squadron of frigates, and he was particularly enjoined to keep a strong force off Boston, a favourite port for the American navy and one difficult to blockade.[31]

---

[29] See Croker to Warren, 20 March, 1813, *ibid.*, p. 343; also letters of Croker, 31 May, 17 June, 1814, Adm 2/1380, pp. 177–9, 196.
[30] Adm 2/1375, pp. 276–8, 337–8; 2/1376, pp. 179–81, 320–22; 1/503, p. 109; CO 43/49, pp. 262–3, 280–83; 43/50, pp. 39–40.
[31] Croker to Warren, 17 May, 1813, Adm 2/1377, pp. 14–16.

In spite of all the warnings American vessels succeeded in leaving port, and were still able to win engagements. The most dramatic cruise was that of the frigate *Essex* (32), under the command of Captain David Porter, which had left the Delaware in late October 1812 before Britain had begun her strict blockade in that area. Porter had been ordered into the South Atlantic, and cruised off the coast of South America until January 1813. He then decided to round Cape Horn, and attack British vessels, particularly the whaling fleet, in the Pacific. As usual the rounding of Cape Horn produced great hardship and shortage of provisions, but the frigate arrived safely at Valparaiso in the middle of March. Porter ran down the coast of Chile and Peru, and then sailed to the Galapagos Islands. All through the summer the *Essex* cruised in that area, seizing a dozen ships and causing chaos among the British whale fishers. It was not until October 1813 that the ship left the Galapagos to sail to the Marquesas for refitting, and by that time she had shattered British merchant shipping in the Pacific. It was to be 1814 before the British finally caught up with Captain Porter.[32]

Another American vessel free in the South Atlantic in the late fall of 1812 was the sloop *Hornet* (18), in the command of Captain James Lawrence. In February 1813 while sailing northward close to the coast of British Guiana she encountered the British brig *Peacock* (18), under the command of Captain William Peake. After manœuvring for position, the two vessels first exchanged broadsides at fifty or sixty yards, and the action was over in less than half an hour. The *Hornet*, after badly damaging the *Peacock* with her first broadside, took up a position on the starboard quarter of the British vessel. From there Captain Lawrence was able to bring his whole broadside to bear, while the *Peacock* could only reply with two afterguns. Soon every man at the after-guns of the British vessel was killed or wounded by the grape and small shot fired from the muskets and swivels in the American's tops. The *Peacock*'s topsails and gaff halyards were shot away, and the mainsail rendered useless. Captain Peake was wounded, staggered to his feet to take command of his ship and was then killed by a cannon shot. The battle

---

[32] Porter to Jones, 3 July, 1814, Brannan, *Official Letters*, pp. 347-9.

continued, but with six feet of water in the hold the British surrendered; the senior lieutenant having to wave his hat as the ensign had fallen into the water with the gaff.

The *Peacock* had been at a considerable disadvantage in this engagement. She was armed with only 24-lb carronades as against the 32-pounders of the *Hornet*, but she also suffered from the ineffectiveness of her gunnery. The rigging and sails of the *Hornet* were much cut, but her hull received little or no damage. The *Peacock* was so damaged that she went down with men from both crews still aboard; 8 British and 3 Americans drowned. Apart from this the British lost 9 killed and 28 wounded out of 122 men; the Americans 1 killed and 2 wounded out of 135. On receiving this news *The Times* thought it would be worth discovering whether the Americans had some secret in the management of their guns, or in the making of their shot and powder, but also attacked 'the imbecility displayed by Ministers in the conduct of the maritime war against America'.[33]

The difficulties of effectively blockading the American coast became fully apparent in the spring of 1813. When the *Constitution* slipped back into Boston at the end of February, nearly two months after defeating the *Java*, Admiral Warren was able to point out that his blockading squadron had been driven out of position in very heavy weather and driving snowstorms, but it was difficult to advance a similar excuse at the end of April. On 23 April Commodore John Rodgers sailed from Boston in the *President*, accompanied by the *Congress*. The *Congress* had an uninspiring cruise, but was not intercepted by the British in eight months at sea. The *President* had a far more dramatic voyage, and caused much more embarrassment to Warren. Rodgers sailed to the Azores, the Shetlands, the Orkneys, around Ireland, and across to the Newfoundland banks before returning to Newport, Rhode Island, in September. He had taken a dozen prizes. The *United States* and the *Macedonian* were less fortunate. They managed to escape from New York at the end of

---

[33] *Times*, 17, 18 May, 1813. Accounts of the action are in Frederick A. Wright to Warren, 26 March, 1813, Adm 1/503, pp. 244–7; Lawrence to Jones, 19 March, 1813, SN, CL, 1813, vol. 2, p. 61.

May, only to be chased back into New London, Connecticut, by a British squadron.[34]

When the news reached England that the *President* was out, and it was also feared for a time that the *United States* and the *Macedonian* had escaped, there was considerable criticism of Warren, and also fear that another blow would be delivered to British naval prestige. In July orders were again sent that no British frigate should engage an American frigate single-handed, and when the *President* was reported north of Britain the Admiralty found that the American war was becoming an even bigger burden. Ships had to be detached from other stations to go in chase of her; all to no avail.[35]

Rarely in the wars against France had the Admiralty waited so anxiously for news of a successful naval action to silence critics at home, and at last in the summer of 1813 came the news of the long-awaited victory. The British frigate *Shannon* (38), under Captain Philip Broke, had been watching the port of Boston, and waiting hopefully for a contest with an American frigate. Broke was an excellent captain, who took a far greater interest in gunnery than many officers in command of British ships at this period. At a later date Captain John Pechell, who commanded the *San Domingo* (74) on the American station, argued that Broke's methods should be a model for the British navy in this regard, that Broke had personally directed the mounting of the guns so that they threw in one horizontal line, and that his men were more effectively trained and understood gunnery better than any he had ever seen. The often casual methods of other British commanders in this regard, argued Pechell, was because in recent years the British had encountered few enemies at sea who were equal to them; thus had sprung up the idea, proved mistaken, that a British frigate could take on anything with one deck.[36]

---

[34] Warren to Croker, 8 March, 1813, Adm 1/503, p. 296; also see 1/504, pp. 87–8; 2/1377, p. 88; Rodgers to Jones, 27 Sept., 1813, SN, CL, 1813, vol. 6, p. 100.

[35] Admiralty concern is shown in Adm 2/1377, pp. 140–49, 159–71, 240–49, 264–7; also Warren to Croker, 4 Sept., 16 Oct., 1813, Adm 1/504, pp. 111–12, 210.

[36] Warren to Croker, 10 May, 1814, and enclosure, Adm 1/505, pp. 380; 387–94.

In Boston harbour was the American frigate *Chesapeake* (38), under the command of Captain James Lawrence, late of the *Hornet*. The *Chesapeake* was not one of the largest class of American frigates, and was about equal in strength to the *Shannon*, although its crew was somewhat larger. Both Broke and Lawrence were anxious for a fight, and although Broke issued a formal challenge on 1 June, Lawrence had sailed before the challenge reached him. There was no evasion. As the *Chesapeake* came out, the *Shannon* hove-to and waited for her. The first broadsides caused severe losses on both sides, killing the American sailing master, and mortally wounding Captain Lawrence. As he was carried below he told his men 'Don't give up the ship'. The first broadsides had severely damaged the *Chesapeake*'s rigging, and within little more than ten minutes the *Chesapeake* fell on board the *Shannon*, and Broke ordered the vessels to be fastened together. An arms chest on the American's quarter deck was blown up by a hand grenade thrown from the British ship, and Captain Broke led a boarding party on to the American ship. Sword in hand he took the *Chesapeake*'s quarterdeck. The hand to hand struggle was soon over; the whole action had only lasted fifteen minutes.[37]

Losses were heavy in the engagement. The British had 24 killed and 58 wounded, the latter including Captain Broke, who received a severe sabre wound. American losses were even more numerous; 61 killed and 85 wounded.[38] Both ships were seaworthy after the engagement, so decisive had been the initial accurate gunnery of the British ship and the élan with which Captain Broke had led the boarding party. The defeat was a severe blow to the Americans, who had almost come to believe that they could not be beaten in single-ship engagements. American victories were now, however, to be far rarer than in those first six months of the war when the British grossly underestimated their adversary.

Two months after the defeat of the *Chesapeake*, the American

---

[37] Broke to Captain Thomas Capel, 6 June, 1813, Adm 1/503, pp. 322-5; George Budd to William Jones, 15 June, 1813, SN, OL, 1813, vol. 2, p. 138; also D. L. Dennis, 'The Action between the Shannon and the Chesapeake', *The Mariner's Mirror*, 45, (1959), pp. 36-46; Adams, *History*, VII, 285-301.

[38] Adm 1/504, p. 8; Roosevelt, *Naval War of 1812*, I, 230-31.

brig *Argus* (16) met the same fate. The *Argus* had sailed to France with the American Minister to that country, and had then cruised in the chops of the Channel and around Cornwall, seizing twenty prizes, and causing great excitement, along with amazement, that this could be allowed to happen on the very coasts of Britain. On this occasion, however, the Americans had overreached themselves. On 14 August the British brig-sloop *Pelican* (18), under Captain John Maples, sighted the American vessel. The *Pelican* was a little better armed than the *Argus*, and carried a slightly larger crew, 116 against 104. The American vessel could probably have escaped, but chose to wait and fight. The action began at 6.00 a.m. within musket range. In a few minutes the American captain, William Henry Allen, had his leg shot off; he was carried below and later died in England. The action was fiercely fought, but on this occasion the American gunnery was again less accurate than that of the British; within thirty minutes the *Argus* was unmanageable. The brigs fell together, but, before the British could board, the American vessel struck her colours. She had lost 11 killed and 12 wounded. It was not a distinguished action from the American point of view; their gunnery had been below the standard they had set in earlier battles, and they had struck their colours before attempting to repel the British boarders.[39]

With the victories over the *Chesapeake* and the *Argus*, and a far more effective blockade around the American coasts, the British in the spring and summer of 1813 gradually began to regain some of the confidence and authority they had lost in 1812. American privateers were still active, and the British could still lose single-ship engagements, as in the loss of the brig *Boxer* (12) to the American *Enterprise* (14) off Maine early in September, but for the most part the British began to assert the naval dominance expected of them when the war began.[40] This great superiority of force began to have particularly destructive effects for the United States on her own

---

[39] W. H. Watson to B. W. Crowinshield, 2 March, 1815, Brannan, *Official Letters*, pp. 485–7; Mahan, *Sea Power in its Relations to the War of 1812*, II, 216–19.

[40] Adm 1/504, pp. 152–4; Edward R. M'Call to Isaac Hull, 7 Sept., 1813, SN, CL, 1813, vol. 6, p. 19.

coasts. Although many individual American vessels still escaped to harass the British merchant fleets, the Americans had no means of preserving their own shores from amphibious operations by the British. For the rest of the war this was a constant danger to the Americans – they had simply not provided a large enough navy in the pre-war years to pose any real threat to an enemy carrying out landings.

The area that suffered most from British attacks was Chesapeake Bay. In the spring and summer of 1813 the British raided at will on the shores of Virginia and Maryland. In April Warren sent Rear-Admiral Sir George Cockburn to the head of Chesapeake Bay with orders to enter the rivers and destroy anything that might help the American war effort. The American defences were so weak that the largest ship sent on the expedition was a frigate, and the force consisted of only 180 seamen, 200 marines, and a small detachment of artillery. On the night of 28 April part of the force went up the Elk River towards the village of Frenchtown. After going the wrong way in the dark, the British arrived the next morning, quickly drove off the few American defenders, burnt a large quantity of stores and some small vessels in the river, and retreated with only one man wounded.[41]

On 3 May Admiral Cockburn sent his force against an American battery at Havre de Grace. After a bombardment from the ships, the British marines landed, and the Americans fled through the town into the woods. Cockburn burned the houses of those Americans who had fled with the militia to show them 'what they were liable to bring upon themselves by building batteries'. From Havre de Grace Cockburn's force proceeded a few miles up the Susquehanna River, and spent most of the day wrecking machinery in an American cannon foundry. Once again the British had only one man wounded, although this small body of men was carrying out its operations on the line of communications between Philadelphia and Baltimore.[42]

Cockburn rounded off his expedition by sending his boats up the

---

[41] Warren to Croker, 28 May, 1813, Cockburn to Warren, 29 April, 1813, Adm 1/503, pp. 328, 330–33.
[42] Cockburn to Warren, 3 May, 1813, Adm 1/503, pp. 334–8; *ASP, MA*, I, 365–7.

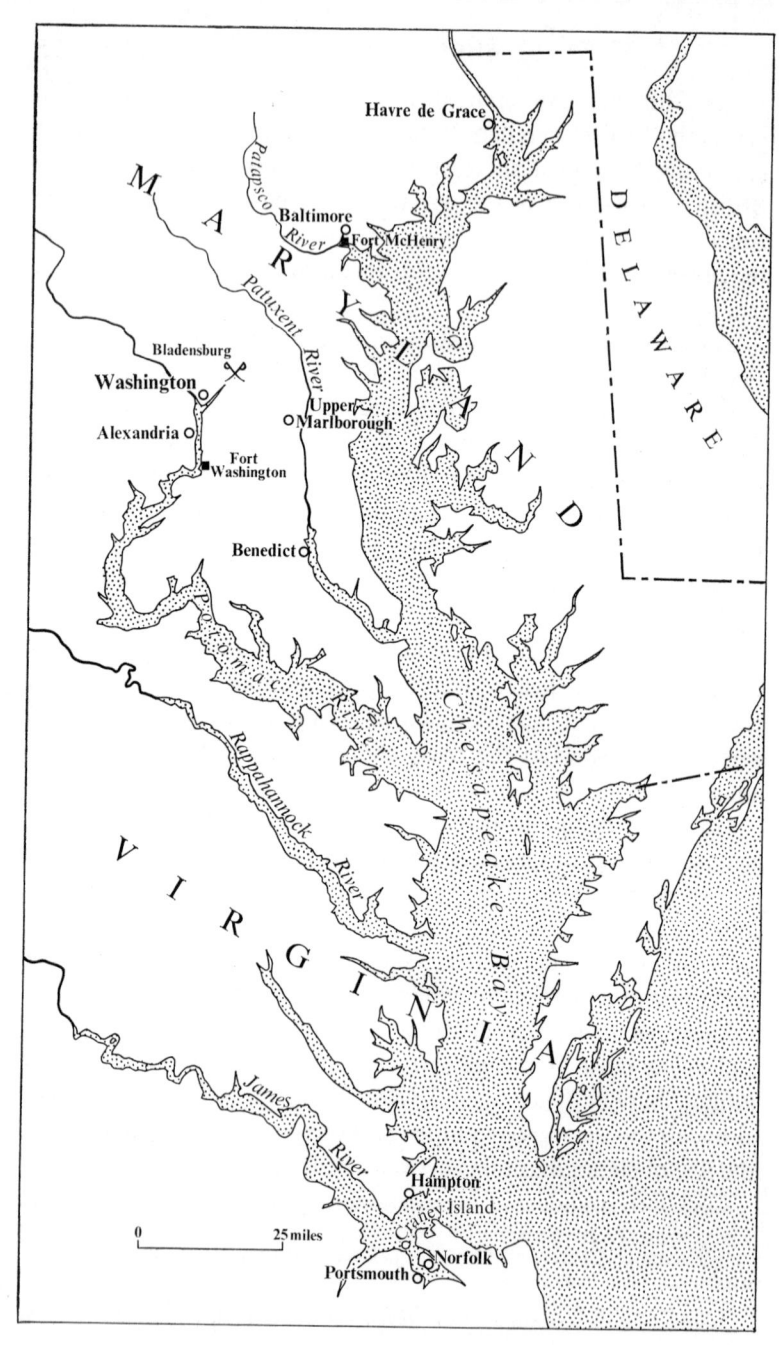

MAP 3 The Chesapeake Bay Region

Sassafras River to Georgetown and Fredericktown on the night of 5 May. The British lack of local knowledge again caused them to be delayed, and it was late morning before they reached their objective. They met some resistance from the American militia of the area, and as a result destroyed all the houses in the two villages except those in which the inhabitants had stayed. In general this was the pattern followed by the British. If the inhabitants resisted, their homes were destroyed and their property seized. When the inhabitants co-operated and made no resistance, the procedure was usually forced purchase of supplies rather than seizure. In any event the British fleet blockading the Chesapeake was kept supplied in cattle and provisions by the raiding parties operating along the shores of the bay. Warren's comment to the Admiralty on this region was that he had never seen a country so vulnerable and so affording the means of support for an enemy force.[43]

In this second campaigning season of the war, the British government was prepared to commit a limited number of additional men to amphibious operations in the hope of providing a diversion of advantage to Canada and of striking more destructive blows against the American coastline. To achieve this it was planned that Warren should use some 2,400 men. The major part of this force consisted of two battalions of Royal Marines (each of 842 officers and men) sent from Britain, but Warren was also given the use of some 300 British Troops from Bermuda, and another 300 men in two 'independent Companies' of foreigners. These two companies consisted mainly of French prisoners-of-war who had been recruited into the British service. In each marine battalion there was also a company of marine artillery, and more fire power was provided by the *Mariner*, a vessel fitted out with an assortment of Congreve's rockets, and carrying marine artillerymen trained in their use. Along with Warren's own naval resources, including marines, this gave him a useful attacking force.[44]

The overall control of the British amphibious operations and the

---

[43] Cockburn to Warren, 6 May, 1813, Warren to Croker, 28 May, 1813, Adm 1/503, pp. 278-80, 339-42; *ASP, MA*, I, 359-63.

[44] Croker to Henry Goulburn, 17 March, to Warren, 20 March, 1813, Adm 2/1376, pp. 146-8, 358-62.

choice of the point of attack was given to Admiral Warren, and the land force was put under the command of Colonel Sir Thomas Sydney Beckwith, a renowned soldier, who after serving in India had distinguished himself in the Peninsula. The secret instructions sent to him in the middle of March stated that the main object of the expedition was to effect a diversion in favour of Upper and Lower Canada, and that it was not intended that he should occupy any area. He was merely to raid and re-embark as soon as the object of a particular raid was accomplished. All government stores, harbours, and shipping were to be destroyed, but Beckwith could accept money or supplies from the inhabitants in return for not destroying their private property. He was given particular instructions not to encourage the slaves to rise against their masters, although he could allow individuals to come with him if they feared vengeance because of helping the British. In this case they were not to be looked upon as slaves, and if they wanted they could enlist in one of the British 'Black Corps' which had previously been raised in the West Indies.[45] As the raids increased in Chesapeake Bay, many slaves fled to join the British.

While the Secretary for War, Earl Bathurst, looked upon the expedition primarily as a means of providing relief for Canada, the Admiralty, thinking of their own problems, told Warren that if possible he should choose an objective which would cripple the American naval force.[46] Warren took this advice to heart, and decided that the British would first attack the major American naval base at Norfolk in Chesapeake Bay. Of major interest was the American frigate *Constellation*, which was in the Elizabeth River under the protection of two forts. The approach to Norfolk lay through Hampton Roads, and at the entrance to the Elizabeth River the Americans had placed a battery and 700 troops on Craney Island, and a line of gunboats strung out across the channel. To enter the Elizabeth River to attack the forts and the town of Norfolk, the British would first have to take Craney Island.

The troop ships from Europe arrived at Bermuda late in May, and in June the expedition set out for the Chesapeake. The attack

---
[45] Bathurst to Beckwith, 18 March, 1813, CO 42/23, pp. 97–8.
[46] Croker to Warren, 20 March, 1813, Adm 2/1376, p. 364.

on Craney Island took place on the 22nd. It was intended that while Beckwith landed on the mainland, and approached the island from the rear, other troops would assault the island in boats. The attack was poorly executed, and once again the British suffered from their lack of detailed knowledge of local conditions. The boats launching the sea attack found the approach waters too shallow, and grounded, while the troops attempting to flank the island from the mainland found that there were creeks too deep to ford. Both attacking forces withdrew, although total British casualties amounted only to some forty killed, wounded, and missing. The problem of naval commanders choosing ground on which the army should fight continued to plague the British on the American coasts.[47]

In an effort to secure at least some minor success, Warren now decided to attack the village of Hampton, near to Norfolk on the James River. This was a minor sortie after the attempt on Norfolk, for there was little else at Hampton other than an American battery and several hundred militia. The British troops landed on 25 June, drove off the militia, took the American guns, and re-embarked after pillaging the village. The houses were not burned, but the contents were seized or destroyed, and women were raped. The worst excesses were carried out by the French companies. Lieutenant-Colonel Charles Napier, commanding part of the British force, said that 'every horror was committed with impunity, rape, murder, pillage: and not a man was punished'. He also stated that his regiment, the 102nd, almost mutinied at not being allowed to join in the sack of the town. Napier later wrote to his sister that he disliked strongly one necessary part of his job – the 'plundering and ruining the peasantry'.[48]

Despite Napier's complaints that the Frenchmen had not been punished for their outrages at Hampton, Colonel Beckwith had in

---

[47] Warren to Croker, 24 June, 1813, Adm 1/503, pp. 371, 373; John Cassin to Jones, 23 June, 1813, SN, CL, 1813, vol. 4, p. 107; Lossing, *Pictorial Field Book*, pp. 675–80.

[48] There are accounts of the attack in Warren to Croker, 27 June, 1813, and enclosure, Adm 1/503, pp. 387–92; *ASP, MA*, I, 379–80; also see Guillard Hunt, ed., *Forty Years of Washington Society* (London, 1906), p. 90. Napier's comments are in Napier, ed., *Life and Opinions of Charles Napier*, I, 221–2, 225.

fact already decided that he would have to dispense with their services. He told Warren that they were constantly insubordinate, and that many were deserting to the enemy. Warren agreed early in July that the two independent companies would have to be sent to Halifax, ready to be embarked for Britain.[49]

To this point the supposedly major British diversion on the southern coasts of America had been little more than a minor piratical raid, in which one American village had been pillaged. This type of warfare continued in the following weeks, and Rear-Admiral Cockburn was detached with the 102nd Regiment to raid farther south along the American coast. On 12 July the British attacked Ocracoke Island and Portsmouth, North Carolina, captured two American vessels, and forced the inhabitants to sell cattle and provisions to the invading force. Meanwhile, Warren continued in the Chesapeake, obtaining supplies and causing local damage, but making no major attacks. In August he left the bay with his ships and troops, and sailed north to Halifax to escape the fevers that were besetting the British.[50]

The naval ascendancy which brought devastation to the population of Chesapeake Bay also brought difficulties to other parts of the American coast, even though the British generally attempted to avoid offending their many friends in the north-east. Sir Thomas Hardy, late of the *Victory*, commanded off New York, and kept Stephen Decatur's squadron blockaded first in that port, and then in New London, Connecticut, where it had taken refuge when the British had blocked its attempt to escape. In 1813 as the unexpected American naval successes of the previous year were succeeded by a gradual tightening of the blockade around the American coast, it became increasingly obvious that to hurt the British the Americans would have to carry out a successful invasion of Canada. It was on the Canadian border that the Americans had always hoped to win success, and during the winter of 1812–13 plans were made which it was hoped would redeem the disasters of 1812.

---

[49] Beckwith to Warren, Warren to Croker, 5 July, 1813, Adm 1/504, pp. 44–6.
[50] Cockburn to Warren, 12 July, 1813, Warren to Croker, 14 Aug., 1813, Adm 1/504, pp. 11–14, 47; also *ibid.*, pp. 70–73, 124, 171; Lossing, *Pictorial Field Book*, pp. 668–91.

4
America Tries Again

The loss of Detroit and the failure of Hull's campaign was a bitter disappointment to the enthusiastic westerners. They hoped for a quick reversal of fortunes, and for this placed their faith in William Henry Harrison, territorial governor of Indiana and victor of Tippecanoe. He was an astute leader, who won the confidence of his troops. At the end of August the Kentuckians appointed him major-general in their militia, but for a time there was uncertainty whether Harrison or Brigadier-General James Winchester should have overall command of the north-western army. Winchester was a Revolutionary veteran, an older man than Harrison, and had been given a regular appointment as brigadier-general in March. The problem was resolved in the middle of September when President Madison appointed Harrison brigadier-general and commander-in-chief of the north-western army, which was to consist of 10,000 men; Winchester chose to serve under Harrison rather than be transferred to the Niagara front.[1]

Even before Harrison had received his federal commission he had taken steps to end the rapid deterioration of the American position south of Detroit. His first task was to relieve Fort Wayne in north-eastern Indiana, which was besieged by the Indians. Early in September he sent an advance force of some 900 men from Piqua, Ohio, to the relief of the besieged fort. Harrison soon followed them, and relieved the fort with over 2,000 men.[2] This minor success on the western front at least checked the continual British and Indian successes, and Harrison was soon further encouraged by the news

---

[1] Harrison to Eustis, 28 Aug., 1812, WD, LR, Reg. Series; Eustis to Harrison, 17 Sept., 1812, Secretary of War, Letters Sent, Military Affairs (hereafter cited as SW, LS, MA).
[2] Harrison to Eustis, 21 Sept., 1812, WD, LR, Reg. Series.

that early in September two of the small American forts on the Wabash and upper Mississippi – Fort Harrison and Fort Madison – had repulsed Indian attacks. At Fort Harrison Captain Zachary Taylor was in command. He managed to keep the Indians out, although they set fire to part of the fort, and showed some of the confidence necessary in a future President when he told Harrison that 'my presence of mind did not for a moment forsake me'. At Fort Madison the attack lasted from 5 to 8 September. On the first day a soldier was killed and scalped within twenty-five paces of a sentinel, and on the next day his head and heart were held up on sticks before the garrison. The fort was not taken, but it was obvious that the American position west of Lake Michigan and north of St Louis was flimsy in the extreme.[3]

After the relief of Fort Wayne, General Winchester late in September advanced down the Maumee. On their march the Americans encountered a force of British who had been sent by Colonel Procter to join the Indians who were still believed to be besieging Fort Wayne, but these troops retreated without engaging the Americans. Winchester advanced to the site of old Fort Defiance at the junction of the Maumee and Auglaize rivers.[4]

On 24 September Harrison received the news of his appointment as commander-in-chief of the north-western army. He had already thought of a rapid strike with mounted troops against Detroit, but now devised a general plan of operations to capture that post. His intention was to have three columns converge on the rapids of the Maumee before advancing to attack Detroit; Winchester's force would form the left of these three columns, the centre column was to advance along Hull's route from Ohio, and the right was to advance from Upper Sandusky with the artillery.[5] Harrison certainly had more than enough troops to defeat the British on the Detroit frontier, but he did not have the command of Lake Erie, and, like Hull, by the time his army reached the Detroit River his land line

---

[3] Taylor to Harrison, 10 Sept., T. Hamilton to Lt-Col D. Bissell, 10 Sept., 1812, Brannan, *Official Letters*, pp. 61–5.
[4] Winchester to Eustis, 7 Oct., 1812, WD, LR, Reg. Series; Horsman, *Matthew Elliott*, pp. 198–201.
[5] Harrison to Eustis, 21, 24, 27 Sept., 1812, WD, LR, Reg. Series.

5a. Battle between the *Constitution* and *Guerrière*

5b. *Constitution* meets *Guerrière*, 1812

6. Massacre of American prisoners at Frenchtown on the River Raisin, 1813

of communication would stretch out tenuously through a wilderness, and would be vulnerable to the attack of hostile Indians. Attempts to quell the Indians of the region had been singularly unsuccessful. In September, after relieving Fort Wayne, Harrison had ordered the burning of the villages of the hostile Indians in the region, but his troops had found them deserted, and more ambitious efforts in October and November also had little result. In October Brigadier-General Samuel Hopkins led some 2,000 Kentucky troops to attack Indian villages in the Illinois country, but became lost and found nothing. Hopkins had a little more success in November when he burned Prophet's Town on the Tippecanoe, but again he had not been able to bring any major Indian force to battle. These raids were in any case unlikely to prove decisive, as the hostile Indians were being provisioned by the British at Malden, and were avoiding any large-scale engagements except when accompanied by British troops. It was quite obvious that to convince the Indians of British power the Americans would have to win back their position along the Detroit River.[6]

Impelled by the desires of the westerners, Harrison had decided to continue operations at a most unsatisfactory season of the year, but it quickly became apparent that any swift advance on Detroit was impossible. The heavy autumn rains soon delayed Harrison's centre and right columns. Provisions could not be moved over the muddy tracks through the forest, and on the Maumee Winchester's force settled down to await the coming of winter with insufficient food and clothing. By the middle of October they had rebuilt Fort Defiance and rechristened it Fort Winchester. Before there could be any large-scale gathering of troops on the Maumee, Harrison had to find a means of supplying them. Meanwhile, his troops gathered in Ohio, with little chance of speedy action, and American hopes of even regaining the pre-war position on the Canadian frontier became more distant.[7]

Harrison's last hope for prompt results was that as winter brought

---

[6] Harrison to Eustis, 21 Sept., 15 Nov., 1812, WD, LR, Reg. Series; Gilpin, *War of 1812*, pp. 147–50; Brannan, *Official Letters*, pp. 95–7

[7] Harrison to Eustis, 13, 22, 26 Oct., 9, 15, 20 Nov., 1812, WD, LR, Reg. Series.

snow and ice to the Old Northwest he could advance using sleds, and eventually cross the Detroit River on the ice to attack Fort Malden. Before Harrison could move enough troops to the rapids to begin this operation, General Winchester had shattered American plans. In January Winchester had at last been able to move his force down the Maumee to the Rapids. While there he began to receive messages from some of the inhabitants at Frenchtown on the River Raisin south of Detroit, saying that the village was a place of deposit for a considerable quantity of supplies, and that these could easily be secured as there was no large British force in the vicinity. Winchester had some 1,300 men at the Rapids, nearly all Kentuckians, and decided to send part of them to the River Raisin to secure the supplies and answer the request of the inhabitants for assistance.

On 17 January nearly 700 men marched from the Rapids for the River Raisin. Arriving there on the next day, they met stiff resistance from a small British force of militia and Indians. By nightfall they drove them off, and took possession of the settlement, losing 12 killed and 55 wounded. Winchester, although already well in advance of the main American base on the Sandusky, had now split his army, and had his advance less than twenty miles from the British on the Detroit River. On the 19th he left for the Raisin, taking some 250 men as reinforcements, and leaving the rest to guard his camp. Winchester had just under 1,000 men at the Raisin, but his position was a most dangerous one. The original force was behind pickets, but the reinforcements, who now formed the right wing of the small army, encamped in an open field. Winchester knew he was in considerable danger, but apparently thought that it would be several days before the British could react.

At Malden General Henry Procter acted swiftly when he heard of the American occupation of Frenchtown. On 21 January he crossed the Detroit River on the ice with nearly 600 regulars and militia and several hundred Indians. That night he camped within five miles of the American position, incredibly still undiscovered by the Americans, who in their exposed position should have been constantly patrolling the possible routes from Fort Malden. Before dawn on the 22nd the British troops advanced, dragging with them three 3-pounders and some howitzers. The British were only discovered when actually forming their lines for a bombardment and attack. The Americans still had a chance, as Procter had failed to send his troops into immediate attack to catch the Americans asleep, but the unfortified right wing was outflanked by the Indians and Canadian militia, fell back, and finally fled in panic. General Winchester was captured, and although the Americans within the pickets were still resisting, the American commander decided that if he did not surrender there was danger of a general Indian massacre. While a prisoner, therefore, he surrendered on behalf of the remainder of the men still fighting.

After the battle Procter immediately withdrew to Malden, and took with him some 500 American prisoners; the American wounded were left at the Raisin. By failing to provide sufficient protection for these men Procter earned for himself the undying hatred of the Kentuckians. On the next morning the Indians fell upon the wounded who were sheltering in the houses of the settlement. The houses were set on fire, and the wounded shot, tomahawked, and scalped. Probably thirty or forty died in this way.

At Frenchtown the American force had been destroyed. Over 500 were captured, a hundred or so killed, and only a remnant found their way back to the Maumee. The British in their attack had lost 24 killed and 158 wounded. Once again an American attempt to regain the initiative had ended in disaster. Harrison now abandoned any hope of making a sudden winter blow against the British on the Detroit River, and during the winter contented himself with building a new fort – Fort Meigs at the rapids of the Maumee.[8]

With the abject failure of Harrison's campaign, the only decisive question of the winter was whether American preparations for the spring and summer campaigns would be sufficient to overcome British defensive plans and produce a decisive result. Both sides in this winter of 1812–13 realized that the lakes were of vital importance, and began to consider how superiority could be achieved. During the first summer of the war the British had held a superiority

---

[8] Harrison to Eustis, 12 Dec., to Monroe, 4, 6, 24 Jan., 1813, WD, LR, Reg. Series; Horsman, *Matthew Elliott*, pp. 203–5; WO 1/96, pp. 52–5.

of force on both Lakes Erie and Ontario. If the United States was to conquer Upper Canada, it was essential that this situation should be reversed on at least one of the lakes.

At the beginning of September 1812 Commodore Isaac Chauncey was appointed commander of American naval forces on all the lakes except Champlain. He had a good reputation as a regular naval officer, and had served in the war with Tripoli. He decided to establish his headquarters at Sackett's Harbor on Lake Ontario, and arrived there in October. That summer the United States had used a force comprised of the *Oneida* (16) and six schooners on the lake, and had been faced by a much more powerful squadron of six British vessels; the four largest rated 22, 16, 14, and 10. This discrepancy assured that the Americans could not take control of the lake in 1812, but the British advantage had to some extent been dissipated by the inefficiency of the officers and seamen on the British ships. Many of them were Canadian landsmen, and as late as March 1813 a British officer commented of the British Lake Ontario squadron that 'I do not Conceive there is one Man of this Division *fit* to Command a Ship of War'. Taking advantage of this situation Chauncey was able to cruise on the lake after his arrival at Sackett's Harbor in October. The British squadron was superior in strength, but it proved unwilling to meet him in any serious engagement. Meanwhile, the Americans began to bring in carpenters and seamen from the East to increase their naval strength. The *Madison* (24) was launched in November, more schooners were purchased, and work began on the *General Pike* (28).[9]

The Americans had also started to plan a naval force on Lake Erie after Hull's defeat. A few vessels had been gathered at Black Rock in the autumn of 1812, and during the winter construction of new ships began at Presque Isle (now Erie, Pennsylvania). This effort increased after John Armstrong became the new Secretary of War in February 1813, and after the appointment of Oliver Hazard Perry, a young but experienced sailor, to command the new Lake

---

[9] Chauncey to Hamilton, 3, 26 Sept., 8, 21, 22, 27 Oct., 4, 5, 6, 26 Nov., SN, CL, 1812, vol. 3, pp. 14–192 *passim*; Roosevelt, *Naval War of 1812*, I, 191–6; A. Gray to Prevost, 12 March, 1813, CO 42/150, p. 108 (comment of British officer).

Erie fleet. Perry arrived at Presque Isle in late March 1813, and in spite of the efforts of the shipbuilders it was quite obvious that it would be well into the summer before the United States could contend effectively for the control of Lake Erie.[10]

While the Americans strove to remedy the paucity of their prewar naval preparations on the lakes, the British in Canada realized that a successful defence of Canada depended upon the maintenance of naval supremacy. To achieve this the lake navy needed not only new ships to match the American building programme but also regular officers and sailors to replace the Canadian landsmen. In late October 1812 Prevost warned the British government of American naval preparations, and argued that experienced naval officers and seamen would have to be provided from outside Canada; from England or from Admiral Warren's North American station. While asking the British government for regular seamen, Prevost also ordered the construction of new vessels at York and Kingston on Lake Ontario and at Amherstburg on Lake Erie, and asked the government in England to send the necessary supplies and ordnance.[11]

A major difficulty in organizing an efficient British navy on the lakes was that initially it was under the control of the Governor through the army Quartermaster General's Department rather than under the direction of the British Admiralty. Prevost realized the weakness in this, and when in the autumn of 1812 he asked the British government for seamen and naval supplies, he also asked that the lake navy should become the responsibility of the Admiralty. The British government realized the necessity of naval strength in Canada, but the delays in communication, and the other demands for supplies and seamen, made it difficult to give prompt satisfaction to Prevost. In any case, any reinforcements sent before the spring

---

[10] Jones to Perry, 5, 8, 23 Feb., 1813, Secretary of the Navy, Letters Sent to Officers, vol. 10, pp. 246, 248, 277, National Archives. Also see Ernest A. Cruikshank, 'The Contest for the Command of Lake Erie in 1812-13', in Morris Zaslow, ed., *The Defended Border: Upper Canada and the War of 1812* (Toronto, 1964), pp. 84-90.

[11] Prevost to Bathurst, 26 Oct., 21 Nov., 1812, 8 Feb., 1813, CO 42/148, pp. 3-15, 50-52; 42/150, pp. 37-43.

would have to travel overland, because of the ending of navigation on the lakes and the St Lawrence. It was not until March 1813 that Admiral Warren sent a small number of officers from his command to help ease the officer shortage on the Great Lakes, and in the same month the British government decided that the Admiralty would assume partial responsibility for the Great Lakes, and send out officers and seamen.

Sir James Lucas Yeo was ordered to proceed from England to Canada with over four hundred officers and men to take command of the lake navy. Yeo was a young officer, only thirty in 1813, but he had seen considerable service since first going to sea in 1793. It was emphasized in his instructions that his task was essentially defensive, and that he was to assist in the preservation of the North American colonies. The Admiralty had been anything but enthusiastic to assume new responsibilities in Canada, and although they agreed to send out as many naval supplies as possible with Yeo and to ask Warren to supply what he could, the army in Canada would continue to provide the lake navy with its basic supplies. The navy agreed to supply what ordnance it could, but the Admiralty argued that other demands were too great, and not enough notice had been given, for the navy to assume total responsibility. As a result of this, there was still a deficiency of guns when Yeo and his men joined the lake navy in May, and in the early summer land batteries at Kingston had to be dismantled to provide guns for the new ships. It was also obvious that because the United States had increased her lake navy still more British seamen would be needed; Yeo needed all he had for Lake Ontario and could do little for Lake Erie.[12]

Although both sides realized the importance of increasing their lake naval strength in the winter of 1812–13, and began the construction of new ships, neither side could hope to obtain a decisive advantage by the following spring. It was clear that the control of Lake Ontario would be in the balance in the early campaigns of 1813, while for the time being Lake Erie would still be decisively in

---

[12] Adm 1/503, pp. 178–9, 271; 2/1376, pp. 131–3, 183–5, 191–5, 249–64 (Yeo's instructions).

control of the British; Perry did not even assume his new command there until the end of March.

In spite of this lack of naval advantage the United States had no choice but to commit its land forces against Canada in 1813, for public opinion demanded some action after the disasters of 1812. As soon as the new Secretary of War Armstrong took office he presented to the cabinet his plans for the spring. These plans were based on the American expectation of the arrival of British reinforcements in Canada once navigation reopened, and on Armstrong's recognition that his land forces on the Lake Champlain front were inadequate for an attack on Montreal. In February 1813 the American army still numbered less than 20,000 men, and of these only 2,400 were on the Lake Champlain front. There was no hope of increasing this force sufficiently to attack Montreal before the expected arrival of British reinforcements on the reopening of the navigation of the St Lawrence in the middle of May.

As the United States lacked the troops to attack Montreal, Armstrong hoped to launch an attack to sever the St Lawrence route further to the West, and isolate Upper Canada. This would be effected by an attack against the British at Kingston, at the entrance of the St Lawrence from Lake Ontario, the defeat of its garrison, and the destruction of the British ships in its harbour. Armstrong then hoped to attack York, destroy the ships being built there, and lastly attack Forts George and Erie on the Niagara frontier. As Lake Ontario was normally free from ice by 1 April, but the St Lawrence did not become navigable until 15 May, Armstrong wanted to attack in that six-week period during which Prevost could not reinforce his garrisons.[13]

On 10 February Armstrong informed Dearborn of the campaign he was expected to carry out against Kingston, York, and the forts on the Niagara River. To carry out the first two objects 4,000 troops were to be assembled at Sackett's Harbor, and for the attack on the forts these would co-operate with another 3,000 men who were to be assembled in the neighbourhood of Buffalo. To assist the build-up

---

[13] Armstrong to Cabinet, 8 Feb., 1813, *ASP, MA*, I, 439; Adams, *History*, VII, 148–9.

of troops on Lake Ontario two brigades were to be transferred from Lake Champlain. In theory, it now seemed that the Americans had sensibly estimated their own deficiencies, and had formulated a plan which was best designed to give them success. In practice, the following weeks saw the vacillation and doubts that had helped to bring disaster in 1812.[14]

Within two weeks of telling Dearborn what his plan of campaign should be, Armstrong suggested a completely new method of accomplishing it. He now decided that a winter attack across the ice of the St Lawrence might be practicable. One of his main reasons for reaching this conclusion was that Captain Benjamin Forsyth, in command of the American garrison at Ogdensburg on the St Lawrence, had early in February successfully attacked a Canadian militia post at Brockville across the river. This limited success was short-lived, for the British were perturbed by the threat the American garrison at Ogdensburg presented to their supply lines. On 22 February, two days before Armstrong, on the basis of Forsyth's earlier success, suggested the possibility of a winter attack on Kingston, the British counter-attacked across the frozen St Lawrence. Lieutenant-Colonel George Macdonell led a force of some 480 regulars and militia from Prescott about 7.00 on the morning of the 22nd. They were slowed down by the depth of the snow, and the field pieces were for a time stuck on the banks of the St Lawrence, but by 9.00 a.m., after brisk fighting, the Americans were driven from the town and the fort, and the British had taken 70 or so prisoners, after losing 8 killed and 52 wounded. The Americans had 20 killed, and the remainder of the American force retreated towards Sackett's Harbor.[15]

The British sortie against Ogdensburg had been a useful victory, but hardly substantial enough to justify any basic change in American plans, yet it served to increase Dearborn's innate caution. Combined with the information that Prevost was visiting Upper Canada,

---

[14] Armstrong to Dearborn, 10 Feb., 1813 (extract), *ASP, MA*, I, 439–40.
[15] Forsyth to Dearborn, 8 Feb., 1813, WD, LR, Reg. Series; Armstrong to Dearborn, 24 Feb., Forsyth to Macomb, 22 Feb., 1813, *ibid.*, pp. 440–41; Prevost to Bathurst, 27 Feb., Macdonell to the Adjutant General, 22 Feb., 1813, CO 42/150, pp. 76–81; Edgar, ed., *Ten Years of Upper Canada*, pp. 175–8.

actually to inspect the military posts but in Dearborn's mind to plan a major attack, it served to change Dearborn's thinking from offensive to defensive. He now thought of his reinforcements from the East as urgently needed defenders rather than the additional force which would enable him to take Kingston, and he urged them to come with all possible speed to his assistance. By 3 March Dearborn had convinced himself that Prevost had assembled 6,000 or 7,000 men at Kingston, and that an attack might be expected on Sackett's Harbor within forty-eight hours. In reality, the British had nowhere near the force estimated by Dearborn at Kingston, and Prevost had not the slightest intention of attacking Sackett's Harbor across the ice. Dearborn, however, used his unjustified fears of British attack to reject Armstrong's plans for a prompt attack on Kingston, and in the middle of March began to suggest an easier, and less useful campaign, for the first major endeavour of 1813.

Dearborn's new plan put off the attack on the powerful post of Kingston. He now proposed that first York should be attacked, and the United States given complete control of the lake by the destruction of the ships there; he would then link up with the American troops from the Buffalo region to take the British forts on the Niagara frontier, and lastly the whole force would attack Kingston. Although it was generally agreed that the United States could conquer Canada only by attacking the St Lawrence as far to the east as possible, Dearborn was again, in these first campaigns of 1813, avoiding the main problem, and giving the British time to use the opening of navigation to reinforce and redistribute her forces along the St Lawrence.[16]

By the time Dearborn was able to organize his forces for the attack it was well into April. On the 22nd some 1,700 troops were embarked on Chauncey's vessels, but because of bad weather it was not until the 24th that they finally got under way. Many of the troops still thought that the attack was to be against Kingston or Niagara, but on the night of the 26th they came in sight of York, and lay off the town throughout the night. The British knew they were there, but were in no position to repel any sizeable enemy force. Major-General Sir

---

[16] Dearborn to Armstrong, 3, 9, 16 March, 1813, *ASP, MA*, I, 441-2.

Roger Sheaffe had under his command some 700 regulars and perhaps a hundred or so Indians, and York itself was poorly fortified.

The American troops, under the immediate command of Brigadier-General Zebulon Pike, began disembarking at 8.00 a.m. on the 27th. Strong winds drove the boats off course, and they came under severe fire from Indians under Major James Givins, but a bombardment from the American ships helped the American troops effect a landing. Fighting continued throughout the morning, but British resistance was weakened when the magazine of one of their batteries blew up, causing thirty or more casualties. After taking this battery, the Americans pushed forward, seemingly advancing to victory without undue loss. Yet, as the British retreated to the town, they blew up the main magazine. Its explosion caused many casualties among the American troops. The American commander, General Pike, was hit by a large block of stone and later died, and in all nearly 40 were killed and over 200 wounded. 'My wound, they say, is a very good one,' wrote one American officer who lost his leg, 'but it has maimed me for life.' The wounds from the debris of the magazine were particularly severe, and a surgeon wrote of the medical men who 'waded in blood, cutting off arms, legs, and trepanning heads'. On his part, he 'cut and slashed for 48 hours without food or sleep'.[17]

In spite of the shock from the explosion of the magazine, the Americans were in sufficient strength to continue their advance into the town. Sheaffe realized that his position was hopeless, and decided to retreat eastward, leaving a militia officer to obtain the best terms he could for capitulation. Before they marched away the British destroyed the naval stores, and a large ship building on the stocks, but the brig *Gloucester* (10) fell into the hands of the Americans. By the terms of capitulation it was agreed that public property

---

[17] Surgeon's quotation is in Myer, *Life and Letters of Beaumont*, p. 44, see also pp. 35–43. The comment of the American officer is in Stephen H. Moore to his brother, 15 May, 1813, Brannan, *Official Letters*, p. 152. For account of voyage and action see Chauncey to Jones, 28 April, 1813, *ibid.*, pp. 146–7; Dearborn to Armstrong, 27, 28 April, 1813, WD, LR, Reg. Series; Sheaffe to Prevost, 5 May, 1813, CO 42/354, pp. 132–5. Information from these sources is also used in the following paragraphs.

would be given up, while private property was guaranteed to the residents. In later months there was considerable argument between the British and the Americans regarding the treatment of the captured town, and American conduct at York, the capital of Upper Canada, was subsequently used as an excuse for British depredations at Washington in 1814. Even the defenders and residents had different views of American conduct, and one British emigrant who was at York even spoke highly of the conduct of the Americans: 'They used the people with great civility. They did not allow their men to plunder any property that could be prevented. In the night they put a sentry over every store but they could not keep the inhabitants from it who made shameful work in some people's houses. But the Americans were greatly praised for their good conduct.'[18]

The militia major who was left to surrender to the Americans was far more critical of American actions, arguing that the inhabitants were 'exposed to every sort of Insult and Depredation'. For the most part, although individual troops stole property, the Americans concentrated on the destruction of public property. The Parliament building, the residence of the lieutenant-governor, as well as part of the barracks, were burned, the government printing press was destroyed, and about £2,000 in the public treasury was taken. It had been hidden, but the Americans threatened to burn the town unless it was given up. Major-General Sheaffe had little reason to be pleased by the American definition of public property, as they took his baggage which he had left in his hasty flight; a few weeks later at Niagara Sheaffe's effects, including 'his most superb Scarlet coat', were sold at an auction. The Americans also destroyed all the possessions of Major Givins and his family, being particularly bitter against those who led the Indians.[19]

---

[18] Terms of capitulation, 27 April, 1813, are in CO 42/150, p. 163; quotation is from Isaac to Jonathan Wilson, 5 Dec., 1813, in Edith G. Firth, ed., *The Town of York, 1793–1815: A Collection of Documents of Early Toronto* (Toronto, 1962), p. 293.

[19] Major W. Allen to Sheaffe, 2 May, 1813, CO 42/150, p. 162; John Strachan to Dr James Brown, 27 April, 1813, Firth, ed., *Town of York*, p. 296; Sheaffe to Bathurst, 13, 15 May, Francis de Rottenburg to Bathurst, 25 Oct., 1813, CO 42/354, pp. 107, 109, 350–51; Myer, *Life and Letters of Beaumont*, pp. 45–6 (Sheaffe's coat).

The attack on York had been an embarrassment to the British, and had resulted in the loss of stores and property, but it was not a decisive victory in the struggle for the control of Lake Ontario. Ultimately, the American raid was far more important for the struggle on Lake Erie. Naval stores and provisions intended for Lake Erie had been destroyed, and before the British could replace them the Americans had severed communications on the Niagara River.

After the attack on York, the American troops were taken to the Niagara River, hopefully to help carry out the second stage of Dearborn's plan and capture the British forts in that region. The British knew that they were soon likely to be under severe pressure there, and when late in May the Americans began to bombard Fort George Prevost attempted a diversion by attacking Sackett's Harbor. He sailed from Kingston with about 800 men, and launched an attack early on the morning of 29 May. The British troops had difficulty effecting a landing. The boats assembled near Sackett's Harbor during the night, but they drifted in the current, and it was after daybreak before the troops could be landed. By that time the American defenders, consisting of 400 regulars and several hundred militia, were waiting to receive them. The British managed to land under fire, but when the Americans retreated to their block houses and fort the British advance stalled.

The American defence was ably conducted by Major-General Jacob Brown, a militia officer with very little experience, and indeed Colonel Edward Baynes, who commanded the actual British assault force, later admitted that the American defences could not be taken by direct attack. Prevost was never one to take risks, and when he realized that the British advance had halted before the American positions, he decided to re-embark his troops and return to Kingston. His casualties had been heavy – 48 killed, 195 wounded, and 16 missing – and he had achieved nothing by his attack on Sackett's Harbor. The Americans had suffered about 100 casualties, but they had put up an effective resistance to the British attack.[20]

---

[20] Prevost to Duke of York, 1 June, 1813, WO 1/96, p. 59; Prevost to Bathurst, 1 June, 1813, Baynes to Prevost, 30 May, 1813, CO 42/150, pp. 175–81, 183 (casualties); Jacob Brown to Dearborn, 29 May, 1813, WD, LR, Reg. Series.

Prevost was a remarkable optimist if he really expected that his ill-supported attack on Sackett's Harbor would divert American attention from the Niagara frontier. In reality, the Americans attacked in that region before Prevost actually launched his diversionary manœuvre. Dearborn put his attacking force under the command of Colonel Winfield Scott, and preparatory to its advance across the Niagara River the American fleet under Chauncey bombarded the British positions. On the morning of 27 May several thousand American troops landed about two miles from Fort George, British batteries near the landing point having been put out of action by the American fleet. The British commander, Brigadier-General John Vincent, had a total strength of nearly 2,000 regulars defending the Niagara frontier, along with a few hundred militia. He at first resisted the American attack, but on realizing that he was faced by 4,000 or 5,000 men decided to abandon Fort George and retreat towards the head of Lake Ontario. Vincent ordered the guns of the fort to be spiked and the ammunition destroyed, gathered together his men from Forts Erie and Chippawa, and retreated in good order. The British casualties had been quite heavy – 52 killed and over 300 wounded or missing against the total American casualties of some 150.[21]

The Americans had won control of the forts along the Niagara River, but the British force was still intact and able to base its operations on Burlington at the head of Lake Ontario. To win a complete victory in the region the Americans would have to engage and defeat Vincent's army. When Prevost heard of the retreat from Fort George he sent the British fleet under Yeo, with supplies and about 200 men, to support Vincent's army.[22] Within a few days it became clear that the support was hardly needed, for yet again the Americans made a fiasco of their advance into Canada.

At the beginning of June General Dearborn sent a part of his army westward from the Niagara River towards Burlington. The

---

[21] Morgan Lewis to Dearborn, 27 May, Dearborn to Armstrong, 27 May, 1813, Brannan, *Official Letters*, pp. 161-2; Prevost to Bathurst, 3 June, Vincent to Bathurst, 28 May, 1813, CO 42/150, pp. 185-7, 189-93.
[22] Prevost to Duke of York, 3 June, 1813, WO 1/96, p. 60.

advance was led by Brigadier-General William H. Winder, but on 5 June he was joined by Brigadier-General John Chandler, who took command. Chandler, who had served both on land and sea in the Revolution, was a politician who had seen long service in the Massachusetts militia before accepting a commission in the United States army in November 1812. After he had joined Winder he had a total force of some 2,000 men, and he immediately advanced to Stoney Creek and made camp for the night of 5–6 June.

At Stoney Creek the Americans were less than ten miles from General Vincent's army, and one would have expected considerable caution, but yet again an American army was taken by surprise. That night about 11.30 Vincent quietly moved forward with some 700 men. In the early hours, while it was still dark, the British troops charged into the American camp. It was a very dark night, and there was complete confusion. Chandler was hurt in falling from his horse, wandered over to a party he thought to be Americans, and was captured by the British. Winder also was captured, and among 125 American prisoners there were 2 brigadier-generals and 7 other officers; the Americans also lost 55 killed and wounded. British casualties were heavy – 23 killed, 136 wounded, and 55 missing – but when the British broke off the engagement before daylight, the demoralized American force fell back. Once again an American invasion force was in retreat.[23]

On 7 June when Major-General Morgan Lewis took command of the American army at Forty Mile Creek he was quickly under pressure, for the British fleet under Yeo appeared off the coast, and on the following day Indian skirmishers harassed his outlying posts. That morning the American army retreated to Fort George, followed by the Indians and militia. All this proved too much for Dearborn, who for some time had been complaining of his health. He now gave up the direct command of his armies, leaving General Lewis with the task of dealing with an increasingly sorry situation, for a stalemate was again developing on the Niagara frontier. The

---

[23] Vincent to Prevost, 6 June, 1813, CO 42/151, pp. 20–24, 26; Chandler to Dearborn, 18 June, Dearborn to Armstrong, 6 June, 1813, *ASP, MA*, I, 445, 448.

Americans still held Fort George, and concentrated their troops there, but it was more a prison than a bastion as the British advanced from the head of the lake to regain the ground they had previously evacuated. The Americans had abandoned Forts Erie and Chippawa, placing all their hopes on Fort George.[24]

The main American attempt to venture forth from Fort George in June resulted in another severe setback. On 23 June 540 men were sent to attack a British advanced post at Beaver Dam. On the morning of the 24th the Americans were attacked by Indians. At first they drove them off, but with several hundred Indians renewing their harassment of the American troops, the American commander, Lieutenant-Colonel C. G. Boerstler, decided to surrender his whole force to a small party of British troops rather than risk an Indian massacre. Early in July the Secretary of War agreed that for reasons of health Dearborn should give up his command.[25]

An additional and major embarrassment to the Americans on the Niagara frontier was that in spite of all their efforts they had not won naval control of Lake Ontario. Of major importance had been the launching of the British *Wolfe* (23) at Kingston in the spring; this had given the control of the lake to the British and enabled Yeo to sail to aid the British armies on the Niagara frontier while Chauncey sheltered in Sackett's Harbor. The British advantage would have been more lasting but for the failure of Prevost's attack on Sackett's Harbor at the end of May, for the British failed to destroy the *General Pike* (26), which was under construction. She was ready to sail by the latter part of July, and with this additional force Chauncey was once again able to risk leaving Sackett's Harbor. At the end of the month he first sailed to Niagara, and then to York, which the British were no longer attempting to defend. On 31 July York was again occupied by the Americans, storehouses were burned, and some property seized, but there was practically no public property left in the town. When Chauncey sailed from York it seemed likely

---

[24] Prevost to Bathurst, 14 June, 3 July, 1813, CO 42/151, pp. 16-18, 46-8; Lewis to Armstrong, 14 June, 1813, WD, LR, Reg. Series.

[25] Dearborn to Armstrong, 25 June, 1813, Brannan, *Official Letters*, pp. 173-4; C. Bisshopp to Vincent, 24 June, 1813, CO 42/151, pp. 52-3, 58 (prisoners taken).

that a naval engagement to decide the control of Lake Ontario would soon take place.[26]

Yeo sailed from Kingston with his squadron at the beginning of August, and on the morning of the 7th came up to the Americans anchored off Fort Niagara. The American squadron was slightly superior in force, although it was exceedingly difficult to take advantage of this owing to the inefficient sailing qualities of the schooners that formed a large part of the American squadron. In the long run neither Chauncey nor Yeo were prepared to take the risks necessary to win a decisive victory, and losses were more by accident than design. During the night of 7–8 August, after considerable manœuvring, two of the American schooners overturned and sank in a heavy squall. On the following two days evasion continued, neither commander wanting to risk losing the engagement. Yet the British took advantage of errors, when the Americans allowed two more of their schooners to be cut out and taken. When the two squadrons separated, the advantage rested with the British, but Yeo had not done enough to satisfy the British land forces. They had hoped he would win command of the lake, and join them in the reduction of Fort George.

Throughout the summer both Yeo and Chauncey claimed they were seeking action, but either one or the other on each possible occasion found sufficient reason to avoid an engagement. Apart from the caution of both commanders, the likelihood of an action was lessened by the circumstance that the Americans, with a predominance of long guns, wanted to fight at long range, while the British, with a majority of carronades, wanted to close.[27]

The inability of either side to win a decisive victory on Lake Ontario was of most benefit to the British. Their aims in the war were essentially defensive. The United States hoped to capture

---

[26] Roosevelt, *Naval War of 1812*, I, 267–83; Prevost to Bathurst, 8 Aug., 1813, CO 42/151, pp. 106–8. British naval force on Lake Ontario in July 1813 is listed in *ibid.*, p. 100. Chauncey to Jones, 12 June, 5, 8 July, 4 Aug., 1813, SN, CL, 1813, vol. 4, pp. 57, 156, 170, vol. 5, p. 69.

[27] Yeo to Warren, 10 Aug., 1813, Adm 1/504, pp. 168–9; Prevost to Bathurst, 25 Aug., 1813, CO 42/151, pp. 141–2; Chauncey to Jones, 19 Aug., 1813, SN, CL, 1813, vol. 5, p. 119; Roosevelt, *Naval War of 1812*, I, 269–74; Brannan, *Official Letters*, pp. 195–8.

7. The capture of the *Chesapeake*, 1813 (Aquatint by Teakes after Lee)

8a. Oliver Hazard Perry, American commander on Lake Erie

8b. Battle on Lake Erie, 1813 (Line by Tanner after Barralet)

Canada and force Britain to change her maritime policies. While stalemate existed, American desires were being thwarted and British defensive policy a success. Throughout the summer and autumn the Americans retained possession of Fort George, but their hold on the British side of the Niagara frontier was a precarious one, and the British army was still intact. American rewards in this area were simply not commensurate with the efforts expended.

While Americans were faltering on the Niagara front, General Harrison had begun his efforts to reconquer Detroit and advance into Upper Canada. The defeat of Winchester at Frenchtown in January had ended any hopes of a winter campaign, and in February most of Harrison's militia returned home after six months' service. The force that was left in the unfinished Fort Meigs on the Maumee was more worried about being overwhelmed by a sudden British attack than concerned with the invasion of Canada.[28]

Secretary of War Armstrong, whose plans for Kingston and the Niagara front had been rejected by Dearborn in the spring, found similar opposition on the western front. Early in March Armstrong suggested an attack against Malden, in which the troops would be transported by water from Cleveland at the mouth of the Cuyahoga River, and would land on the north shore of Lake Erie below Malden. The plan depended on naval control of the lake. Harrison, who had already decided that he wanted to advance against Malden around the west end of Lake Erie, objected to Armstrong's plan. He pointed out that he already had large deposits of stores on the Maumee for the coming campaign, and that until the United States won naval control of Lake Erie troops and supplies would have to be transported laboriously across Ohio by land. Harrison wanted to advance on Malden by land while the baggage of his army would be sent by water down the Maumee and along the edge of the lake; this might well be possible even if the British navy continued to control Lake Erie. Harrison also spoke out strongly for a large force, arguing that the initial enthusiasm had been lost, and he would have to make up for quality by numbers.[29]

---

[28] Harrison to Armstrong, 11, 18 Feb., 1813, WD, LR, Reg. Series.

[29] Armstrong to Harrison, 5 March, 1813, SW, LS, MA; Harrison to Armstrong, 17 March, 1813, WD, LR, Reg. Series.

During the winter General Procter could probably have inflicted another blow on the demoralized Americans along the Maumee, but he held off until the spring. In April he decided to strike at Fort Meigs before Harrison could set in motion his 1813 campaign against Upper Canada. By this time the fort had been reinforced, and was much stronger. Procter advanced from Malden by water with just under 1,000 regulars and militia, and about 1,200 Indians. The attack on the fort was a laborious affair. For several days in heavy rain the British worked to erect batteries on the north bank of the river to bombard the fort on the opposite bank. From the morning of 30 April they were under fire from the American fort. They were, however, soon able to return the fire, and on the night of 3 May were able to use another battery very close to the American position on the south side of the river. In spite of all this, even Procter later admitted that his artillery was making very little impression on the American defences, and it seemed likely that the expedition would prove a failure. That it was able to achieve a moderate success stemmed yet again from American blunders.

On the night of 4 May an American officer reached Fort Meigs to inform Harrison that Brigadier-General Green Clay, who had come down the Auglaize River with a reinforcement of 1,200 Kentuckians, was within two hours of Fort Meigs. Harrison immediately decided to launch a sortie against the British besiegers. He ordered Clay to attack the batteries across the river with 800 men. They were to spike the guns and retreat, while Harrison sent a detachment from the fort to attack the British guns on the south bank of the river.

The American attack took place on the morning of the 5th. It seemed likely that it would bring success, and that Procter would suffer for having allowed Clay's force to advance to the Maumee without harassment. The initial attack of the Kentuckians, led by Colonel William Dudley, overran the British batteries on the north bank. The guns were spiked and the objects of the sortie achieved, but when the Kentucky militia were ordered to withdraw they delayed too long, and were overwhelmed by a sudden British and Indian counter-attack. 500 Kentuckians were taken prisoner, and probably another 150 were either killed in the engagement or massacred afterwards by the Indians. As at the River Raisin the British did not take sufficient care of their prisoners. Some who were taken to the ruins of old Fort Miami after the engagement were tomahawked by the warriors, and the massacre only ended when Tecumseh himself rode in to stop it.

The Americans were more successful on the south bank. A detachment from the fort overran the British guns and took 40 prisoners before retreating into the fort. Yet the whole episode had been yet another defeat for the Americans. American losses were quoted in very vague terms, but the total in killed, wounded, and prisoners in these first days in May undoubtedly approached 1,000. On 5 May the British had lost only 15 killed, 46 wounded, and 41 prisoners, and they had lost few more on the whole expedition.

The ill-executed affair of the 5th tended to obscure the fact that Procter's siege of the fort was a failure. It had become obvious that his guns were making no impression on the fort and that he dared not risk a direct assault. Immediately after the American sortie against the guns Procter also ran into trouble from his militia and the Indians. On the 6th the militia officers petitioned to be allowed to return home. They pointed out that they had been unable to plant extensive crops the previous fall, and that the present campaign had already prevented the planting of spring wheat. They thought it essential that they should be able to plant corn to prevent famine the following winter. Militiamen were already leaving the camp, and by 7 May only about half of them remained. The Indians were also leaving in great numbers. To them the victory had been won on the 5th; they were now returning to their villages with their plunder from the Kentuckians, and prisoners they had not handed over to the British. On the 9th Procter abandoned his position, carrying away with him all his supplies and ordnance. The siege had been a failure, but luckily he could report a victory.[30]

Harrison's caution increased after the events at Fort Meigs, and he

---

[30] For campaign against Fort Meigs see Procter to Prevost, 14 May, 1813, CO 42/151, pp. 3–6, also pp. 7, 9, 12–14; Alexander C. Casselman, ed., *Richardson's War of 1812: With Notes and Life of the Author* (Toronto, 1902), pp. 148–176; Harrison to Armstrong, 5, 13, May, 1813, Clay to Harrison, 13 May, Brannan, *Official Letters*, pp. 149–51, 156–60; Horsman, *Matthew Elliott*, pp. 206–7.

now showed more willingness to accept Armstrong's suggestion that the advance against Fort Malden would have to depend on the United States attaining naval ascendancy on Lake Erie. In the meantime he built up his supplies at Upper Sandusky and Cleveland. The delay was no help to Procter. In the spring and summer he was facing a severe shortage of supplies. Apart from feeding his own troops, he had the considerable task of distributing rations to a host of Indians and their families. As the normal routine of the Indians had been interrupted by the demands of war, they depended on the British for their needs. By July it had become essential to relieve the pressure on supplies at Fort Malden, and Procter decided once again to move against Fort Meigs, hoping to occupy the Indians, and to live as much as possible off the country and from American depots.

On 20 July the British arrived before Fort Meigs, but the position had hardly changed, except that the fort was now stronger than before. It seemed an aimless campaign, and there was a hint of desperation in an attempt to lure the Americans out of the fort by the Indians fighting a supposed battle against non-existent American reinforcements. When this attempt failed, and the Indians began to leave for their villages, Procter decided to go down the Maumee, along Lake Erie, and up the Sandusky to Fort Stephenson. This posed a severe threat to Harrison, as his main supply depot was beyond Fort Stephenson on the Sandusky. The fort itself was a weak one, defended by only 160 men under 21-year-old Major George Croghan. Harrison decided to abandon the fort, and make his main attempt at defence near to the supply depot. Croghan, however, disregarded Harrison's order to withdraw, and at the beginning of August the British and their Indian allies appeared before the fort. As Procter had only light guns, he attempted to persuade the defenders to surrender by using the method employed effectively by Brock at Detroit. He sent word that unless the Americans surrendered he could not guarantee them safety from the Indians. Croghan refused to heed this request, and Procter decided on an assault.

The attack took place on 2 August, but the Indians would not advance into the American fire. The Indian warriors showed their usual dislike for attacking entrenched positions: they expected their

British allies to provide the guns to reduce forts. The attack of the British troops was beaten off, and they suffered nearly 100 casualties against American losses of 1 killed and 7 wounded. It was an inglorious episode for the British forces. The army returned to Malden with its morale reduced and the problem of supplies critical.[31]

For all the marching and counter-marching of these armies on the western front of the war, it was to be naval superiority that decided the fate of the Detroit frontier. Since Master Commandant Oliver H. Perry had arrived at Presque Isle at the end of March he had pressed forward with the completion of a fleet to challenge the British on Lake Erie. At Presque Isle were being built two 20-gun brigs, a schooner, and three gunboats, and at Black Rock there was a captured brig, the *Caledonia*, three schooners, and a sloop that had been purchased for the government. When the British had to retreat from their forts on the Niagara to the head of Lake Ontario at the end of May, the blockade of Black Rock was lifted, and in the middle of June the Black Rock vessels joined the rest of Perry's fleet in Presque Isle.[32]

To supply and provision his fleet Perry was able to depend on a supply route from and through Pittsburgh. In 1783 Pittsburgh had been a tiny frontier outpost of log cabins, fur traders, and drunken Indians, but by 1813 it was the main industrial centre of the West. Although still small it was supplying manufactured goods throughout the Ohio Valley, and had the advantage to Perry at Presque Isle of being reasonably accessible by way of French Creek and the Allegheny River. What could not be supplied at Pittsburgh came west from Philadelphia, or even, in the case of some of the guns, from Washington.[33]

---

[31] For second siege of Fort Meigs and attack on Fort Stephenson see Gilpin, *War of 1812*, pp. 202–7; Casselman, ed., *Richardson's War of 1812*, pp. 177–9, 185–8, Brannan, *Official Letters*, pp. 181–6.

[32] Chauncey to Jones, 9, 16, 23 April, 16, 29 May, 24 June, 1813, Perry to Chauncey, 29 March, 12 June, 1813, SN, CL, vol. 2, p. 159, vol. 3, pp. 1, 39, 143, 196, vol. 4, p. 103.

[33] Perry to Chauncey, 10 April, 1813, SN, MCL, 1813, p. 46; also C. P. Stacey, 'Another Look at the Battle of Lake Erie', in Zaslow, ed., *Defended Border*, pp. 109–11.

While Perry was preparing his fleet for action, the British were doing too little to maintain their naval ascendancy on Lake Erie. Their main vessels were the *Queen Charlotte* (18) and the *Lady Prevost* (12), and their main hope for the retention of naval control lay in the *Detroit* (20), which was being rushed to completion at Amherstburg in the early summer. The British commander on Lake Erie, Captain Robert Heriot Barclay, had a variety of problems. He had been sent by Admiral Warren from the North American squadron to help the British on the lakes, but when he arrived to take up his Lake Erie command in June he found that his ships were woefully short of seamen and supplies. Barclay, who had lost an arm at Trafalgar, was an experienced officer, but he had little support. The British commander on the lakes, Sir James Yeo, had brought experienced seamen with him from England, but he kept these with him on Lake Ontario, and ignored Barclay's acute shortage of sailors.

Barclay was also in a critical position in regard to the equipping and provisioning of his ships. Ordnance, ammunition, and other supplies for Lake Erie had been stored at York and been burned or taken by the Americans, and the retreat of the British from Fort George made it exceedingly difficult to send any other stores from Lower Canada. Barclay's supply line stretched all the way east through the lakes, down the St Lawrence, across the Atlantic to Britain; it made Perry's difficulties seem slight. When Barclay in the middle of July informed Prevost that he had no seamen, ordnance, or supplies to put in his new vessel the *Detroit*, Prevost sent an urgent request for seamen to Admiral Warren, but as Warren was in Chesapeake Bay when the letter reached him, it was late in August before emergency measures to send seamen from Halifax were taken. In the meantime Prevost ordered 40 seamen, who had formed the crew of a troopship, to proceed as rapidly as possible to Amherstburg.[34]

While Perry, in June and July 1813, prepared his fleet in Presque

---

[34] *Ibid.*, pp. 107–9. British naval strength on Lake Erie in July 1813 is in CO 42/151, p. 83. Prevost to Bathurst, 20 July, 25 Aug., 1813, Barclay to Prevost (extract), 16 July, 1813, CO 42/151, pp. 78–81, 138–44; Prevost to Warren, 24 June, 1813, Warren to Croker, 21 Aug., 1813, Adm 1/504, pp. 140–43.

Isle, Barclay was prevented by a sand bar across the mouth of the harbour from sailing in and raking the American ships. If Barclay had maintained a continuous, tight blockade, the Americans could not have risked dragging their vessels across the bar, but for a few days Barclay inexplicably and disastrously left the port unblockaded. He apparently thought the Americans were not ready to come out in his brief time away. Perry, however, took advantage of Barclay's temporary absence, arduously dragged his vessels over the bar, and sailed into Lake Erie.[35]

The initiative had now passed to the Americans. Perry controlled the lake, while Barclay attempted to solve his problems of seamen and supplies at Amherstburg. His task was complicated by the dire situation of the British army and their Indian allies. The shortage of provisions was becoming critical, and by the beginning of September there was practically no corn or flour left in the stores. The nearest depot of provisions was at Long Point on Lake Erie, and Procter exerted pressure on Barclay to sail and obtain those supplies. Barclay knew that to establish safe communication with Long Point he would first have to meet and defeat Perry's fleet.[36]

Barring some unforeseen stroke of fortune, Captain Barclay was doomed to defeat. He had six vessels – the *Detroit*, the *Queen Charlotte*, the *Lady Prevost*, the *Hunter* (10), the *Little Belt* (2), and the *Chippewa* (1). The *Detroit* had been armed with guns taken from Fort Malden, and the whole squadron lacked power: they carried no 32's and less than twenty 24's. Barclay was even worse off in regard to his crews. He had 364 men, of whom 214 were soldiers provided by General Procter. Perry's force was considerably stronger. He had nine vessels, of which by far the largest were the *Lawrence* and the *Niagara*, each rated at 20 guns. The American vessels carried fewer total guns than the British, but there was a marked difference in calibre: over forty 32's were carried on the American ships. Perry had some of the difficulties of Barclay in obtaining crews for his vessels. Although he originally had over 500 men, there were more than 100 unfit for duty by the time of the battle.

---

[35] Perry to Jones, 4 Aug., 1813, SN, MCL, 1813 14, p. 93.
[36] For the situation at Amherstburg see CO 42/151, pp. 150, 152; Adm 1/505, pp. 188–9, 201–2.

At Procter's request Barclay finally sailed from Amherstburg on 9 September. The Americans were at anchor at Put-in-Bay in the Bass Islands in Lake Erie, and sighted the British force on the morning of the 10th. There was a light south-westerly wind, and having the weather gauge Barclay attempted to bear down and bring Perry to action among the islands. This hope was frustrated when the wind shifted to the south-east, bringing the Americans to the windward of the British squadron.

Perry cleared the islands by about 10.00 a.m., and bore up to the British in line abreast. At 11.45 a.m. the British began to fire a few long guns, and about ten minutes later the Americans also began the action. Much of the British fire was directed at Perry's own ship the *Lawrence*, but Perry continued to close as fast as possible in order to make full use of his carronades. By 12.30 p.m. the *Lawrence* was within musket shot of the *Detroit* and was supported by two of the smaller American vessels – the *Ariel* and the *Scorpion*. The other main American vessel, the *Niagara*, under the command of Captain Jesse D. Elliott, did not follow Perry, and with her supporting vessels engaged the British *Queen Charlotte* at long range. As the *Queen Charlotte* was unable to use her carronades at that range, she came to join the *Detroit* in engaging Perry's flagship the *Lawrence*. Elliott still did not close with the British squadron, and for a time it seemed that the undoubted superiority of the Americans in metal was to be wasted.

The *Lawrence* continued to receive most of the British fire, and by 1.30 p.m. was so disabled that she could no longer be managed. By 2.30 she had no guns that would fire. Perry now made a decision that won him the battle; he was rowed from the *Lawrence* to assume command of the *Niagara*. Soon after he left, the *Lawrence* struck her colours. The British commander considered that to this point the day was going against Perry, but generously conceded that the American 'made a noble, and alas, too successful an effort to regain it.' The *Niagara* made all possible sail, supported by the smaller vessels, and bore down on the British, passing through their line. The situation had altered dramatically. Barclay's flagship, the *Detroit*, had been badly damaged in the engagement with the *Lawrence*, and many of the small number of able seamen on the British vessels were now dead or wounded. The captain of the *Queen Charlotte* had fallen early in the engagement, and under the inexperienced provincial officer the ship tangled with the *Detroit*. Barclay himself was so severely wounded that he had to relinquish his command, and his first lieutenant was killed. With few experienced officers and seamen left on their feet, the British were in no position to resist the more heavily-armed Americans, particularly as the matches and tubes taken on at Amherstburg were so bad that all through the action the British had to fire pistols at their guns to set them off. The two tangled British vessels were raked by the American guns, and were so disabled when they finally got clear that before 3.00 p.m. the British struck their colours.

Losses on both sides were heavy, and on the American side clearly demonstrated the nature of the action. Of the American total of 27 killed and 96 wounded, 83 were on the *Lawrence*, including 22 dead. British losses of 41 killed and 94 wounded were more evenly distributed than those of the Americans: heaviest were on the *Detroit*, 11 killed and 38 wounded (2 later died of their wounds). The controversy surrounding the part played by Captain Elliott of the *Niagara* persisted well into the nineteenth century; there seems little doubt that had he closed rapidly at the beginning of the action the Americans would have carried the day more easily and swiftly. But it was a bravely fought engagement, and it left the Americans in complete command of Lake Erie.[37]

The British troops at Fort Malden and Detroit were now in a desperate situation. Procter had persuaded Barclay to commit his inefficient force to action because of the absolute necessity of opening his supply lines to the east. The officer responsible for supplying the British and their Indian allies had written on 5 September that the

---

[37] British naval strength and losses in the battle are given in Adm 1/505, pp. 87, 196-7; Barclay to Yeo, 12 Sept., 1813 (Barclay quotation), Lt George Inglis to Barclay, 10 Sept., 1813, Adm 1/505, pp. 190-95. For Barclay's Court Martial proceedings, 9 Sept., 1814, see *Perry's Victory Centennial Number* (*Journal of American History*, VIII, no. 1, Jan.-March, 1914), pp. 129-46. American reports are Perry to Jones, 10, 13 Sept., 1813, *ibid.*, pp. 11-16, and extract from the log-book of the *Lawrence* in *ibid.*, pp. 119-21.

situation was 'truly alarming'.[38] There was practically no food left in the store, and such was the shortage of ready cash that the troops had often remained unpaid. What made the situation even worse was that Procter had stripped his heavy guns from Fort Malden to arm the *Detroit*, and these had been lost to Perry along with 200 British troops. There is considerable discrepancy in the British records regarding the number of troops Procter still had under his command, but it was not more than 800 to 900, including sick. On the day of any battle the actual number of effectives he could utilize would of course be much less. This made it essential that Procter, if he fought a battle, should make full use of his Indian allies. On the eve of Perry's victory, there were several thousand Indian warriors in the neighbourhood of Malden, as well as a great number of women and children.

As General Harrison could now transport his troops with ease to the Detroit River, and as the British expected him to bring more than enough troops to match the total British force of regulars and Indians, Procter's only choice was either to retreat eastward overland to link up with the British at the head of Lake Ontario, or to stand and fight a battle against Harrison at Fort Malden. As he had very few supplies, and as even a victory over Harrison would not free the lake, there was little choice but retreat. The major complication was the Indians. To them it was most difficult to understand why the loss of a fleet on Lake Erie should mean the desertion of the area they knew best. It was quite obvious that should the British abandon Fort Malden and Detroit there would be widespread defections from the British cause, even though it was now certain with the victory of Perry that the British could no longer supply the Indians and their families unless they retreated eastward.

By 11 September Procter knew that the fleet was lost, and he immediately decided that he would have to retreat. He was perturbed not only by the lack of supplies, but also by the consideration that with naval control of Lake Erie Harrison could turn his flank at will. Once this decision had been taken it was essential that the retreat should take place in a swift and orderly manner to avoid any chance

---

[38] CO 42/151, p. 152.

of being overtaken by the Americans while disorganized, and without prepared positions. Any hope of this was shattered by the indecision and eventual panic induced in Procter by his precarious situation and the opposition of his Indian allies.[39]

On 13 September Procter ordered the dismantling of Fort Malden. This began on the 14th, and the Indian leader Tecumseh immediately stormed off 'in a violent passion' to protest to Indian agent Matthew Elliott.[40] Tecumseh was no ordinary Indian chieftain. Since 1805 he had travelled widely throughout the Mississippi Valley in an effort to organize an Indian confederacy to resist the American pressure for land. Although his hopes of a firm confederacy had been shattered at the battle of Tippecanoe in November 1811, his reputation remained very high. He was spoken of with great respect by the American and British leaders with whom he came into contact. He had been born in Ohio, his home had always been on the Ohio–Indiana frontier, and he did not intend to yield without a struggle. In the following days Procter held two conferences with Tecumseh in an effort to persuade the Indians that a retreat was necessary. In the first of these meetings Tecumseh told Procter that 'We must compare our father's conduct to a fat animal that carries its tail upon its back, but when affrighted, it drops between its legs and runs off'.[41] The protests of the Indians and of their friends in the Indian department were to no avail; Procter insisted he must retreat, but was apparently driven by the Indian protests to say he would fortify and make a stand in the forks of the Thames as he retreated eastwards along that river. It appears unlikely that Procter had any real intention of seeking a major battle on that spot, but he apparently thought that if a battle were to occur he would have secured his retreat by having it on the Thames rather than at Fort Malden, where he feared he could be flanked by an American landing.

---

[39] Considerable information on the proceedings of the British forces from the time of Perry's defeat to the battle of the Thames has been obtained from the extensive evidence of the court martial of Procter in WO 71/243. Other sources are indicated where relevant.
[40] WO 71/243, p. 6.
[41] Casselman, ed. *Richardson's War of 1812*, p. 206.

The arguments with the Indians, Procter's attempts to appease them, and the preparations for the retreat, took over a week after the news of Perry's victory reached the British, and there was ample reason for haste when on 21 September Procter reported to Prevost that the American fleet and army had been reported among the islands in Lake Erie, and could soon be expected at Fort Malden. By this time Procter had already sent off the women and children by boat to travel on the Thames, and many of his stores had also been sent in advance.[42] On the following day the dockyard at Amherstburg was burned, and on the 23rd the public buildings were destroyed and Procter's army marched to Sandwich, opposite to Detroit. With the Americans near, a prompt retreat was essential, but Procter was still encountering considerable resistance from his Indian allies. Indian agent Matthew Elliott had been threatened with violence by the Indians, and there was considerable difficulty in persuading the warriors and their families actually to begin the retreat. The Indians also objected to plans for destruction of bridges on the line of march, and such was Procter's indecision on this point that the American army eventually found bridges intact when pursuing the retreating British.

On 27 September Procter, still at Sandwich, received word that the Americans were actually landing at Amherstburg, less than fifteen miles away. General Harrison had been on the Sandusky River when on 12 September the terse message arrived from Perry that 'We have met the enemy; and they are ours'. Harrison acted promptly. He arranged to be transported on the lake to Fort Malden with 4,500 men, while Richard M. Johnson went overland to Detroit with 1,000 mounted Kentucky infantry. While Harrison's troops disembarked at Amherstburg on 27 September, Procter at Sandwich made hasty preparations for immediate retreat. That night Major Adam Muir destroyed the public buildings in Detroit, and crossed the river with his troops to join the retreating British army; they were withdrawing along the Detroit River and Lake St Clair to the Thames. Along with the British went some 1,200 disillusioned Indians, many of them ready at any moment to join those others who

---

[42] CO 42/151, pp. 217–18.

had already deserted the British forces to make their own separate peace with the Americans.[43]

In the retreat from Sandwich not only the Indians but also the British troops lost all confidence in their commander. Procter's action on the retreat, and his subsequent confused report to Prevost on the manner in which he conducted it, leave little doubt that he panicked. For most of the retreat Procter was ahead of his troops, attempting to survey the country and find suitable places for possible resistance to the Americans. As at the same time he showed great concern for his family and personal baggage, the natural conclusion of the troops was that he was looking out for his own affairs. At Procter's subsequent court-martial the evidence of his second-in-command, Lieutenant-Colonel Augustus Warburton, made it quite clear that for much of the retreat Procter failed to provide instructions to his officers while he was absent. As a result the army retreated along the Thames in a desultory and confused manner.[44]

At the time Harrison landed at Amherstburg he expressed the opinion that there was 'no prospect of overtaking' the retreating British, and in the following days he proceeded in an unhurried manner. It was not until 2 October that the Americans finally left Sandwich in pursuit of Procter's force. Harrison took with him some 3,500 men, leaving behind Brigadier-General Duncan McArthur with a force to garrison Detroit. Harrison found Procter's conduct of the retreat so strange, including bridges left intact, that he later expressed the opinion that Procter must have thought that the Americans were staying at Sandwich.[45]

The first major crisis of the British retreat came at the forks of the Thames on 3 October. Procter had ignored his promise to Tecumseh that he would fortify the forks, and was in advance of the army viewing the situation around the Moravian Town on the banks of the

---

[43] Perry to Harrison, 12 Sept, 1813, *Perry's Centennial Number*, p. 109; Harrison to Armstrong, 15 Sept., 1813, WD, LR, Reg. Series; Harrison to Armstrong, 22 (extract), 23 Sept., Perry to Jones, 24, 27 Sept., 1813, Brannan, *Official Letters*, pp. 214–15, 220–21.

[44] WO 71/243, pp. 6–46 (examination of Warburton).

[45] Harrison to Armstrong, 23 Sept., 1813, Brannan, *Official Letters*, p. 214; Harrison to Armstrong, 9 Oct, 1813, WD, LR, Unregistered Series.

Thames. Tecumseh was in a rage, and agent Elliott 'extremely agitated' (one officer reported that the old frontiersman was in tears). Elliott came to tell the British officers that he could no longer answer for the consequences. Lieutenant-Colonel Warburton's urgent request to Procter for instructions was ignored, and on 4 October, after the Indians had skirmished with the advancing Americans, the retreat was continued. Tecumseh and his Indians now determined to fall back on the Moravian Town. So many Indian women and children were trudging along the road in retreat that the British column on several occasions had to be halted.[46]

On the morning of the 5th came the news that the British boats carrying supplies and ammunition had been captured by the Americans who were now on the heels of the retreating force. The retreat had become so confused that the boats had been allowed to remain in the rear rather than in advance of the army. The British officers were now expecting to fight in the Moravian Town, as the heights near there would be suitable for defence, and most of Procter's remaining ordnance had been removed there. But as the army was on its march about two-and-a-half miles from the village, it was met by Procter. He had heard the Americans were in close pursuit, and had decided to turn and face them before being overtaken. In addition, he apparently wanted to use a wooded area to impede the American cavalry, and was also disturbed by the fact that the women and children and the sick accompanying the army were still in the Moravian Town.

The ground on which Procter had decided to make his stand had certain advantages. His left was on the Thames and his right in thick woods bordering a swamp. Within a few yards of the river was a road, and on this road Procter stationed his only gun in the action, a six-pounder. To the right of the gun, forming the left of Procter's line, were the British troops. What with the losses on the retreat, and the general confusion, the first line of British regulars of the 41st Regiment numbered only some 280 men. About a hundred yards in their rear was drawn up a second line of 80 men, and near to this second line was a small body of dragoons, with whom Procter

---

[46] WO 71/243, pp. 11–12, 50 (quotation).

stationed himself at the beginning of the action. The right of the British line was formed by some 500 Indians, all that was left of the great force of warriors who had gathered around the British at Fort Malden. The situation was excellent for their mode of fighting, as they were positioned in thick woods; the trees thinned out towards the river.

After Procter had given the order to halt and face about rather than proceed to the Moravian Town, the troops waited for two or three hours while the Americans came up to them. Procter's indecision as to whether to retreat rapidly from Amherstburg, deserting the Indians and marching to the head of Lake Ontario, or whether to appease the Indians by making a stand and fighting a battle with Harrison's force, had resulted in a disastrous compromise. He had neither retreated fast enough to escape the American force, nor had rallied the troops and Indians by making a firm stand in a fortified position. The British troops were demoralized by a disorganized and faltering retreat, and most of the Indians had deserted the British. As a result Procter found himself waiting for an American army of over 3,000 men in an unfortified position, with one six-pounder, and a total force in the field not exceeding 1,000.[47]

When General Harrison first saw the position the British had chosen to fight in, he intended to use his infantry, but after his scouts had discovered that the first line of British troops was so thin that they were drawn up in open order, he decided to charge with Richard M. Johnson's mounted Kentucky infantry. It was most unorthodox to use mounted troops over a wooded terrain, but Harrison knew that his westerners were well used to riding in this type of country. The battle was a rout. The American horsemen charged straight through the first British line, most of the British infantrymen firing only one shot before fleeing. The gun was taken before it fired at all, and with the officers of the first line trying to rally the troops around the second, Procter was already leaving the field after a brief attempt to urge the troops back into action. The second line was soon overwhelmed as the Americans flanked it on both sides. So ineffective had been the British resistance that

---

[47] *Ibid.*, pp. 13, 51–2, 67, 160–61, 257.

Harrison later reported that the mounted Kentuckians had suffered only three wounded in breaking the first British line.

The only real resistance was put up by the Indians on the British right. They fought with all the bravery and desperation induced by their long sufferings. To them this was not a battle in the War of 1812, but one episode in a continual struggle to protect their villages and hunting grounds from the voracious appetites of the American farmers. Even while the British troops were fleeing from the battle, part of the Indian force was advancing to engage the American infantry. But as the left of Procter's line had collapsed, the mounted infantry were soon in the rear of the Indians, and in the desperate fighting Tecumseh was killed, the Indians broke, and the battle was over.

The casualty figures well reflected the sad demoralization of Procter's regulars. In the battle they lost only 18 killed and 25 wounded, while in the general retreat and on the field over 600 were taken prisoner. The Americans found 33 Indians dead, but the Indians always took away as many of their casualties as they could. The fate of Tecumseh's body was uncertain, but the Kentuckians carried away mementos of their victory in the form of strips of skin from a body they believed to be his. The Americans lost only 7 killed and 22 wounded, although 5 more subsequently died of wounds. With good reason Procter was subsequently court-martialled for his conduct following Perry's victory on Lake Erie, and was sentenced to loss of rank and pay for six months; after this he remained on the unattached list of the army.[48]

Procter retreated to the head of Lake Ontario with his remaining troops, some 250 men. Eventually 2,000 Indians, many of them women and children, joined him there. The Detroit frontier was left in the hands of the Americans. As it was late in the season, Harrison

---

[48] For American account of action see Harrison to Armstrong, 5, 9, 11 Oct., 1813, WD, LR, Unreg. Series; Harrison to Governor Meigs, 11 Oct., 1813, Brannan, *Official Letters*, pp. 239–40. For British reports see Procter to De Rottenburg, 23 Oct., 1813, CO 42/152, pp. 66–9; Matthew Elliott to William Claus, 24 Oct., 1813, Claus Papers, MG 19, Series F 1, vol. 10, pp. 111–13, Public Archives of Canada, Ottawa; also WO 71/243, pp. 13–18, 34–43, 52, 149, 155; Casselman, ed., *Richardson's War of 1812*, pp. 204–24.

planned no further action, and left Michilimackinac in the possession of the British. Late in October, after sending many of the Kentucky militia home, he sailed to Buffalo on the Niagara frontier with over 1,000 troops.[49] For the conquest of Canada the Americans still needed victories farther east; all the efforts on the Detroit frontier had done little more than regain what had been lost in the first summer of the war.

---

[49] Return of Right Division of British Army, CO 42/152, p. 59; Harrison to Armstrong, Nov. 8, 14, 16, 1813, SW, LR, Reg. Series.

5

Failure

The American advance across the Niagara River in the early summer had not resulted in any decisive change in the balance of land forces in the region. The British had retreated in good order to the head of Lake Ontario, successfully resisted any American attempt to pursue them, and had won back control of the ground between Burlington and Fort George. In July and August 1813 the Americans on the British side of the Niagara River were isolated in Fort George. Rather than undertaking any major advance to bring the British to battle, the American troops had to confine themselves to minor sorties to cut off British pickets.

There was also similar lack of decisive action on the Lake Champlain front in these summer months. An American gunboat sortie to the vicinity of the Isle aux Noix early in June only resulted in the capture of the *Eagle* and the *Growler* by the British, and in July they were turned against the Americans. Prevost decided that a minor forward movement on Lake Champlain might help to take some of the pressure off the fronts farther to the west. He appropriated the 50-man crew of the sloop *Wasp* then at Quebec, and sent them to man the British gunboats on Lake Champlain. With 800 men they went south along Lake Champlain, raided Plattsburg and other American settlements, destroying arsenals, block-houses, barracks, and all possible supplies. Such was the ineptness of the American defensive preparations in this region that the British suffered no losses.[1]

---

[1] For the Niagara front see *ASP*, *MA*, I, 450-51; David R. Williams to Armstrong, 3 Aug., 1813, WD, LR, Reg. Series; Brannan, *Official Letters*, pp. 199-200. For Lake Champlain front see Prevost to Bathurst, 7 June, 1, 8 Aug., 1813, CO 42/150, p. 208; CO 42/151, pp. 95-8, 110; also CO 42/150, p. 212; Adm 1/504, pp. 160, 162.

In August Secretary of War John Armstrong at last came forward with additional plans for the invasion of Canada. His hopes for the spring and early summer had been thwarted by the weakness of American military forces and the resistance of Dearborn, but Armstrong was again ready to insist on the necessity of attacking from Kingston eastwards rather than dissipating strength in attacks along the Niagara frontier and farther west. He now had different generals to carry out his plans, but they were hardly such as to inspire confidence. The new commander-in-chief in succession to Dearborn was Brigadier-General James Wilkinson, who had earlier been serving in New Orleans. Wilkinson was the most controversial figure in the early American army. For a time he had been in the pay of Spain, he had been deeply embroiled in the Aaron Burr conspiracy, and had made all manner of enemies. Unfortunately, one of them was Major-General Wade Hampton, a rich South Carolinian whom Armstrong appointed to be commander of the Lake Champlain front. Hampton agreed to serve on the specific understanding that he should have his orders directly from the War Department, and that he would come under Wilkinson's orders only in the event of combined operations. As combined operations were what Armstrong had in mind, his new appointments were hardly auspicious.[2]

Early in August Armstrong suggested two possible plans of campaign to Wilkinson. He first pointed out that the utmost American success in the Fort George region would only give the United States control over the Niagara Peninsula, and even that would be of diminished importance if (as happened in September and October) Harrison won control of the Detroit frontier. In view of this Armstrong wanted American forces to be gathered at Sackett's Harbor. From there they could attack Kingston, and open up the entrance to the St Lawrence from Lake Ontario, while Hampton led a diversionary attack northwards along Lake Champlain. If the British rushed forces west to defend Kingston then Hampton's diversionary movement could become a real attack on Montreal. Alternatively, Armstrong suggested the possibility of bypassing Kingston, landing

---

[2] Hampton to Armstrong, 22 Aug., 1813, WD, LR, Unreg. Series; Adams, *History*, VII, 173–6.

the army on the north bank of the St Lawrence, and attacking Montreal in combination with General Hampton.[3]

Wilkinson, like Dearborn, promptly pointed out some of the realities of the situation to Armstrong. He thought Kingston should be attacked from Sackett's Harbor only if a large enough army could be assembled, and if, and this was essential, naval control of Lake Ontario could be assured. To this point in the war neither side had succeeded in achieving naval dominance on Lake Ontario. Wilkinson presented an alternative plan in the event that the force gathered was insufficient to attack Kingston. In that event he thought Fort George should be strengthened, the British on the Niagara frontier attacked, and, if Harrison had not yet succeeded, a force could march westwards to capture Malden. Neither Dearborn nor Wilkinson showed any enthusiasm for attacking Kingston, or moving against the British troops in the St Lawrence. Armstrong replied immediately to Wilkinson's letter, and made it quite clear that he was not prepared to accept another of the western diversions carried out by Dearborn in the spring. Armstrong insisted that if Wilkinson considered his force too weak to attack Kingston then he should bypass it and proceed down the St Lawrence; above all, Wilkinson was not to engage in operations from Niagara west.[4]

Although Wilkinson had ample reason to fear that Armstrong would not supply him with the men and materials necessary for the major attack he was ordered to undertake, Canada in this second summer of the war would still have been vulnerable to a determined attack. American failures had stemmed more from their own weaknesses than from the strengths of the British defensive position. The United States had the men and resources to take Canada if only she could bring them to bear in an effective manner. Prevost constantly bewailed the lack of detailed instructions from home, and regretted the lack of reinforcements, but to this point in the war the Americans had offered no serious threats to the main settled areas of Canada.

A potential advantage to the Americans, which they had wasted by

---

[3] Armstrong to Madison, 23 July, to Wilkinson, 5 Aug., 1813, *ASP, MA*, I, 463.

[4] Wilkinson to Armstrong, 6 Aug., Armstrong to Wilkinson, 8 Aug., 1813, *ibid.*, 463-4.

their ineptness in the first summer of the war, was the lack of enthusiasm for the war among much of the Canadian population. There were of course many loyal militiamen who fought bravely throughout the conflict, but there was also a large French-Canadian population who could hardly be expected to throw themselves enthusiastically in support of the British, and a considerable number of American immigrants who now found themselves with divided allegiance. The war was a great burden on the whole Canadian population. When the militia were called out to resist American attacks, their farms went untended and their families often suffered. The Assembly of Upper Canada petitioned the Prince Regent for relief in March 1814, pointing out that in Upper Canada, along a frontier of 800 miles, only 10,000 men were able to bear arms. Nearly half of these were embodied in 1812 for the first campaigns of the war, and a large proportion of them for most of the campaigns of 1813. This had brought considerable hardship and shortage of supplies throughout the region. The Assembly of Lower Canada petitioned for relief in a similar vein, observing that as 10,000 men were constantly employed in the militia, public works, and transportation, agriculture had suffered, and the inhabitants had experienced considerable distress. The militiamen also suffered severely. They were frequently short of provisions and adequate clothing, and were paid in an erratic manner, and whatever the chances of being killed in action there was always the danger of dying of disease.[5]

At a time when the farms were losing so many men, the demands of the British commissariat upon them were very heavy. In the summer of 1813 the problem of supplying the British troops at Kingston and at Prescott (on the St Lawrence) became acute. British supply officers and agents had great difficulty in persuading the farmers to sell provisions for the troops and forage for the horses, and their difficulties were compounded by the general lack of specie. Prevost's attempt to counteract the lack of bullion by the issuing of 'army bills' backed by the government had helped to offset the lack of a circulating medium, but the farmers were reluctant to sell except for gold or silver.

---

[5] Address of House of Assembly, Upper Canada, 14 March, 1814, Petition of Lower House, [March 1814], CO 42/355, pp. 40-42; CO 42/156, pp. 223-7.

By the late summer of 1813, as the Americans were preparing for what they hoped would be a great blow against Kingston and Montreal, the difficulty of supplying the British garrisons reached a point of crisis. The Canadian population was simply unwilling to sell what supplies it had to the British troops, and in November Major-General De Rottenburg was obliged to resort to a modified martial law. Provisions and forage were obtained from the farmers by forced purchase, and in an attempt to offset protests the prices were fixed by the magistrates. When Lieutenant-General Sir Gordon Drummond assumed the command of Upper Canada in December 1813 he soon repealed De Rottenburg's proclamation, but in the next few months quickly discovered that the farmers were still unwilling to part voluntarily with their produce. By April 1814 he had to resort to forced purchase, although in March the Assembly passed a vote of censure on De Rottenburg. Such was the bitterness of the Canadian population that prosecutions were brought against the officers and agents of the commissariat, but the authorities in Canada were given the support of the British government in London.[6]

A strange irony is that instead of the Americans attacking vigorously, weakening the Canadian will to resist, and taking advantage of the tension between the British army and many of the farmers, the Americans themselves helped to offset the British shortage of supplies. When in January 1814 Thomas Ridout of the British commissary department left Prescott to take charge of supply at Cornwall farther down the St Lawrence, he commented that there were 1,600 troops there to be fed and 'the country is so excessively poor that our supplies are all drawn from the American side of the river'. The Americans were driving cattle from the interior on the pretence that they were going to the American army

---

[6] For the difficulties over specie see Prevost to Bathurst, 10, 18 March, 1814, CO 42/156, pp. 133-4, 195-203. The supply problem is discussed in William M. Weekes, 'The War of 1812: Civil Authority and Martial Law in Upper Canada', Zaslow, ed., *Defended Border*, pp. 191-204. Also Drummond to Bathurst, 5 April, 2, 28 May, 1814, Bathurst to Drummond, 23 Aug., 1814, CO 42/355, pp. 49-50, 73-4, 82-4; CO 42/40, pp. 386-92; *Letters of Veritas*, pp. 79-80.

on the Salmon River, on the south side of the St Lawrence, and then were crossing over to the Canadian side at night. In the same way they were supplying flour to the British troops. In June 1814 Ridout commented in a letter to his father that he had contracted with a 'Yankee magistrate' to supply the post at Cornwall with fresh beef. The inhabitants of the north-eastern states did not give up their trade with Canada in the War of 1812, and the British army depended a great deal upon American supplies. Rather than increasing the tension between the British troops and the Canadian farmers, the Americans assuaged it.[7]

The greatest British concern regarding the Canadian population was in those districts which had been heavily settled by American immigrants in the years since the American Revolution, particularly Upper Canada and the region between Kingston and Cornwall on the St Lawrence. When Colonel Edward Baynes, commander-in-chief of the Glengarry Fencibles, in June 1814 summed up his difficulties of recruitment in the first two years of the war he wrote particularly of the large number of settlers who had returned to the United States rather than serve in the Canadian militia. He also spoke of the high rate of desertion among all the troops serving on the American frontiers, but pointed out that at least the French-Canadians when they deserted did it to get home rather than to cross over to the enemy. Baynes was exaggerating when he wrote that two thirds of the inhabitants of some of the most populous parts of Canada had absconded to the enemy, but his comments clearly demonstrate American opportunities in their invasion of Canada. Baynes very much wanted to encourage loyal settlers to offset 'the American interloper, industriously undermining the fidelity of his neighbours, by deseminating democracy, affording intelligence to the Enemy, and frequently concluding his career by going over to him'.[8]

Those residents of Canada, whether originally from the United States or not, who crossed over to the American side and served in

---

[7] Thomas G. Ridout to his father, 19 Jan., 1814, Edgar, ed., *Ten Years of Upper Canada*, pp. 269, 282; also *ibid.*, pp. 275, 279.

[8] Baynes to Prevost, 18 June, 1814, CO 42/355, pp. 404-9; see also CO 42/355, pp. 3-5, 118; 42/156, pp. 131-2.

the American forces ran a considerable risk. Their actions were treasonable. Yet, risk or not, residents of Canada did serve in the American forces in the War of 1812. A few had joined Hull on his invasion of Canada, but the problem of disaffection became somewhat more serious in the campaigns of 1813. On the two raids against York, in April and July, the Americans received aid from a few of the inhabitants, but perhaps most bitterness was engendered along the Niagara frontier. Here Joseph Willcocks, who had come to Canada from Ireland in 1800 and in the years preceding the War of 1812 had been a member of the Upper Canadian legislature, went over to the Americans in 1813 and organized a corps of Canadian volunteers. To the disgust of other members of the legislature he was one of two of their number who threw in their lot with the Americans. Willcocks had over 100 men by the end of August 1813, and his force was part of the garrison of Fort George. The numbers grew in the fall, and the Canadian traitors became notorious for their conduct along the British side of the Niagara frontier; as in other parts of Canada they helped to identify militia leaders and other prominent loyalists who were then seized as prisoners-of-war. Willcocks and his followers continued to serve the Americans throughout the campaigns of 1814, and he was eventually killed at the siege of Fort Erie in the fall of 1814.[9]

As Canadian traitors were also prominent in the raids east of Detroit after Harrison had won control of that frontier, the British authorities made determined efforts to dissuade those who might consider joining the Americans. In the session of the Upper Canadian legislature in February and March 1814 General Drummond secured the agreement of the legislature to a suspension of *habeas corpus*, and to the confiscation of the possessions of those who had deserted to the enemy. The culmination of these efforts came in the spring of 1814 when nineteen Canadian residents who had been captured in the ranks of the enemy were tried for treason at Ancaster. One pleaded guilty, fourteen others were convicted, and eventually on 20 July, 1814, at Burlington Heights, eight of those convicted were

---

[9] See Ernest A. Cruikshank, 'A Study of Disaffection in Upper Canada in 1812–15', Zaslow, ed., *Defended Border*, pp. 208–21; Speech of Drummond, Feb. 1814, CO 42/355, pp. 21–4.

hanged, drawn, and quartered for their allegiance to the Americans. British rule was not to be taken lightly.[10]

The British authorities even hoped to proceed with charges of treason against those citizens of Britain who had emigrated to the United States and subsequently served in the American forces in the invasion of Canada. Of twenty-five who were originally in the fall of 1812 chosen to be charged for bearing arms against the British, twenty-one were originally Irish. This group was sent to Britain to be tried, but the trials never took place because of the American threat of reprisals. The United States had never accepted the British doctrine of inalienable allegiance; as a nation of immigrants such a doctrine was inconceivable.[11]

As the Americans prepared to invade Canada in August and September 1813, the core of British resistance was provided by the regular troops, who could well expect to be outnumbered by the American invading forces, and who even yet could expect little help from Europe. Earl Bathurst indicated in August that the demands of the Peninsula were so great that few reinforcements could be spared. The 70th Regiment was sent from Ireland, but on their arrival in November their commander reported to Prevost that 'we are very young and very small', and that the best men had been left behind on furlough or on recruiting service. He reported his regiment as altogether in 'a very infant state'.[12]

The opportunity was there, but a successful invasion of Canada in the fall of 1813 depended upon the ability of General Wilkinson to carry out Armstrong's strict orders to strike eastwards at Kingston or along the St Lawrence. Wilkinson arrived at Sackett's Harbor on 20 August. In conference with his officers he soon decided not to risk a direct attack on Kingston, but rather to sail with his main force down

---

[10] See Cruikshank, 'The County of Norfolk in the War of 1812', Zaslow, ed., *Defended Border*, pp. 224-40; William Renwick Riddell, 'The Ancaster "Bloody Assize" of 1814', *ibid.*, pp. 241-50. There is considerable information in CO 42/355, pp. 103-16; 42/157, pp. 45-8.

[11] There is extensive correspondence on this subject in the British records. See, for example, CO 42/148, p. 46; 43/49, pp. 296-7; 42/151, pp. 70-71.

[12] Bathurst to Prevost, 13 Aug., 1813, CO 43/23, p. 118; Major McGregor to Prevost, 6 Nov., 1813, CO 42/152, p. 23.

the St Lawrence, join up with General Hampton, and attack Montreal. He hoped to set out by the middle of September, but quickly discovered that the organization of his army, and the difficulty of ensuring naval control of Lake Ontario, was going to delay him.[13]

Early in September Wilkinson went to Niagara to arrange for the transfer of the regulars on that frontier to Sackett's Harbor. As this involved the movement by water of over 3,000 men, it was essential to ensure they would not be intercepted by the British fleet. Neither side yet had a clear ascendancy on Lake Ontario, and as the Americans were intent on offensive warfare it was essential that they should attempt to bring the British to battle. In September, while Wilkinson attempted to gather troops at Niagara for embarkation, Chauncey tried to engage the British fleet. In this he was unsuccessful. From 7 to 12 September he chased Yeo's force around the lake, but allowed him to escape into Amherst Bay near Kingston. Late in September Chauncey again sailed in pursuit of the British force. He had heard it was at York. On this occasion Chauncey did manage to bring Yeo to action, but once again the British escaped, this time after inflicting damage on the American squadron. The *General Pike* lost 27 killed and wounded, most of them from the bursting of a gun, and had her main top-gallant mast shot away. The British *Wolfe* also suffered damage, losing her main and mizen topmasts.

At the end of September over 3,000 troops had been embarked in the Niagara River, and with the British unwilling to risk the loss of their naval force on the Lake, the troops were able to sail to Sackett's Harbor at the beginning of October. At this time Chauncey again chased after the British fleet with no success, but on 5 October captured five British troopships on their way from York to Kingston with nearly 300 men. Meanwhile, Wilkinson had arrived at Sackett's Harbor with his troops, there to be met by Secretary of War Armstrong who in September had come in person to the scene of these vital operations. Thus, there was to be not only the usual tension between Wilkinson and the other army officers, but also a discussion

---

[13] Wilkinson to Armstrong, 21 Aug., Armstrong to Wilkinson, 6 Sept., 1813, *ASP, MA,* I, 465-6.

of tactics in the field between the Secretary of War and his commander.[14]

In the first part of October Armstrong and Wilkinson were again beset with doubts as to whether or not to attack Kingston, but at last decided that it would be bypassed: Wilkinson would lead 8,000 men down the St Lawrence against Montreal. The first men were embarked on 17 October, but it was not until the beginning of November that the total force had been moved to the first gathering place at Grenadier Island (less than twenty miles away) at the entrance to the St Lawrence. It was so late in the season that the force was buffeted and drenched by the strong winds and heavy rains. As early as 28 October Wilkinson was writing that 'all our Hopes have been very nearly blasted'. Yet, in the first days of November, he was ready to begin his advance down the St Lawrence to join with General Hampton in the attack on Montreal.[15]

Had Wilkinson known of Hampton's proceedings he would have been even more depressed as he attempted to gather his troops at the entrance to the St Lawrence. General Hampton had been on the Lake Champlain front throughout the summer. He was disgusted at being put under the command of Wilkinson for the main attack, and had already expressed his intention of retiring at the close of the campaign. He had some 4,000 men under his command. The New England militia was sadly missed. This was a pathetically weak little army to send north on the vital Lake Champlain route. In the middle of September the force moved forward towards the Canadian frontier, and marched westward to the Chateauguay River. Hopefully, Hampton could then proceed down the Chateauguay to the St Lawrence for the attack on Montreal. On 21 October, on Armstrong's orders, the movement began.

The British knew that the Americans were assembling a force on the Lake Champlain front. At the end of September Prevost left

---

[14] Chauncey to Jones, 13, 25 Sept., 1, 6, 8 Oct., 1813, SN, CL, 1813, vol. 6, pp. 43, 92, 115, 126, 147; Adams, *History*, VII, 176–9; Yeo to Warren, 29 Sept., 1813, Adm 1/504, pp. 325–6; Wilkinson to Armstrong, 27 Sept., 1813, Brannan, *Official Letters*, pp. 219–20.
[15] Wilkinson to Armstrong, 19, 28 Oct., 1 Nov., 1813, WD, LR, Unreg. Series; Adams, *History*, VII, 180–86.

Kingston to take up his command at Montreal, and even by that time Major-General Sir Roger Sheaffe had called out 3,000 militiamen to augment the British regular troops. This brought the number of militia in the field in the vicinity of Montreal to some 8,000. When Prevost arrived he increased this to nearly 13,000. As Sheaffe could also call on some 5,000 regulars to help in the defence of Montreal, even a united Wilkinson–Hampton army would be engaged in an exceedingly risky operation. Nevertheless, on 21 October Hampton's men advanced down the Chateauguay towards the St Lawrence. They moved very slowly, and a road was completed to secure a supply line for the American troops. The British force on the Chateauguay was comparatively small, consisting mostly of militia and Canadian fencible regiments. Lieutenant-Colonel Charles de Salaberry had constructed wooden breastworks in the woods alongside the river, and had manned the position with 400 men. He had also placed another 160 men on the other side of the river to cover a ford in the rear of the main Canadian line, and there were somewhat over a thousand troops in reserve behind the main British position.

Hampton moved to the attack on the night of 25–6 October. His plan was for Colonel Robert Purdy to cross the river with 1,500 men, march through the woods to the rear of the enemy position, and re-cross the river at the ford. The rest of Hampton's force was to advance directly against the British position, which would be simultaneously attacked in the rear by Purdy's troops. The attack was a fiasco. The guides who were supposedly leading Purdy's men to the ford became hopelessly lost in the dark, they never recrossed the river, and both American columns retreated without seriously engaging the enemy. Total American losses were not more than fifty, and those of the British no more than twenty-five. Such was the eastern wing of the great invasion of Canada. Worried that nothing had been heard of Wilkinson, and afraid that the British might attack, Hampton decided to withdraw up the Chateauguay.[16]

Wilkinson finally managed to leave Grenadier Island and enter the St Lawrence early in November. The dilatoriness of the whole

---

[16] For the American operations on the Lake Champlain front see Hampton's letters in *ASP*, *MA*, I, 458–62. The British side can be followed in Prevost to Bathurst, 8, 30 Oct., CO 42/151, pp. 163–72, 210–13.

expedition had been compounded by the strong winds and heavy rains experienced since leaving Sackett's Harbor. The British of course were fully aware of Wilkinson's movements. His flotilla was harassed by the bombardment of British gunboats, and the Americans tried to keep close to their own bank of the St Lawrence. The Americans should have been able to use their superior resources and much more numerous population to launch a major threat against Canada, but Wilkinson's force was hardly of overwhelming strength. There were no more than 8,000 men, they had sufficient supplies for less than a month of campaigning, and all in all were placing far too much dependence on the problematical resources of the Americans on the Lake Champlain front.

The first major obstacle to the American army was the British post of Prescott on the St Lawrence; here the guns of Fort Wellington were able to range over the river. Wilkinson waited here until the night of 6–7 November, and after disembarking most of his troops tried to pass the post in the dark. The British spotted them, but their fire inflicted little damage on their vessels. To this point it appeared that the excitement of positive action after so much delay had increased Wilkinson's confidence. On the 6th he wrote to General Hampton telling him that they should meet at St Regis, and from there proceed to attack Montreal. Hampton was also ordered to provide two or three months supply of provisions as Wilkinson had only enough for two or three weeks on hand. Wilkinson, of course, as yet had no knowledge of Hampton's retreat.[17]

Beyond Prescott the Americans were bothered so much by the fire of the Canadian militia that troops had to be landed to sweep aside the resistance, but – more important for the Americans – these were now being followed by a detachment of British regulars. As soon as it became obvious that the Americans were not going to attack Kingston, a 'corps of observation' was detached to follow the movements of Wilkinson's army. This corps originally consisted of not many more than 600 regulars from Kingston under the command of Lieutenant-Colonel Joseph W. Morrison. The naval force which transported and escorted it was commanded by Commander William

---

[17] Wilkinson to Armstrong, 3 Nov., to Hampton, 6 Nov., 1813, WD, LR, Unreg. Series; Lossing, *Pictorial Field Book*, pp. 648–50.

Howe Mulcaster, a regular British naval officer. Leaving Kingston on the night of 7 November, the British proceeded as rapidly as possible to Prescott. There the total force was increased to between 800 and 900 men, and they sailed in pursuit of Wilkinson on 9 November.

Beyond Prescott, Wilkinson met in council with his officers, and decided that while the flotilla went through the Long Sault Rapids, Major-General Jacob Brown would march along the Canadian shore with 2,500 men to overcome the resistance of the Canadian militia on the way to Cornwall. It quickly became apparent that troops would also be needed to protect the American rear, as Morrison's force was rapidly gaining on the American army. In order to thwart any possible threat, Brigadier-General John P. Boyd was given command of a large portion of the American army; he was eventually able to join battle with the pursuing British with some 2,000 men.

General Brown was able to overcome Canadian militia resistance at the rapids with little difficulty, but Wilkinson was becoming increasingly concerned about the situation in his rear. Morrison had landed his troops close behind Wilkinson's army at the rapids, and had established his headquarters at Crysler's farm. This provided an area of cleared fields, flanked by the St Lawrence on the right and woods on the left. Neither commander was sure of the intentions of the other, and both overestimated the strength of their opponents. Wilkinson became convinced that the British were preparing to attack, and on the morning of 11 November ordered his rearguard under General Boyd to move against the pursuing British force.

Colonel Morrison had skilfully distributed his meagre forces in the best positions to resist an American attack. His main force of some 450 regulars was drawn up behind a log fence which ran along a road jutting out at right angles from the St Lawrence. They were supported by one six-pounder. In advance of this contingent, and to its right, were part of the remaining British troops. They were positioned on the Montreal road which ran parallel to the St Lawrence. Their right was on the river, and they were protected by two gullies as well as being supported by two six-pounders. Still further in advance were three companies of Canadian voltigeurs who were acting as skirmishers, and in the woods on the British left were about thirty Indians.

As the British had no entrenched positions or fortifications, and were much inferior in numbers, the Americans should have carried the day decisively. Certainly, if this American army was to have any chance of capturing Montreal it would have to cope with far more than a 'corps of observation'. General Boyd appeared to have no particular plan for the attack. His orders from Wilkinson had told him to form three columns, and his first attack consisted of little more than sending the three columns directly against the British front. He made no real effort to take advantage of his more numerous troops, his superiority in artillery, or his cavalry contingent. His advancing columns drove in the British skirmishers, but then faltered as they attempted to advance across the open fields of the farm against the calm volleys of the well-disciplined regulars. Boyd attempted to counter this effective British fire against the American frontal attack by sending a column to turn the British left on the fringes of the woods while his main body advanced against the British centre. Again the Americans wavered under the fire of the British troops. Boyd was meeting the British on ground of their own choosing, and had formulated no clear plan to overcome their resistance.

Even more surprising and destructive to American morale, the British troops now turned to the attack, and drove the demoralized Americans from the field. British casualties were 22 killed, 148 wounded, and 9 missing, while the Americans lost 102 killed, 237 wounded, and had over 100 taken prisoner. Wilkinson could hardly view the future with confidence. He was pushing deeper and deeper into the heart of Canada with only two or three weeks' supplies, and was hoping to defeat an army more numerous than his own that would certainly be gathered to defend Montreal. Yet, a large portion of the American army had been defeated by a British 'corps of observation' of less than 1,000 men. It was enough to appal the most optimistic and energetic of generals, and Wilkinson was neither. He had long doubted the wisdom of striking east along the St Lawrence, and by this time he was ill and confined to his bed. The long-awaited assault on Canada was again collapsing.

In spite of Boyd's defeat Wilkinson's flotilla ran the Long Sault Rapids on the next morning, and the despondent American army united near Cornwall. There, only the day after the battle of

Crysler's farm, Wilkinson received General Hampton's reply to his orders for a meeting at St Regis. Hampton said this could not be done, and put the whole blame on Wilkinson's critical supply position. His argument was that as he could not bring more than each man could carry he would only increase Wilkinson's supply problems. Thus, with no emphasis on the failure at Chateauguay, he told the commander-in-chief that he could not meet him, and was withdrawing.

With this news from Hampton, Wilkinson really had no choice other than to abandon the operation. Wilkinson's critics have been quick to point out that this gave him the excuse he needed after the defeat at Crysler's farm, yet even without that action Wilkinson would have courted complete disaster to have continued to Montreal with no hope of reinforcements. At a council with his officers the decision was taken to withdraw immediately to the American shore, and to take up quarters at French Mills on the Salmon River.[18]

This attempt to invade Canada had been sadly mismanaged from its inception. Secretary of War Armstrong and the American administration knew that the major blow should be struck against Kingston or eastward down the St Lawrence, but it was obvious to those in actual command of the troops that however desirable this might be, it was extremely doubtful whether the Americans had the army in the field to undertake it. The delays in recruiting and in transporting supplies meant that the expedition sailed in unfavourable weather, too late in the season, and with too few men. There was never adequate unity between the eastern and western wings of the attack, the notorious Wilkinson was distrusted by many of the officers, and Hampton only half-heartedly agreed to take his orders. Above all, Hampton had under his command only 4,000 men. If this eastern wing of the attack could have been launched in force then there would have been a major threat to the British at Montreal, but given

---

[18] For the American side see letters in *ASP, MA*, I, 462–3, 475–80 (most of the original letters are in WD, LR, Reg. and Unreg. Series). British reports are in Morrison to De Rottenburg, 12 Nov., Prevost to Bathurst, 15 Nov., 1813, CO 42/151, pp. 7–15; also Edgar, ed., *Ten Years of Upper Canada*, pp. 255–6; Ronald L. Way, 'The Day of Crysler's Farm', Zaslow, ed., *Defended Border*, pp. 61–3.

the indifference and even the outright opposition of the New England states to the war, it was not possible to raise and adequately support an army. This effort at invasion ended in another crushing blow to American morale. Prevost was able to report to England early in December that the threat of invasion had ended, and that the American armies had to 'seek for winter quarters under circumstances so highly disadvantageous as to have produced in both of them discontent, desertion, and disease'.[19]

At French Mills, far from any centres of American settlement, the soldiers who had expected to attack Montreal now had to build huts to stand the rigours of a northern winter. Lacking adequate clothing, bedding, or even medical supplies they suffered bitterly in the freezing weather. Eventually, in February 1814, the army destroyed their flotilla which was frozen in the ice of the St Lawrence, burned their block-houses and barracks, and retreated. Most of the army marched to Sackett's Harbor, while part of it went with Wilkinson to Plattsburg. A small British detachment followed Wilkinson's retreating army to within a few miles of Plattsburg, and made it obvious that the American failures had not taken away the attractiveness of the United States for British troops; ninety of them deserted on this service. Most of them were from the 103rd Regiment which had recently arrived in Canada. Prevost complained that much of this was due to the type of men being sent to his command; too many of the 103rd, he asserted, were convicts taken from the hulks to be soldiers. Even 'the repeated infliction of capital punishment' was not stopping the desertion which had always plagued the British army along the Canadian frontier.[20]

The effort to supply Wilkinson with troops, which had dragged on throughout the late summer and early autumn, had also created a precarious situation for the Americans along the Niagara frontier, although this was not immediately apparent. The Americans continued to occupy Fort George on the British side of the river throughout the summer, and it was stated in the middle of September that

---

[19] Prevost to Bathurst, 12 Dec., 1813, CO 42/152, pp. 78–80.
[20] Wilkinson to Armstrong, 11, 12, 19 Feb., 1814, WD, LR, Reg. Series; Lossing, *Pictorial Field Book*, p. 657; Prevost to Bathurst, 10 (quotation), 12 March, 1814, CO 42/156, pp. 134–9.

the British were losing eight or ten men daily by desertion to the Americans.[21]

Even the departure of General Wilkinson with most of the regulars at the beginning of October produced no immediate crisis. There were still some 800 regulars under Colonel Winfield Scott to augment the New York militia under the command of Brigadier-General George McClure. Wilkinson had ordered these regulars to leave the Niagara frontier and support him if the British abandoned their positions. In the early part of October Scott attempted to strengthen Fort George, and all seemed well on the 9th when the British precipitously retreated to the head of Lake Ontario. Major-General John Vincent had heard of Procter's defeat on the Thames, and had decided to gather his forces at Burlington in order to counter any attempt of Harrison to march overland to the Niagara frontier. At the head of the lake Vincent was joined by the remnants of Procter's defeated force, and about 2,000 Indians, many of them women and children. Seemingly, the Niagara frontier was safely in American hands, and on 13 October Colonel Scott and nearly all the regulars crossed the river and marched away.[22]

In these first weeks of October the Americans held the dominant position all along the Canadian side of the Niagara frontier, and the militia, aided by the British traitors, pillaged the inhabitants. In the middle of the month General McClure issued a proclamation regretting this pillage, but surprisingly asserted openly that he could not 'promise complete security'. McClure's position at this point depended more on the British concern with other fronts than on his own inherent strength. With the departure of Scott he was left with only 1,000 militia, a few regulars, and some 250 pro-American Indians. Temporarily the situation was considerably improved on 24 October when Harrison arrived at Buffalo with over

---

[21] Thomas to George Ridout, 16 Sept., 1813, Edgar, ed., *Ten Years of Upper Canada*, p. 226.

[22] Daniel D. Tompkins to McClure, 27 Aug., 1813, Hugh Hastings, intro., *Public Papers of Daniel D. Tompkins, Governor of New York, 1801–1817* (3 vols., New York, 1898–1902), III, 373–9; McClure to Tompkins, 6 Oct., Scott to Wilkinson, 11 Oct., 1813, Brannan, *Official Letters*, pp. 230–31, 241–4; also *ibid.* pp. 210–11, 228; Edgar, ed., *Ten Years of Upper Canada*, pp. 228, 237–9.

1,000 men from the west, but this reinforcement was short-lived. Late in November Harrison and his troops left for Sackett's Harbor.[23]

McClure's position now deteriorated rapidly. Although it had been made quite clear to him that on the departure of the regulars the defence of the Niagara frontier was to be his responsibility, he had failed to make the energetic efforts necessary to gather more militia. Early in December, when the militia under his command reached the end of their terms of enlistment and crossed the river to go home, he had no one to take their place. The garrison of Fort George now consisted of sixty effective regulars. McClure had allowed himself to be placed in an untenable position, and he decided to evacuate Fort George and retire across the river to the American Fort Niagara.

In making the decision to withdraw, McClure compounded his own earlier folly by deciding to burn the Canadian village of Newark before he crossed the river. In doing this he was able to cite the authority of Secretary of War Armstrong who at the beginning of October had given him the power to destroy it should the defence of Fort George make it necessary. This was hardly the time to use the authority given to him, even if he had no qualms about its morality, as the American side of the Niagara River now had very few troops to defend it. Yet, on the night of 10 December, after a warning to the inhabitants, the whole village of some 150 houses was burned to the ground. In forcing the inhabitants out into the bitter cold and snow of the Peninsula, McClure was presumably hoping to deny shelter to the British forces who would now reoccupy the frontier, but it was a most ill-advised act, and one that was subsequently disavowed by the American government. Ironically, the British advanced so rapidly on hearing of the American plundering, that the Americans failed to destroy Fort George; it was stronger when reoccupied than when originally abandoned by the British.[24]

---

[23] McClure to Armstrong, 23 Oct., 17 Nov., 1813, WD, LR, Reg. Series; McClure Proclamation, 16 Oct., 1813, McClure to Public, 1 Jan., 1814, Brannan, *Official Letters*, pp. 244–6, 290–92.

[24] Tompkins to McClure, 26 Nov., 1813, *Public Papers of Tompkins*, III, 400–401; Armstrong to McClure, 4 Oct., 1813, Brannan, *Official Letters*, p. 229; McClure to Armstrong, 10 Dec., 1813, WD, LR, Reg. Series; Murray to Vincent, 12 Dec., 1813, CO 42/152, p. 84; Wilkinson to Prevost, 28 Jan., 1814, CO 42/156, pp. 103–4; *Letters of Veritas*, p. 93.

The balance on the Niagara frontier had now shifted dramatically against the Americans. The British had no need to fear the outcome on other fronts. There was no danger of the Americans advancing in strength from the Detroit frontier, Kingston was safe, and Wilkinson had abandoned his attempt against Montreal. Practically all the American regulars had left the Niagara frontier, and by insufficient preparation McClure had left himself without militia. As the British troops occupied Fort George, and viewed the ashes of Newark, the Americans had ample reason to fear a sad end to a year from which they had expected so much.

In the middle of December Lieutenant-General Gordon Drummond arrived on the Niagara frontier to assume the civil and military control of Upper Canada in succession to Major-General de Rottenburg, who was given command of the troops in Lower Canada. In a further reshuffling of British commanders Major-General Phineas Riall accompanied Drummond to take over the immediate command of the troops, and his predecessor Major-General John Vincent was transferred to Kingston. Both Drummond and Riall had seen previous action outside Canada, although Drummond was by far the more experienced. Drummond was ordered by Prevost to take advantage of any weakness caused by the withdrawal of the American troops.[25]

Drummond decided to attack immediately across the Niagara River. The first object of the attack was to be Fort Niagara, and for this purpose Lieutenant-Colonel John Murray was given the command of some 550 regulars. Originally, Drummond hoped that the troops would cross the river on the night of 17 December, but great difficulty was experienced in bringing boats from Burlington. The weather was extremely cold, there was snow on the ground, and during the first part of the journey, on Lake Ontario, the boats had to contend with a gale. After the boats had been landed in a very heavy surf, they then had to be dragged overland on sleighs to the river. This took so long that it was impossible to act on the 17th, and the crossing was made on the following night. The troops were landed three miles above Fort Niagara, and moved to the attack at about 5.00 a.m.

---

[25] Prevost to Bathurst, 6 Jan., 1814, CO 42/156, pp. 11–14.

There was ample reason for the Americans to expect a British attack. British troops had advanced quickly to reoccupy Fort George, and on 18 December at his headquarters at Buffalo General McClure issued an address to the American inhabitants of the region asking for immediate volunteers. He stated openly that he had heard that the enemy were concentrating all their forces at Fort George, and that they would attack Fort Niagara on the following night. The American fort was defended by over 400 men under the command of Captain Nathaniel Leonard; on the night of the attack Leonard was at home with his family in a house three miles away. Early on this bitterly cold winter's morning the British advanced swiftly, seized the American pickets and sentries, learned the password from them, and with fixed bayonets dashed through the open main gate. Most of the Americans were asleep. The British had expressed their intention of seeking revenge for the burning of Newark, and this was reflected in the unusual American casualties of 65 killed and 14 wounded. There were also nearly 350 Americans taken prisoner. The negligence was remarkable even for the War of 1812. At a time when an attack was expected at any moment, the Americans had allowed themselves to be completely surprised. British casualties were only 6 killed and 5 wounded. Within this ineptly defended fort were nearly thirty pieces of cannon, three thousand stands of arms, and great quantities of other supplies.

Drummond, hardly expecting so pathetic an American resistance, had provided a reserve for Murray's force. This reserve consisted of a detachment of regulars under Major-General Riall, and several hundred Indians led by Colonel Matthew Elliott of the Indian Department. Elliott, an Irishman who had emigrated to America before the Revolution, was now well over seventy. He had fought the Americans since the Revolution, his eldest son had been killed on the Maumee early in the war, and he had been obliged to desert his home and farm at Amherstburg when Procter retreated. Before the attack Drummond had ordered Elliott to assemble the Indian chiefs, and impress upon them that no atrocities should take place; this assurance had been given by the Indians.

Riall and the reserve were ordered to cross after Murray, give him any support that might be needed, and also independently attack the village of Lewiston where some American batteries had been constructed. Riall's force was not needed at Niagara, and on the morning of 19 December marched on Lewiston. Most of the inhabitants had wisely fled. The town was destroyed, and the Indians, having found liquor in some of the houses and got drunk, killed some of the residents they found in the vicinity, in spite of the efforts of the officers of the Indian Department to stop them. General Drummond expressed his great concern over the outrages in his report to Prevost, although the destruction of Lewiston and other small settlements in the vicinity was looked upon as retaliation for the burning of Newark. The British government in London later approved this retaliation, but Bathurst in March 1814 expressed the hope that no more would be necessary.[26]

On receiving the dismal news from the Niagara frontier, the governor of New York, Daniel Tompkins, immediately appointed Major-General Amos Hall to succeed McClure in command of the Niagara frontier. Volunteers had been joining the American forces, but they were neither numerous enough nor sufficiently organized to put up an effective resistance. On the night of 29 December General Riall crossed the river. This time he had over 1,000 troops, mostly regulars, and some 400 Indians. The object of the attack was the villages of Black Rock and Buffalo. Buffalo had flourished in the years immediately preceding the war, but it was now ill-defended.

The militia and volunteers under General Hall were swept aside when they attempted to resist the British advance, and on the morning of the 30th Black Rock and Buffalo were burnt to the ground. The fighting was somewhat more severe than in the earlier engagements, and the British lost 31 killed and 72 wounded. The American side of the Niagara frontier was now practically depopulated, for

---

[26] Drummond to Prevost, 18, 20 Dec., Series C, Military, C 681 4/1813 Public Archives of Canada; Murray to Drummond, 19 Dec., Riall to Drummond, 19 Dec., 1813, CO 42/156, pp. 19–22; also *ibid.*, p. 26 (casualties); Bathurst to Prevost, 5 March, 1814, CO 43/23, pp. 144–5; McClure to Armstrong, 22, 25 Dec., 1813, WD, LR, Reg. Series; Tompkins to McClure, 24 Dec., 1813, *Public Papers of Tompkins*, III, 403–4; Lossing, *Pictorial Field Book*, pp. 633–5.

the settlers had abandoned their possessions and fled eastward.[27]

With the exception of the distant Detroit frontier, the Americans had made no inroads on Canada in the one-and-a-half years of war; in fact their own possessions now seemed in danger. The autumn which had started so optimistically with the victories of Perry and Harrison, and had brought hopes of the capture of Montreal, had ended in complete failure for the American forces. The possibilities for the coming spring and summer campaigns of 1814 seemed particularly bleak. For eighteen months the United States had failed in its attempts to conquer Canada, although during the whole of that period the British had regarded the war as only a side-show compared to the war against Napoleonic France. It seemed now that the time of reckoning was near. By the end of 1813 it was becoming obvious that Napoleon was finished. During the year the Russians had thrust into Germany from the east, and Napoleon's reluctant allies had seized the chance to desert him. In Spain Wellington had won his decisive victory at Vittoria in July, and broken the French hold on the Peninsula. By the beginning of 1814 France was encircled and invaded, and in spite of Napoleon's brilliant rearguard actions the allies could not be stopped. Paris fell at the end of March, and in April Napoleon capitulated. As France collapsed in the winter of 1813–14 the Americans could well wonder what the campaigns of 1814 would bring.

---

[27] Tompkins to Hall, 24 Dec., to Armstrong, 25 Dec., 1813, 2 Jan., 1814, to Madison, 3 Jan., 1814, *Public Papers of Tompkins*, III, 402–3, 405–13; Hall to Tompkins, 30 Dec., 1813, Brannan, *Official Letters*, pp. 289 90; Riall to Drummond, 1 Jan., Drummond to Prevost, 2 Jan., 1814, CO 42/156, pp. 31–7, 39 (casualties); Lossing, *Pictorial Field Book*, pp. 635–7.

6

British Naval Supremacy 1813-14

At sea the British had not waited for the collapse of France to treat the war against the United States with the utmost seriousness. The American victories of 1812 had forced the Admiralty to look upon the American ships and sailors with great respect, and by the summer of 1813 the increase of British strength on the North American station had enabled a much tighter blockade to be placed around the American coastline. The Admiralty had also begun to use its resources to build up British naval strength on the Great Lakes.

Even before Perry's victory on Lake Erie in September 1813 provided a sudden stimulus to British efforts on the other lakes, the British government was making an effort to direct naval resources to Canada. At the end of July 1813 Bathurst ordered 300 seamen to be sent from England, and another 300 to be transferred by Admiral Warren from the North American station. The seamen from Britain were at Quebec in early November, and by that time the disaster on Lake Erie had caused fresh demands to be made on Warren. At the end of October two battalions of marines, two companies of marine artillery, and a company trained to use Congreve rockets arrived in the St Lawrence from Warren's command. British successes on land in the late autumn of 1813 did not diminish the efforts at increasing naval strength on the Lakes in the winter of 1813-14. Early in December the commander on the lakes, Sir James Yeo, asked for between 200 and 250 seamen to be sent overland from Halifax to Quebec so that they would be available on the opening of navigation in the spring of 1814. To meet this request four ships were laid up at Halifax, and their complements, numbering over 200 men, marched

BRITISH NAVAL SUPREMACY, 1813-14

west through the snow, not arriving at Kingston until late March.[1]

The repeated demands for emergency reinforcements obviously threw a great strain on the North Atlantic station, and in January 1814 it was at last agreed that the British Admiralty would take complete charge of the naval establishment on the Great Lakes. The Admiralty had been reluctant to assume this responsibility, but with the rapid collapse of France the British government clearly felt that this obligation would not impose too great a strain on Admiralty resources.[2] There was already on the Great Lakes a British naval force of reasonable size. On Lake Ontario there were six vessels (the largest the *Wolfe*, of 23 guns), but under construction were the *Prince Regent* and the *Princess Charlotte*, which were intended to carry 58 and 43 guns respectively. The largest of the four vessels on Lake Champlain carried only 13 guns, but the *Niagara* (16) was being built at the Isle aux Noix. There were also between twenty and thirty gunboats ready or being built on the two lakes, and on the St Lawrence above Montreal. It had also been agreed late in 1813 that two frigates and two sloops would be built in frame in Britain, and sent to Canada on the opening of navigation in the spring.[3]

With the Admiralty in complete command, and in the position of having to face direct criticism should there be further disasters on the lakes, preparations for the summer of 1814 continued rapidly. It was immediately ordered that the second battalion of marines in Canada should be broken up and distributed among the lake ships according to Yeo's directions, and in March a convoy sailed from Britain carrying 600 sailors and dockyard workers, the ships in frame, ordnance, and stores for the lake service. By that time a third large vessel had been laid down on Lake Ontario. All this effort considerably strengthened the British on the lakes for the campaigns

---

[1] Information on reinforcements for the lakes is scattered throughout Adm 1/504, 1/505, 1/506, 2/1377, 2/1378, and there is also material in CO 42/151, 42/152, and 43/23.

[2] Bathurst to Prevost, 20 Jan, 1814, CO 43/23, pp. 140-42; Croker to Yeo, 29 Jan., 1814, Adm 2/1379, pp. 130-35.

[3] There is a detailed list of British naval strength on the lakes in Jan. 1814 in Adm 1/505, pp. 336-7. See also CO 42/151, p. 172; 43/23, pp. 133-7; Adm 1/504, pp. 367-8; 2/1379, pp. 65-6. The *Niagara* was renamed *Linnet*.

of 1814, but a major problem developed in that Prevost could not spare the men and resources needed to transport westward from Quebec the four ships sent in frame from Britain. Not until July was he able to report to Bathurst that a contractor had agreed to transport the frame and equipment of one frigate westward from Quebec on reasonable terms.[4]

The Americans were dilatory on Lake Ontario in the winter of 1813-14. They did not begin enough construction at Sackett's Harbor during the winter to achieve even a balance of power in the early summer. Two new 22-gun brigs were laid down in February, as well as a large frigate, the *Superior*, originally intended to mount over 60 guns but actually given less. Another frigate, the *Mohawk* (42), was begun in May, and when this was completed in mid-summer the eight main United States vessels on Lake Ontario were slightly superior in force to the British squadron. Neither side, however, was able to obtain a decisive advantage, and this was also the case on Lake Champlain.[5] In view of the rapid French collapse in Europe, this was becoming more of a disadvantage to the British than to the Americans. It was becoming obvious that rather than the Americans conquering Canada they were in danger of being invaded themselves, and a decisive invasion depended upon definite naval superiority. The United States had suffered from the lack of this in 1812 and 1813 when Britain had been content to fight a defensive war on the Canadian frontier, but if Britain turned to the attack then the United States would benefit by a naval balance of power.

The difficulties on the Great Lakes, where the Admiralty had to build its ships, were not present on the oceans of the world. If Britain was successful in Europe, then such ships as were needed from her huge navy could be used on American service. Even by the summer of 1813 the increase of force on the North American station had imposed far greater controls on American trade, but the Admiralty had long shown a lack of confidence in Admiral Warren's conduct of affairs. There had frequently been sarcastic replies to his constant requests for additional force, and he had been rebuffed

---

[4] Adm 2/1379, pp. 112-13, 292-4, 254-5; 1/506, p. 299; CO 42/156, pp. 241-2.
[5] Chauncey to Jones, 7, 14, 19 April, 11 June, 1814, SN, CL, vol. 2, pp. 128, 144, 156, vol. 4, p. 54; Roosevelt, *Naval War of 1812*, II, 86-90.

earlier in the year when he had suggested that his North American station be relieved of responsibility for the Jamaica and Leeward Island commands. The Admiralty did not look favourably upon the unusual situation of a senior officer anxious to narrow the sphere of his responsibility. The West Indies and North American stations had been united at the beginning of the war to give greater unity to British naval operations in the American theatre, but the West Indian islands had constantly complained that their defence was neglected. Warren's main attention had been devoted to the North American coast, and he had based himself on Bermuda and on Halifax. American privateers had severely hindered the West Indian trade, and there were constant demands by West Indian merchants and officials for more efficient naval protection.

In the late fall of 1813 the Admiralty managed both to give a more direct supervision to the Jamaica and Leeward Island stations, and at the same time remove Warren. On 4 November Secretary of the Admiralty Croker informed Warren that it had been decided to separate the different stations now under his command, and that as this narrower command needed a less senior officer he was to return to Britain. In his place the Admiralty appointed Vice-Admiral Sir Alexander Cochrane. The new commander-in-chief had seen much experience in the West Indies since 1800, and from 1810 to 1814 had served as governor of Guadaloupe. He assumed his new post in March 1814 at a particularly favourable moment. French resistance in Europe was coming to an end, and Cochrane could expect much more support than his predecessors.

During the winter of 1813–14 the actual command was retained by Warren, although the Jamaica and Leeward Island commands were separated. The division of strength ordered by the Admiralty clearly indicated the respect commanded by United States maritime operations. American naval strength had been scoffed at when the war began, but in November 1813 the Admiralty ordered a strength on the Halifax station of ten ships-of-the-line or 'razees' (cut-down 74's large enough to cope with the largest American frigates), twenty frigates, and twenty-five ships or sloops rated as 20 guns, as well as a variety of smaller craft. In the now separated West India stations, Jamaica was to have a strength of one flagship, three large frigates, fifteen smaller frigates and sloops, and the Leeward Island station was to be set at a strength of one flagship, two large frigates, and twelve smaller frigates and sloops. Owing to the transfer of ships, and the special needs of the moment, these forces were not exactly maintained in the winter of 1813–14, but they formed the basis of the distribution of naval strength among the divided stations. Warren, however, continued to press for additional force; he pointed out at the end of December that there were insufficient ships in the West Indies to perform the necessary convoy services, and that the British still suffered because of the superior sailing qualities of many of the American privateers.[6]

Even with all the British strength, it was impossible to prevent the sailing of some of the few American warships. The frigate *President* (44), under the command of Commodore John Rodgers, managed to slip out of Providence early in December 1813, and cruised through the West Indies. Rodgers had little luck in taking prizes, but in the middle of February he evaded the British blockade to get back into Sandy Hook; the British ship *Loire* (38) could have intercepted the American ship, but followed Admiralty orders and evaded a single-ship engagement. The American frigate *Constitution* also managed to leave port during the winter of 1813–14. On 1 January, under the command of Captain Charles Stewart, she left Boston, and cruised off the West Indies and the coast of Guinea. She made few prizes, but like the *President* was able to evade the British blockade. She slipped into Marblehead on 3 April, in spite of the fact that there were two British frigates off the port. Not all the vessels of the American navy were so fortunate. Late in December, when the schooner *Vixen* attempted to run from Wilmington, North Carolina, to Newcastle, Delaware, to pick up her guns and stores, she was captured by the *Belvidera* (36). The *Vixen* was pierced for 18 guns.[7]

Although no navy could completely seal the bays, harbours, and

---

[6] Croker to Warren, 4 Nov., 1813, Adm 2/1378, pp. 146–51; Lords of Admiralty to Cochrane, 25 Jan., 1814, Adm 2/933, pp. 91–5; Warren to Croker, 30 Dec., 1813, Adm 1/505, pp. 44–5; Captain David Milne to George Home, 2 Jan., 1814, *Report on Home Mss*, p. 160.

[7] Rodgers to Jones, 19 Feb., 1814, Stewart to Jones, 4 April, 1814, SN, CL, 1814, vol. 1, p. 125, vol. 2, p. 117; Roosevelt, *Naval War of 1812*, II, 5–10; Captain Byron to Warren, 3 Jan., 1814, Adm 1/505, p. 136.

inlets of the whole coastline of the United States, the ships that escaped were less important than the total effect of the blockade imposed by the British navy in 1813 and 1814. In November 1813 Warren extended the blockade off America to cover Long Island Sound, and the blockade now stretched around the American coast all the way to the Mississippi River. By this time it was tight enough to have a very severe effect on American trade, and what was particularly infuriating to the American government was that where trade was continuing considerable help was given to the British. The British government had not extended the blockade to New England, hoping by this forbearance to take advantage of the already strong pro-British sympathy.[8]

The American government had good reason for being concerned at trade with the enemy. The British armies in Canada leaned heavily upon British resources, and New England exporters often filled British needs. Yet the method which Madison chose to deal with the problem could only increase the economic problems of his country. On 17 December, 1813, at the request of the President, Congress imposed a strict Embargo which restricted even coastal traffic. The law was never strictly obeyed, and supplies still reached Canada, but combined with the British blockade it helped to produce a commercial crisis in the United States. In the year ending 30 September, 1814, American exports fell to $7,000,000. They had been $45,000,000 in 1811, even though that had been a year of severe restrictions. Certain areas suffered particularly badly. Virginian exports were only $17,851 in 1814, and those of New York $209,000. Partially owing to the great restrictions on trade between sections, prices increased sharply in the latter part of 1813 and 1814, and as governmental revenue fell the financial position of the country became critical, particularly as the commercially depressed population was hardly in a position to lend money to the government. Congress had little choice other than to repeal the Embargo, and this was done in April 1814. As in 1808, the Embargo served as a great stimulus to disaffection in New England.[9]

---

[8] Warren to Croker, 20 Nov., 1813, and enclosure, Adm 1/505, pp. 277-8.

[9] Adams, *History*, VII, 263-4; Mahan, *Sea Power in its Relations to the War of 1812*, II, 176-208.

The arrival of Admiral Cochrane at Bermuda early in March 1814 brought a new energy into the conduct of naval affairs in North American waters. Although Warren, to Cochrane's resentment, did not formally hand over his command until 1 April, Cochrane had already asked the Admiralty for an additional thirty frigates, forty sloops, and twenty armed vessels. He also argued that the ships already on the station were 1,000 men short in their complements, and he asked that these reinforcements be sent out to America.[10]

Cochrane was more fortunate than previous North American commanders in that his letters for reinforcement coincided with the ending of the war in Europe. By the middle of April 1814 the Admiralty was considering which ships should be kept in commission when the French war was over, and at the end of the month announced the end of European hostilities. This meant that in the middle of April a dozen ships of the Mediterranean command were given secret orders to proceed to Bermuda to join Cochrane. In May reinforcements began to cross the Atlantic with a regularity that presaged disaster for the Americans. This increase of force continued throughout the summer, and by October 1,000 new men had been sent out to Cochrane's command. From the time of the new commander's arrival, and the news of the defeat of France, a confidence swept through the British navy. Captain David Milne of the *Bulwark* wrote privately at the end of May that the Americans would now have to yield to any terms offered to them, and that 'at all events they must be made to give up all the lakes in Canada, both Floridas and Louisiana to us. We will then be a barrier between them and Mexico'.[11]

One of the first acts of Cochrane after his assumption of command was the decision to extend the blockade to cover the New England ports. By proclamation on 25 April the whole coast of the United States was declared to be in a state of strict and rigorous blockade. To accomplish this two 74's with supporting vessels were assigned to the area from Long Island Sound to Nantucket, and a similar force

---

[10] Warren to Croker, 7 March, Cochrane to Croker, 8, 31 March, 1 April, 1814, Adm 1/505, pp. 309, 318, 322, 420–21, 434, 440.

[11] See Adm 2/1380, pp. 22–3, 25–7, 75; 2/933, pp. 256–8; Milne to George Home, 30 May, 1814, *Report on Home Mss*, pp. 163–4.

to the coast from Nantucket to New Brunswick. With the war in Europe over, Britain no longer felt the need to encourage trade wherever possible. At the end of May Cochrane denied the request of Halifax merchants to engage in a licensed trade with blockaded American ports. He pointed out that the United States had removed her Embargo because of her critical financial position, and that any trade would help the Americans raise money.[12] In the summer of 1814 the British maintained control of the waters around the United States. This made possible a series of attacks on the American coast, and for the most part throttled the small regular American navy. Only privateers now had any reasonable chance of escaping to threaten British shipping.

In a desperate attempt to break the British blockade support was given to inventor Robert Fulton's efforts at new methods of naval warfare. Late in June 1814 his 'Turtle Boat', long under construction at New York, was launched. The heavily armoured, cumbersome vessel was some 30 by 16 feet, and plated over with iron. She was to be used to fire Fulton's torpedoes against the British blockading squadron, but soon after she was launched she was driven aground on Long Island. The British squadron landed men, and they blew her up. Later in the year, at the end of October, another Fulton invention, the steam frigate, was launched in New York. The war was over before she was finished, but Fulton had demonstrated what was to come in naval warfare.[13]

Whatever the fighting qualities of the ships of the United States navy, it was quite obvious that barring occasional encounters the great days of 1812 and 1813 were over. The element of surprise was gone. No longer were the British overconfident, and the British navy was now assembled in considerable strength. Even in the far off Pacific the British had by 1814 provided for the protection of the whaling fleet and the merchant vessels that plied those waters.

The American frigate *Essex* (32) had carried out a remarkable

---

[12] Cochrane to Croker, 25, 28 April, to Sherbrooke, 30 May, 1814, Adm 1/506, pp. 26, 38–9, 44–5, 242, 244–7.

[13] Captain Burdett to Charles Paget, 29 June, 1814, Adm 1/506, pp. 451–4; H. W. Dickinson, *Robert Fulton, Engineer and Artist: His Life and Works* (London, 1913), pp. 260–64.

cruise since leaving the Delaware in October 1812. Throughout 1813 she had wrought havoc among British ships in the Pacific, and it was not until the latter part of that year that the British had a vessel in that area capable of engaging Captain Porter's vessel. The first moves to send a British ship into the Pacific had been taken early in 1813. The frigate *Phoebe* (36), under Captain James Hillyar, had been given 'most secret' instructions to proceed to Rio de Janeiro with orders for the British commander-in-chief on the South Atlantic station. These orders contained secret instructions for Captain Hillyar of the *Phoebe*; he was not to open them until his ship was thirty miles south of Rio. The original intention was for the *Phoebe* to sail round Cape Horn all the way north to the mouth of the Columbia River, and there 'totally annihilate' any American fur trading establishment on the Columbia, and in its place establish a post for the Canadian North West Company. In fact, after reaching Rio, Hillyar was able to proceed on the more important task of finding the *Essex*, and the North West Company was able to take over John Jacob Astor's trading post by purchase rather than attack.[14]

The *Phoebe* sailed from Spithead in late March 1813, and anchored at Rio on 11 June. It was nearly a month later when she left, now supported by the *Cherub* (18), a sloop-of-war. The arduous voyage around Cape Horn into the Pacific, and a long search for the *Essex*, finally brought results in February 1814 in Valparaiso Bay. The *Essex* had spent the autumn of 1813 refitting in the Marquesas, and had arrived on the coast of Chile in January 1814. Captain Porter decided to wait in the vicinity of Valparaiso for the *Phoebe*; he had heard the British were looking for him. For a week after the British arrival both vessels remained anchored close to each other in neutral Valparaiso Bay. Both crews were in very good spirits. At the top of her fore top gallant mast the *Essex* hoisted a white flag with the motto 'Free trade and sailors right', and was answered by the *Phoebe* with 'God and country; British sailor's best rights; traitors offend both'. Three cheers from the American crew high in their rigging were immediately answered on the *Phoebe* by the playing of God Save the King and three more cheers.

---

[14] Croker to Hillyar, 16 Feb., 12 March, 1813, Lords of Admiralty to Hillyar, 12 March, 1813, Adm 2/1380, pp. 367–79.

On 15 February the *Phoebe* and the *Cherub* put to sea, and for six weeks hovered off the bay waiting for the *Essex*. The American ship was probably a better sailer than the *Phoebe*, and carried forty 32-pound carronades and six long twelves. The *Phoebe* had twenty-six long eighteens, four long nines, and fourteen 32-pound carronades, and the *Cherub* had eighteen 32 and six 18-pound carronades, and two long sixes. The *Essex* was inferior in strength to the combined British force, but stood a good chance of victory if she could manœuvre to bring the *Phoebe* to battle at short range.

Captain Porter was hopeful he might persuade Hillyar to fight a single-ship engagement, but this would have meant Hillyar ignoring specific Admiralty orders, and willingly giving up the chance of bringing superior force to bear. On 27 February Porter set sail to find out if the *Phoebe* would engage him singly, but quickly discovered that Hillyar meant to use both the *Phoebe* and the *Cherub* in the action, and put back into the bay. A month later Captain Porter had immediate action forced upon him. On 28 March a strong wind broke the larboard cable, and dragged his starboard anchor to sea. Porter quickly made sail, and the *Phoebe* and the *Cherub* beat to quarters. Before the battle began the *Essex* suddenly lost her main topmast. It plunged into the sea and drowned the men who were aloft. Porter tried to return to his anchorage, but could not reach it. Instead he anchored in a small bay close to shore in an attempt to repair the damage. Just after 4.00 p.m. the first attempts of the British ships to fire on the *Essex* were of little effect; it was difficult to manœuvre so close to the shore in the strong wind.

By 5.35 p.m. the British ships finally managed to bring their guns to bear on the American vessel. The *Phoebe* had intended to anchor to fire on the *Essex*, but before she could do this Porter cut his cable and made an attempt to close. This attempt failed, and with the *Essex* heavily damaged and on fire Porter made a desperate attempt to run on shore and destroy his ship. A shift in the wind made this impossible, and the thousands of spectators on the surrounding hills were able to see American sailors diving overboard in an attempt to swim to shore. At 6.20 p.m. Porter struck his colours. His losses had been very heavy. Out of a crew of 255 the *Essex* had 58 killed, 66 wounded, and 31 missing (probably drowned). The *Phoebe* had lost only 4 killed and 7 wounded, and the *Cherub* 1 killed and 3 wounded. It was not until November 1814 that the *Phoebe* moored in Plymouth Sound. She had been away for twenty months.[15]

Early in 1814 American shipbuilders had completed three new sloops-of-war: the *Frolic*, the *Peacock*, and the *Wasp*; they each carried twenty 32-pound carronades and two long eighteens. The *Frolic*, commanded by Joseph Bainbridge, sailed from Boston in February with a crew of over 170 men. Unfortunately on this, her first cruise, she encountered the British frigate *Orpheus* (36) and schooner *Shelburne* (12) on 20 April off Cuba. The American ship made desperate attempts to get away, but after a chase of sixty miles during which every effort was made to lighten the vessel, including the jettisoning of the guns, she was captured. The captain of the *Orpheus* called the American sloop 'a remarkably fine ship'.[16]

The second of the new sloops to sail was the *Peacock*, under Captain Lewis Warrington, who successfully escaped from New York in March. She had a far more distinguished cruise than that of her sister ship, and once again proved to the Admiralty that on anything like equal terms the American navy was difficult to defeat. The *Peacock* sailed south from New York, and intercepted a Havana–Bermuda convoy escorted by the British brig-sloop *Epervier* (18), under Captain Richard W. Wales. The British ship was definitely inferior in strength to the American sloop. The *Epervier* carried sixteen 32-pound and two 18-pound carronades against the twenty 32-pound carronades and two long eighteens of the American sloop. Her crew of 121 was outnumbered by the American crew of 166, and it later became apparent that there was a difference in effectiveness as well as in numbers.

---

[15] Captain's Log of the *Phoebe*, March–Nov. 1814, Adm 51/2675, and Hillyar to Croker, 28 Feb., 30 March, 1814, Gerald S. Graham and R. A. Humphreys, eds., *The Navy and South America, 1807–1823, Correspondence of the Commanders-in-Chief on the South American Station* (Naval Records Society, 1962), pp. 132–3, 141–2; Porter to Jones, 3 July, 1814, Brannan, *Official Letters*, pp. 347–58.

[16] Pigot to Cochrane, 25 April, 1814, Adm 1/506, p. 213; Bainbridge to Jones, 26 April, 3 June, 1814, SN, MCL, 1814, vol. 1, pp. 114, 139; Adams, *History*, VIII, 181.

The action took place off Cape Canaveral (now Cape Kennedy) on 29 April. At 8.00 a.m. the American ship was sighted by the *Epervier*, which immediately put herself between her convoy and the enemy. The action began at 9.50 a.m. at short range, and was over by 11.00 a.m. The first broadsides caused damage to both ships, and the *Peacock* was hampered by having her fore-yard disabled. Yet, that initial blow by the British was followed by very few others. By 11.00 a.m. most of the British larboard guns were out of action, and Captain Wales could not manœuvre to bring his starboard broadside to bear as the rigging and sails had been cut to pieces, the main boom shot away, and the foremast severely damaged, and there was four-and-a-half feet of water in the hold. Although the *Epervier* had extensive damage to her hull, the *Peacock* was practically untouched in vital areas. The British captain was obliged to strike his colours, although he had lost only seven killed and ten wounded; American casualties consisted of only two slightly wounded.[17]

The American sloop had been of superior force, but the discrepancy had not been great enough to account for the complete victory of the American ship. The British vessel had inflicted little damage on the *Peacock*, although the action was fought at very close range. In the subsequent court martial held at Portsmouth in January 1815 it was pointed out that some of the bolts holding the carronades had given way, but that another basic problem had been the inefficiency of the crew. The first-lieutenant thought that not more than twenty had been in action before, and that 'they were a weak crew, and not bred as Seamen'. The Master went further, and asserted that he had never seen a worse crew in his life. Edward Codrington, Admiral Cochrane's Captain of the Fleet, expressed other opinions in a letter to his wife. After pointing out that the British sloop had been cut to pieces while the American had been barely scratched, he asserted that there was too much favouritism in the British service; officers in the small American navy were chosen on merit, and would continue to prevail unless they met the best

---

[17] Wales to Cochrane, 8 May, 1814, Adm 1/506, pp. 564–5; Warrington to Jones, 29 April, 1814, SN, MCL, 1814, vol. 1, p. 114; Lieut John B. Nicholson to Jones, 1 May, 1814, Secretary of the Navy, Officers Letters, 1814, vol. 2, p. 57.

British officers on equal terms. Moreover, even those ships which were reputed to be '*crack ships*' did not do as well as expected, for 'the people, from being tyranically treated, would rejoice in being captured by the Americans, from whom they would receive every encouragement'. It is quite apparent that the lack of trained seamen, the brutal discipline, and a variety of standards for officers, which had not been fully apparent in meeting the French, became far more obvious in facing fast-sailing, enthusiastically-manned American ships.[18]

The third of the new American sloops, the *Wasp*, under the command of Captain Johnston Blakely, left Portsmouth, New Hampshire, on 1 May, 1814. The Irish-born Blakely sailed his ship across the Atlantic, and took up a position in the approaches to the English Channel. Nothing was more infuriating to the British public than American vessels blithely entering the lion's den. The *Wasp* spent the month of June burning and sinking British merchantmen off the British coast, and on the 28th sighted the British brig *Reindeer* (18), under Captain William Manners. It was an unequal contest. The American carried twenty 32-pound carronades and two long eighteens, the British ship sixteen 24-pound carronades, a twelve pounder in the bow, and two long nines. The *Wasp* had over 170 men, the *Reindeer* only 118. This, however, was no *Epervier*, and the bravery of the captain and crew of the *Reindeer* helped to wipe out the British memory of that dismal episode.

There was very little wind, and it took a considerable time for the action to begin. When at last it started, with the British to windward, it was all over in twenty minutes. As the *Reindeer* was inferior in fire power, Captain Manners made every possible effort to close for boarding, but by the time he closed his ship was severely damaged, and he was badly wounded in his legs. A British attempt at boarding was repulsed, and when Captain Manners, in spite of his wounds, attempted to lead another, he was shot through the head and killed. The Americans now quickly took possession of the British ship. The *Reindeer* had lost 33 killed and 34 wounded out of a total of 118 men;

---

[18] Minutes of Court Martial, 20–21 Jan., 1815, CO 42/160, pp. 212–22; Codrington to his wife, 10 July, 1814, Lady Bourchier, ed., *Memoir of the Life of Admiral Sir Edward Codrington* (2 vols., London, 1873), I, 310.

the Americans lost only 5 killed and 21 wounded. The British ship was so severely damaged that the Americans destroyed her on the following day.[19] The *Wasp* went into the French port of L'Orient, refitted, and put to sea again in late August.

The *Wasp* quickly seized two more merchant vessels, and then managed to cut out and seize a ship from a convoy guarded by a 74 before, on 1 September at 6.30 p.m., sighting four more sails. Blakely immediately pursued the ship that was farthest to windward, and came up with her after nearly three hours. The vessel being chased was the British brig *Avon* (18), Captain James Arbuthnot. She was somewhat weaker than the American ship, as she carried only sixteen 32-pound carronades and two long nines, and had a crew of 117. The action began at 9.29 p.m. in the dark. Blakely was, as usual, anxious to bring the contest to an issue, and he placed himself very close to the *Avon*, in her lee, and poured in a heavy fire. Within an hour the British ship had struck. She had seven feet of water in her hold, the magazine was flooded, the tiller, foreyard, and main-boom were shot away, and she was completely unmanageable. The *Wasp* had to flee from the other British ships before the *Avon* could be boarded, and it was just as well, for she soon sank. The *Avon* had lost 10 killed and 32 wounded, the *Wasp* had 2 killed and 1 wounded. Yet again the *Wasp* had escaped with only slight damage, and had again shown superior gunnery. Blakely continued his remarkably successful cruise, and the *Wasp* was last heard of in the Atlantic early in October. Then she disappeared. Nothing was ever heard again of her or her crew.[20]

For all the exploits of the *Peacock* and the *Wasp*, the regular American navy was able to make little impact in 1814. Three small brigs – the *Syren*, the *Enterprise*, and the *Rattlesnake* – also cruised in the first half of the year, taking some prizes, but the *Syren* was captured by a 74, and the *Rattlesnake* by a frigate. In the last months of the year the remaining ships of the American navy were all

---

[19] Blakely to Jones, 8 July, 1814, *American State Papers, Naval Affairs* (Washington, 1834), I, 315; Roosevelt, *Naval War of 1812*, II, 49–55; Adams, *History*, VIII, 184–8.

[20] Arbuthnot to Sawyer, 1 Sept., 1814, CO 42/160, pp. 223–4; Blakely to Jones, 11 Sept., 1814, Brannan, *Official Letters*, pp. 410–13.

blockaded in port, while three 74's were belatedly under construction. The reaction of the Admiralty to these 74's clearly illustrated the attitude of mind induced by American successes early in the war. By a secret circular on 25 November, 1814, it was pointed out that these 74's were actually as powerful as British three-deckers, and that the captains of British 74's should not engage these American ships in single-ship engagements.[21]

Yet, whatever the caution of the Admiralty, in practical terms any American onslaught at sea in the latter part of 1814 depended upon the privateers. At no time in the war did the British succeed in eliminating their menace. In 1813 they had captured over 300 British prizes, and even the increase in British force in 1814 did not prevent their cruises. In September 1814 British merchants and shipowners petitioned the Prince Regent to the effect that there had been an unparalleled destruction of ships and trade by American privateers around the British coasts and in particular in the Channel, 'in which they seem to roam at pleasure'. They expressed astonishment that this could have taken place since the end of the war with France had left ships free to protect the British coasts.[22]

In Parliament, on 1 December, 1814, the government was hard pressed by those who wanted to know, in view of Britain's all-powerful navy, how the Americans had been able to maintain a threat at sea. The chairman of the committee of underwriters at Lloyds, Joseph Marryat, told the House that from the beginning of the war to that time the Americans had captured a grand total of 1,175 British merchant vessels, of which 373 had been recaptured or given up. Also pointed out was the surprising fact that since the end of the war with France losses of ships had increased. The reason for this was that British trade was now flowing again into channels earlier closed, and into areas where the British had not been providing protection. Throughout the summer of 1814 American privateers came into the English Channel and the Irish Sea. As most of them were light-built and fast-sailing schooners, the British navy could not catch them in the light summer breezes. It was not until the

---

[21] Adams, *History*, VIII, 193; Adm 2/1381, pp. 46–8.
[22] Adams, *History*, VII, 320–21; Petition of Merchants etc. of Glasgow and Newark, 10 Sept., 1814, CO 42/160, p. 109.

stronger winds of the autumn that the situation improved in the Channel.[23] To the end of the war the British public found it hard to understand how a power with such a small official navy could so harass British trade. It was hard to convince them that no blockade could completely seal the whole United States coastline, and that American schooners could, in suitable conditions, outsail the more heavily armed vessels trying to take them.

An unusual feature of the War was that by 1814 neither side was satisfied with the naval situation. The British public lamented that the Americans had not been swept from the seas, but the Americans complained that the lack of naval preparations by their government had left the American coastline vulnerable to all manner of British attacks, and the blockade was ruining their trade. Although privateers could still get out, the regular channels of trade were blocked, and if the British wanted to bring a squadron together to attack any spot on the American coast there was no American naval force that could be gathered to resist them. This had been shown in 1813 by the British raids and depredations in the Chesapeake Bay region, and these raids increased in 1814. Throughout the year the whole American coast was vulnerable to British attack. This was most dramatically demonstrated by the major expeditions against Washington and Baltimore in August and against New Orleans in December, but, apart from these major attacks, the Americans suffered from a variety of lesser raids.

In the Chesapeake the situation was fairly quiet in the spring and early summer. Cochrane was expecting major reinforcements of ships and troops from Europe, and until they came he was for the most part content to use his strict blockade to exert pressure on the region. The ships' boats, however, were used to land on the shores of the bay to obtain supplies, and there were occasional minor actions. The boats also provided the means by which slaves fled their masters to join the British forces.

The day after Admiral Cochrane assumed command of the North American station he issued, on 2 April, a proclamation that those who desired 'to emigrate' from the United States would be received

---

[23] *Hansard*, XXIX (1814–15), pp. 640–70.

on board British ships, and could either join the British forces or be sent as free settlers to British possessions in North America or the West Indies. Although slaves were not specifically mentioned, it was obvious to whom Cochrane's appeal was directed. The proclamation later caused Cochrane some difficulty as reports circulated in Britain that some escaped slaves had been sold in the West Indies, or sent to Cochrane's plantation in Trinidad.[24] There appears to be no basis for these accusations, and in the early spring of 1814 Cochrane directed that a corps of 'colonial marines' should be formed from the escaped slaves. By September 300 had joined, and had been paid a bounty of eight dollars. In May the command of this force was given to a senior sergeant of the British marines, who was given an acting rank of Ensign and Adjutant. This new corps distinguished itself in the spring and summer campaigns in the Chesapeake, and in September was united with three companies from the second battalion of regular marines to form a third battalion under Brevet Major George Lewis. At the same time it was proposed that escaped slaves should be given another eight dollars bounty as they had conducted themselves 'with much steadiness and bravery'.[25]

At the end of May a raid was made by some of the boats of the British squadron against an American battery at Pungoteague in the Chesapeake. They were supported by a Rocket Boat and carronades in launches, and the force of sailors, regular marines, and the ex-slave marine force having taken the guns, destroyed the barracks and guard houses. Of the newly raised Negro force it was said 'their conduct was marked by great spirit and vivacity, and perfect obedience'. There were only slight casualties.[26]

A more serious attempt at action was made in the Chesapeake in June. The American naval force in the bay consisted of some thirteen gunboats under the command of Captain Joshua Barney, an officer who had served with distinction in the Revolution. His force was located in the Patuxent River. As most of that river was unnavigable except for the small boats of the British squadron, the

---

[24] Adm 1/508, pp. 562-3, 577-9; 2/1381, pp. 56-7; WO 1/141, pp. 191-4.

[25] Cockburn to Cochrane, 23 June, 1814 (and enclosure), Cochrane to Croker, 28 Sept., 1814, Adm 1/507, pp. 57-60, 248.

[26] Captain Ross to Cockburn, 29 May, 1814, Adm 1/507, pp. 68-70.

American boats could be protected there with the help of the militia on either bank. At the beginning of June Barney tried to escape from the river with his squadron but was chased back again, and on the 9th the British attempted to enter the river with their small craft but were also unable to make any progress. In the hope of luring Captain Barney farther out, where he could be reached by larger British ships, on the following days they raided along the banks of the river. For this task under 200 men were landed, although they were operating within twenty-five miles of the American capital. Among the force were thirty of the ex-slaves. It was commented by the British officer in charge that they 'conducted themselves with the utmost order, forbearance, and regularity that they were uniformly volunteers for the Station where they might expect to meet their former masters'. Although a tobacco store and some houses were burnt, Captain Barney did not allow his force to be drawn out.[27]

Cochrane's first reinforcement for his coastal operations in the south arrived at Bermuda on 6 June. This consisted of nearly 1,000 marines who were sent from Britain early in April. The Admiralty had given Cochrane the discretion to use these men where he thought they would be most effective, although again suggesting that, if possible, they be used to cripple the American navy. Cochrane used the new reinforcements in the middle of July to attack Leonardtown in the Potomac. The British anchored off the creek leading to the town, and on the night of 18–19 July the ships' boats took the marines along the creek. At dawn they were put on shore, and the Americans withdrew without defending the town. Tobacco, flour, and other provisions were brought away by the British, and a variety of military stores were destroyed. This expedition was carried out under the general command of Rear-Admiral Cockburn, who was used by Cochrane for most of his raiding along the Chesapeake in this summer of 1814. American resistance was so weak that he had little difficulty in raiding at will. On the following day Cockburn moved his forces against Nomini Ferry in Virginia. The militia fled after only minor resistance, and the British stayed all night. On the next

---

[27] Captain Barrie to Cockburn, 19 June, 1814, Adm 1/507, pp. 81–6; Mahan, *Sea Power in its Relations to the War of 1812*, II, 336–40.

morning they embarked tobacco, stores, and a large quantity of cattle, and destroyed all the storehouses and buildings. They also sent out parties into the surrounding country to help escaping slaves join the British; 135 Negroes were with the British when they rejoined their ships.[28]

Cockburn's raids continued regularly in the following weeks. On 23 July he sent a force into St Clement's Creek, landed at the mouth of the Wicomico on the 29th, and again early in August, and moved into the Coan River on 7 August. On all these raids stores, tobacco, and cattle were seized when possible, batteries and storehouses destroyed, and schooners and other small vessels brought away. The inhabitants of the Chesapeake suffered greatly throughout the war, and had ample reason to hate the British. They also had ample reason to complain of the lack of protection provided by their own government.[29]

The inevitable destructiveness of these marauding expeditions had been given an official sanction and stimulus in the middle of July when Admiral Cochrane reacted with enthusiasm to a suggestion from Prevost in Canada that the British maritime operations might be directed towards retaliation for American actions in Upper Canada. After the victories of Perry and Harrison gave the Americans the opportunity to raid eastwards from Detroit along the north shore of Lake Erie, the Long Point region had suffered from marauders in the autumn of 1813 and the spring of 1814. In the autumn the raiders had mostly been Canadian renegades, but in the middle of May American troops, guided by a late member of the Upper Canadian legislature, were transported from the other side of Lake Erie to the Long Point region. There they destroyed the village of Dover, and other mills and storehouses. The American commander, Colonel John B. Campbell, argued that this was retaliation for the destruction of Black Rock and Buffalo, but the British pointed out that those places had been burned in retaliation for the destruction of Newark. Although an American court of enquiry later disavowed

---

[28] Croker to Cochrane, 4 April, 1814, Adm 2/1380, pp. 10–12; Cochrane to Croker, 20 June, 1814, Adm 1/506, p. 390; Cockburn to Cochrane, 19, 21 July, 1814, Adm 1/507, pp. 101–7.

[29] Cockburn to Cochrane, 24, 31 July, 4, 8 Aug., 1814, Adm 1/507, pp. 108–18.

the destruction of private property, Prevost had in the meantime written to Cochrane and suggested possible retaliation.[30]

On 18 July Cochrane issued a general order to the senior officers of his blockading squadrons directing them to destroy and 'lay waste' such towns as were assailable on the coast of North America, sparing the lives of the unarmed inhabitants. This policy was to continue until the Americans gave compensation for their Upper Canadian destruction. The full effect of this order, which was partially intended for American consumption, was tempered by the secret memorandum accompanying it. In this it was stated that officers could exempt places that furnished supplies, and that in the case of places that might later be occupied by the British it might be wiser to treat them with lenity and forbearance. The officers were also authorized to levy tribute in return for sparing private property, but harbours, magazines, shipping, and all governmental property were on no account to be spared.

Cochrane's policy of retaliation was approved by the Admiralty, but early in September the American Secretary of State, James Monroe, pointed out that the burning of Newark and the destruction at Long Point were unauthorized by the American government, and that the United States would always be happy to make some reciprocal agreement covering these matters. He also mentioned that the British used the Indians as allies, and had wrought destruction along the Chesapeake since 1813. In response to Monroe's letter the British government on 2 November finally ordered the suspension of the policy of retaliation. By the time this information was received, most of the raids for the year were over.[31]

A new feature of this marauding of 1814 was the extension of the conflict to the coasts of New England. The New Englanders were for the first time feeling the full impact of the British blockade, and

---

[30] Cruikshank, 'The County of Norfolk', Zaslow, ed., *Defended Border*, pp. 230–35; Prevost to Cochrane, 2 June, 1814, Adm 1/506, p. 462.
[31] Cochrane to Croker, 18, 26 July, to Senior Officers, 18 July, to Monroe, 18 Aug., 19 Sept., 1814, Adm 1/506, pp. 460–61, 466–9, 504, 596–7; 1/507, p. 211; Croker to Cochrane, 27 Aug., 1814, Adm 2/933, p. 210; Monroe to Cochrane, 6 Sept., 1814, Adm 1/507, pp. 213–17; Barrow to Cochrane, 2 Nov., 1814, Adm 2/1381, p. 35.

they also had to undergo actual attack. The first moves began early in the spring on the coasts of Connecticut. On 7 April Captain Richard Coote and a party of British seamen and marines, who formed part of the blockading squadron off New London, were ordered to proceed into the Connecticut River to destroy privateers and other vessels that were equipping and under construction. The expedition was made possible by an American traitor who volunteered to guide the British boats on the promise of a handsome reward if the expedition were successful. The British force of 136 men arrived at Pautopaug Point at 3.30 a.m. on 8 April, and destroyed some twenty-seven vessels valued at over $150,000. The same night the British managed to slip past the American militia in the dark and return safely.[32]

The American traitor who made this possible was given $1,000, subscribed for him by the blockading squadron off New London, and Admiral Cochrane directed that an additional $1,000 be sent to him to encourage others to come forward on similar occasions. This striking example of help to the enemy was not completely typical, but, as along the Canadian frontier, the British received considerable help from the inhabitants in the form of provisions; it was quite possible to obtain cattle and vegetables for cash.[33]

In June and July the British gradually exerted greater pressure on the New England coast. On 13 June some 200 men under Lieutenant James Garland were sent from the British ships in Vineyard Sound off Massachusetts to attack vessels at Wareham at the head of Buzzard's Bay. Several vessels and a cotton factory were set on fire without loss to the British, and the boats escaped without harassment by taking some of the local citizens as hostages; they were released when the boats were safe. A few days later, away to the north, boats from the *Bulwark* (74) destroyed vessels at the mouth of the Saco River in Maine, and in the following month a more ambitious expedition was sent to the region. Thinking in terms of future boundaries, Bathurst in early spring had directed the occupation of

---

[32] Coote to Capel, 9 April, Capel to Captain Talbot, 13 April, 1814, Adm 1/506, pp. 273–7, 280; Lossing, *Pictorial Field Book*, p. 888.
[33] Cochrane to Croker, 27 April, 10 May, 1814, Adm 1/506, pp. 47–8, 203.

the islands in Passamaquoddy Bay on the Maine–New Brunswick border. The troops for this operation were provided by the transfer of the 102nd Regiment from Bermuda to Halifax. The naval command was given to Sir Thomas Hardy, who carried his flag in the *Ramillies* (74), and that of the troops to Lieutenant-Colonel Andrew Pilkington. They sailed into the bay on 11 July, and prepared to attack Fort Sullivan at Eastport on Moose Island. As the British had nearly 1,000 men, and the American garrison consisted of only 80 regulars under Major Perley Putnam, and an additional force of perhaps 200 to 250 militia, there was little chance of effective resistance. Putnam yielded without a struggle, and the British occupied Moose Island and took possession of the Passamaquoddy Bay region until the end of the war.[34]

Sir Thomas Hardy left Passamaquoddy Bay, and sailed to join the squadron off New London. The vagaries of naval service had taken him from the high point of British naval history at Trafalgar to the bombardment of a small Connecticut town. The British suspected that the small port of Stonington was active in the preparation and harbouring of Fulton's torpedoes for the sinking of British ships. These were looked upon by the British navy as an infernal, illegal weapon of war. Stonington was thus thought a suitable spot to carry out the retaliation urged in Cochrane's order of 18 July. Captain Hardy was directed to take the *Ramillies* (74), *Pactolus* (44), *Dispatch* (22), and the bomb-ship *Terror*, and destroy the town by bombardment. On 9 August they appeared off the town, and warned the inhabitants to leave within one hour.

Although the women and children were sent out of the town, the men stayed to defend it against the British squadron. Their efforts clearly demonstrated what the United States had lost by the lukewarm New England support of the war on land. On the evening of the 9th many shells and rockets were thrown into the town but there was no loss of life and little damage. Moreover, during the bombardment the inhabitants hauled an eighteen and a six-pounder to the

---

[34] Captain Paget to Cochrane, 14 June, 1814, Hardy to Cochrane, 12 July, 1814, Adm 1/506, pp. 379–83, 456–8; Croker to Cochrane, 29 April, 1814, Adm 2/1380, p. 80; Lossing, *Pictorial Field Book*, pp. 889–91.

end of the peninsula near the town, set up a temporary breastworks, and when they eventually opened fire drove off the barges and a launch from the British ships that were coming in close to shore. On the next morning Hardy ordered the *Pactolus* and the *Dispatch* to anchor as close to the town as possible. The *Pactolus* grounded, and was unable to support the smaller *Dispatch*. By the time she got off the *Dispatch* had been hit by the townsmen's eighteen-pounder, and had lost two men killed and twelve wounded. Soon, however, the Americans ran out of ammunition for their main gun, and spiked it in case the enemy should turn it against the town.

Later in the day more ammunition was found, the gun put back into action, and firing resumed. By this time a considerable number of militia had gathered in the town from the surrounding country. Although the British resumed their bombardment of the town on 11 and 12 August, the whole episode was a singular failure. One American nineteen-year-old who had served the battery eventually died of his wounds, but no one else suffered more than a slight injury. Less than fifty buildings were damaged, and only a handful ruined. After bombarding a small Connecticut town for four days, Hardy's force had suffered more casualties than the defenders.[35]

While some of the New Englanders were showing one reason why the privateers had proved so formidable, for another large group the tight British blockade of 1814 was proving utterly disastrous. The island of Nantucket was only thirty miles from the mainland, but the British controlled the intervening water. Nantucket was an island of seamen and their families, a great port for whalers, and had a population of about 7,000. The soil was infertile. It provided only a small part of what was needed to feed the inhabitants, and no fuel for the icy winters, and both food and fuel had to be imported from the mainland. The British blockade of 1814 placed the inhabitants of Nantucket in an untenable position, with no chance of relief, and in July they petitioned Admiral Cochrane to the effect that the severance of communication with the mainland had produced a great

---

[35] Hardy to Henry Hotham, 12 Aug., Hotham to Cochrane, 13 Aug., 1814, Adm 1/507, pp. 24–8; Lossing, *Pictorial Field Book*, pp. 892–6; George S. Brooks, ed., *James Durand: An Able Seaman of 1812* (New Haven, 1926), pp. 75–8.

shortage of food, and that when the winter came the islanders would face starvation. As the American government could not help them, the petitioners, who said they had always opposed the war, asked permission to import provisions and fuel from the mainland.

Cochrane directed Rear-Admiral Henry Hotham, who commanded the ships from Nantucket to the Delaware, to investigate the condition of the island, and if the inhabitants were as distressed as they claimed to grant them permission to import supplies. In return for this they would have to declare themselves absolutely neutral in the war between Britain and the United States. In the following months a series of most unusual discussions ensued between the British navy and the residents of Nantucket. On 21 August Hotham ordered Captain Vincent Newton of the *Nimrod* to proceed to Nantucket to view the situation. His report was that conditions on the island were even worse than the petitioners had claimed, and the island was 'a scene of the most pitiable distress'. The inhabitants had only two weeks' supply of food and wood on hand.

At a town meeting on the island a committee was elected to talk to Hotham, and these men visited the British commander on the *Superb* (74). At Hotham's request they signed a declaration asserting that 'The Island of Nantucket is hereby declared Neutral', and that none of the inhabitants would take any further part in the war. Any provisions that the islanders might be able to spare in the future would have to be supplied to British ships. In return for this declaration Hotham immediately gave the committee twenty-one passports to permit their vessels to bring provisions and fuel from the mainland. The inhabitants were also given permission to catch what fish they could on the shoals around the island.

Even yet the degree to which Nantucket had severed its connections with the United States was not satisfactory to the navy. On 8 September Hotham wrote again to the Nantucket Committee to tell them that Admiral Cochrane wanted it specifically asserted that the inhabitants would not pay United States taxes. Nantucket was being pressed hard, but still the inhabitants attempted to satisfy the British demands. In the middle of September a town meeting voted to petition Congress to suspend the collection of taxes for the duration of the war, and also persuaded the tax collector to resign. The residents pointed out to Hotham that they did not want to make a public and direct refusal to pay taxes. Hotham, however, was still not satisfied, and late in September a town meeting voted that the citizens would not pay taxes to the United States during the war with Britain. The agreement was now honoured by the British government, and orders were given that the Nantucket men among the American prisoners of war in Dartmoor were to be released from captivity as Nantucket was now neutral.[36]

The British pressure on New England territory reached its peak in the late summer with the decision to take control of Maine from the New Brunswick border to the Penobscot River. The region south and west of the Penobscot was ruled out as being too populous for successful operations with the available troops. The Governor of Novia Scotia, Lieutenant-General Sir John Sherbrooke, was able to use troops that had been sent from the Mediterranean after the victory over France; his total force amounted to some 2,500 men. The naval command of the operation was in the hands of Rear-Admiral Edward Griffith, who spent most of the war in command of the port of Halifax. On 26 August Griffith and Sherbrooke sailed from Halifax on the *Dragon* (74), accompanied by the frigates *Endymion* and *Bacchante*, the sloop *Sylph*, and ten transports. The fleet was off Penobscot Bay by the 31st, and was there joined by the *Bulwark* (74), the frigate *Tenedos*, the sloop *Peruvian*, the brig *Rifleman*, and the schooner *Picton*. Late in the evening of the 31st the fleet sailed up Penobscot Bay.

The American defences were again weak. Castine, the first object of the British on the Penobscot, had a crude redoubt-fort occupied by less than fifty men. Resistance was obviously useless, and on the approach of the British the fort was blown up. British troops landed and took possession of the town without opposition. Some troops were detached to occupy Belfast on the opposite side of the bay, and a more important expedition was sent up the river to Hampden where chance had placed an additional prize within the British grasp.

---

[36] This account of the Nantucket episode is taken from the correspondence in Adm 1/507, pp. 249–61, 453–9, 464; WO 1/142, pp. 415, 419–21, 427–9; also SN, CL, 1814, vol. 5, p. 17; [Charles Andrew], *The Prisoners' Memoirs, Or, Dartmoor Prison* (New York, 1815), p. 145.

On 17 August the American corvette *Adams* (24) had struck a rock, managed to get free, and with her pumps continually working ran into Penobscot Bay and up the river to Hampden. Sherbrooke and Griffith decided that the frigate should be destroyed, and some 700 troops were sent up the river. The naval force was under the command of Captain Robert Barrie. He took with him the sloops *Sylph* and *Peruvian*, the transport *Harmony*, a tender, and a number of launches.

While the British advanced up the river, the American militia gathered in the vicinity of Bangor, just up the river from Hampden. Captain Charles Morris of the *Adams* took the guns from his ship to form a battery, and the Americans eventually gathered some 600 militia, about 200 seamen and marines, and 40 regulars who had retreated from the fort at Castine. On the evening of 2 September the British troops were landed about three miles from Hampden. They advanced on the next morning in a heavy fog. On the approach of the British regulars the militia soon fled, the *Adams* was set on fire by the retreating Americans, and the British took possession of Hampden. The troops then advanced towards Bangor, and it was occupied without resistance. 190 prisoners were taken and paroled, and much property was appropriated by the British, who on the whole operation lost only one killed, eight wounded, and one missing. The expedition had resulted in the destruction of the *Adams* and a variety of other ships, as well as the capture of twelve other vessels. At Hampden a good deal of destruction took place: the village meeting house was wrecked and much property carried away.

The troops who had peacefully taken possession of Belfast were despatched on 6 September, on a longer trip to Machias, the county seat of Washington County, more than half-way back to Passamaquoddy Bay. The expedition was directed by Captain Hyde Parker of the frigate *Tenedos*. The force arrived at Machias on the evening of the 10th, and the troops were landed about five miles from the fort. It was garrisoned by about fifty United States regulars. The British marched through the woods, and took possession of the fort and town without opposition. Rear-Admiral Griffith was able to report to the Admiralty on 27 September that the whole of Maine between Passamaquoddy Bay and the Penobscot River was now under British control.[37]

In 1814 British sea power placed a stranglehold around the American coast. Trade was crushed, the collapse of American finances accelerated, and military landings carried out practically at will. The only solace to the Americans at sea was through the actions of individual ships, and even this consolation was now a rare one. In the first half of the year there were still a few governmental vessels sailing the seas with skill and daring, and there were always privateers willing to carry the war to the heart of British commerce. Yet, these efforts were a nuisance rather than a major threat, and the reality of British naval power placed the whole coastline of the United States at the mercy of British troops. If they were to be stopped they would have to be stopped on land, for there was no American naval force capable of preventing landings.

---

[37] British accounts of this expedition are in Adm 1/506, pp. 539–40; 1/507, pp. 128–37, 304-7; 1/508, pp. 28–32. For American side see SN, CL, 1814, vol. 5, pp. 124, 143; vol. 6, pp. 32, 72; Lossing, *Pictorial Field Book*, pp. 896–903.

7
The Attack from Canada

The comparative positions of Britain and the United States changed dramatically in 1814. At the beginning of the war Britain had been deeply immersed in her struggle against Napoleon. She had looked upon the intervention of the United States as a minor irritant rather than a threat against which major force had to be mustered. For the most part the defence of Canada had been left to the regulars already in the Province and to the local militia. The collapse of France in the spring of 1814 created a new situation. Apart from the great increase in naval strength and in military forces to harass the American coast, Britain was able to plan major invasions of the United States, and to contemplate the transformation of a defensive war into a crushing victory.

For the United States the end of the European war, and the launching of British attacks, could not have come at a worse time. By 1814 the lack of planning and the internal opposition to the war had produced near chaos. The crisis in the American economy brought about by the British blockade injected fresh confusion into a financial situation already bedevilled by the inadequate system of taxation, and by New England's lack of support for government loans. The failure of the government's financial plans had already become obvious in 1813, and in May of that year Secretary of the Treasury Albert Gallatin had obtained a leave of absence to undertake a diplomatic mission; this subsequently led to his resignation. After twelve years at the Treasury he was weary of Congressional resistance and dejected at the failure of so many of his pre-war plans. The Treasury was given over to the temporary guidance of William Jones, the Secretary of the Navy, who did little to avoid the mounting crisis.

The financing of the war in 1813 had depended on loans, as normal income provided less than a quarter of the money needed during the year. In February 1813 Congress authorized the borrowing of $16,000,000, but it was only possible to raise it by letting it out at a 12% discount. New England, by far the most prosperous section of the country, gave very little support, Boston providing only some $75,000 out of $16,000,000. As Congress had also in February authorized $5,000,000 in Treasury notes to replace those issued the previous year, it was essential that something be done to support the financial arrangements of the government. In the summer a special session of Congress finally agreed to impose internal taxes, including a direct tax of $3,000,000 apportioned among the states, as well as a number of excise taxes. Congress also had to authorize a further loan of $7,500,000. Again a considerable discount had to be given to attract lenders.

The government's financing of the war was essentially unsound, and in 1814 the extent of the crisis became fully apparent. When in February Gallatin changed his leave of absence into a definite resignation, considerable difficulty was experienced in securing a new Secretary of the Treasury. Madison eventually had to settle for the makeshift appointment of George Washington Campbell of Tennessee, a man who inspired no confidence among the financial community. He was the man who would have to try to borrow the nearly $30,000,000 that acting Secretary Jones had in January reported as necessary to balance the budget for the year. In March Congress authorized $10,000,000 in Treasury notes and $25,000,000 in loans; in order to spread the impact it was decided to float the loan in three separate instalments. The first of $10,000,000 was almost raised, but the second of $6,000,000 fell more than $3,000,000 short, and there was no chance for the third instalment. Out of $25,000,000 authorized little more than $10,000,000 was raised by mid-summer. The country was bankrupt, and only by the issuing of Treasury notes could the payments be made.[1]

The financial crisis had been caused by the failure of the Republicans to provide an adequate system of taxation for the war, but the actual collapse was precipitated by the attitude of New England.

---

[1] These paragraphs on financial problems are based on Balinky, *Gallatin*, pp. 194–206; see also Adams, *History*, VII, 42–3, 396–7.

Although there was a sizeable minority in New England in favour of the war, the Federalist leaders refused to give the war their support. This opposition had particularly harmful financial effects, as New England was the section with the most money to invest. In 1812 and 1813, while the British blockade tightened around the southern coasts, trade was still allowed to flow through the New England ports. To add to this favourable situation, New England continued to increase its production of manufactured goods, and a country starved of British manufactures was happy to buy from the northeast. While the south and west languished, specie was available in New England. Yet the Federalists who controlled the New England banks did not want to support the war, and for the most part refused to subscribe to government loans. Over $40,000,000 (worth only $28,000,000 in specie) was borrowed by the government by the end of 1814, and of this less than $3,000,000 came from New England, the richest section of the country.[2]

The opposition of New England to the war also created the additional fear in 1814 that the section would give little support to the effort to repel the British attacks. New England had provided many of the volunteers for the regular army, but the states had persisted in the attitude that their militia was only to be used as a defence against invasion, and that the individual state, not the President, would decide when they should be used. The extent to which this doctrine could be taken was well demonstrated in November 1813 when Governor Martin Chittenden of Vermont ordered a brigade of Vermont militia, which had marched to Plattsburg to aid in its defence, to return home. He argued that they were being used to defend New York and that constitutionally they should only defend Vermont. To the credit of some of the officers they refused to obey his order, which carried the idea of the defensive role of the militia to an absurd length. It was quite obvious that a successful British invasion along Lake Champlain and the Hudson Valley threatened the safety of the whole of New England. Nevertheless, should the

---

[2] Adams, *History*, VII, 388–9; Morison, *Life and Letters of Otis*, II, 52–6, 66; Davis R. Dewey, *Financial History of the United States* (New York, 1924), p. 133; Paul Studenski and Herman E. Krooss, *Financial History of the United States* (New York, 1952), pp. 78–9.

British invade in 1814, there seemed ample reason to believe that the New England states would not rally in force to defend areas outside their own actual territorial limits, and there was fear that some prominent individuals would even welcome the invaders. In New England there was widespread bitterness against the Embargo, and talk of a convention to discuss possible steps to resist what was considered unwarranted central government power. Some extremists even talked of secession. The removal of the Embargo in the spring of 1814 helped to defer any idea of independent action, but the disasters of the summer were to bring a revived interest in a New England convention.[3]

At the beginning of 1814 the federal government was obliged to depend on a regular army amounting to some 30,000 men, and such help as could be provided by the militia of the various states. The regulars themselves were, of course, in many cases such recent recruits that they were little better than militia. In January 1814 Congress passed a bill to encourage enlistments, and the bounty of $124 was doubled. Yet, by the end of March, there were less than 6,000 recruits. With these limited military resources the United States had to defend the whole Canadian frontier, and a coastline from Maine to New Orleans.[4]

Late in April 1814, as British ships and troops were gathering to cross the Atlantic to join Admiral Cochrane's command at Bermuda, the Admiralty was also arranging for the transportation of a large body of British troops from the south of France to Canada. These were troops experienced and confident from their victories over the French. The object of the British government in the spring of 1814 was to provide Governor Prevost with 10,000 new troops from Europe, and the first detachments began to cross the Atlantic to Canada in May. On the 9th the 2nd Battalion of the Royal Scots sailed from Portsmouth and the 97th Regiment from Cork, and on the 15th the first detachments from Bordeaux – the 6th and the 82nd Regiments – sailed for Quebec. Altogether these first detachments provided over 3,000 new men for the British army in Canada, and

---

[3] *Public Papers of Tompkins*, I, 38–40; Brannan, *Official Letters*, pp. 261–4; Morison, *Life and Letters of Otis*, II, 85–95; Adams, *History*, VIII, 2–14.
[4] Adams, *History*, VII, 380–84, VIII, 17.

twelve more regiments were to embark in the following weeks, in addition to the troops sent to Sir John Sherbrooke to enable him to occupy a part of Maine. The first of the reinforcements began to arrive at Quebec in June, and more came in July. The whole character of the war was changing, and the British were even able to send Prevost £100,000 in specie to ease Canadian financial problems.

British intentions along the Canadian frontier in this summer of 1814 were clearly outlined in the secret instructions sent by Bathurst to Prevost on 3 June. Prevost was told that he should begin offensive operations with his new troops before the end of the 1814 campaigning season. The first object was to ensure the immediate safety of Canada, but in addition he was, if possible, to provide for the 'ultimate security' of British possessions in North America. To obtain the first Prevost was to accomplish the 'entire destruction' of Sackett's Harbor and the American naval establishments on Lakes Erie and Champlain. For the second he was to retain Fort Niagara and the surrounding area, and also occupy Detroit and the Michigan country. Bathurst's conclusion was that if British successes enabled Britain to retain Fort Niagara and restore Detroit and the whole of the Michigan country to the Indians then the British frontier would be materially improved.[5]

The hope of an Indian barrier state south and west of the Great Lakes, in the American Old Northwest, had long been an ambition of the British government, and had been revived in 1812. Prevost had informed Lord Liverpool in October of that year that for the future safety of Upper Canada a provision for Indian occupation of the Michigan country should be included in any future negotiations between Britain and the United States.[6] Although the British had lost control of the Detroit region, they still in 1814 maintained

---

[5] Bathurst to Prevost, 3 June, 1814, CO 43/23, pp. 150–55; also Croker to Admiral Keith, 27 April, 19, 26 May, 1814, Adm 2/1380, pp. 66–8, 138–42, 170–71; Prevost to Bathurst, 8, 27 June, 12 July, 1814, CO 42/156, pp. 325, 347; 42/157, pp. 21–2. There are numerous letters regarding reinforcements at this time.

[6] Prevost to Liverpool, 5 Oct., 1812, CO 42/147, pp. 207–11; also Brock to Prevost, 28 Sept., 1812, Tupper, *Life and Letters of Brock*, p. 320; Bathurst to Brock, 16 Nov., 1812, CO 43/40, p. 366.

control in the region west of Lake Michigan. With only a few forts scattered over a great wilderness, the support of the Indian tribes gave a great advantage to the few British troops in the region. Since the capture of Michilimackinac in July 1812 the British had been in control. As a result of the British success, Indian warriors from that area were able in 1813 to journey eastwards and reinforce the British on the Detroit frontier – Chippewa, Ottawa, Menominee, Winnebago, Fox, and Sioux all came east to aid Colonel Procter. After Procter's failure to win any decisive advantage along the Maumee, many of these Indians returned home, and the tribes from west of Lake Michigan suffered little in Harrison's victory over Procter at the battle of the Thames in October 1813. That victory, however, meant that the few British west of Lake Michigan were separated by hundreds of miles from the nearest British forces at the head of Lake Ontario.[7]

In the spring of 1814 Governor Prevost despatched Lieutenant-Colonel Robert McDouall to take command at Michilimackinac with a party of some 300 men and with much needed supplies. He arrived there in the middle of May 1814, and was soon obliged to act to retain British control of the region.[8] The Americans had decided to attempt to regain control of the upper Mississippi in the campaigning season of 1814. This was a strange warfare west of Lake Michigan. The whole of the modern states of Wisconsin and Minnesota were untouched by the American settler, and control of areas larger than Britain depended on struggles involving at the most a few hundred British and Americans. Possession of the small strategic posts of Mackinac and Prairie du Chien meant that the surrounding tribes could be overawed.

At the beginning of May 1814 an American force of some 200 men left St Louis, travelled laboriously by barge up the Mississippi, and took Prairie du Chien without resistance. The British had concentrated their forces at Michilimackinac. Colonel McDouall was informed of the loss of Prairie du Chien by 21 June, and he immedi-

---

[7] Horsman, 'Wisconsin in the War of 1812', *Wisconsin Magazine of History*, XLVI (Autumn, 1962), pp. 6–8.

[8] Prevost to Cochrane, 11 May, 1814, Adm 1/506, pp. 171–2; Prevost to Bathurst, 10 July, 1814, CO 42/157, pp. 7–9.

ately despatched an expedition across what is now Wisconsin to retake it. The total force amounted to something over 600 men, most of them Indians, but it included over 100 Canadian volunteers from Mackinac and Green Bay, all under the command of the heavy-drinking fur trader, William McKay. The British discovered on reaching Prairie du Chien that the Americans had built a fort, and were supported by a gunboat anchored in the Mississippi, but after a three-day siege, during which a British three-pounder transported laboriously from Michilimackinac played a decisive part, the American garrison surrendered on 19 July. There were practically no casualties, although a small American force on its way up the Mississippi was badly mauled by the Indians, inspired by the news from Prairie du Chien, and had to retreat to St Louis.[9]

A more serious American threat in this region developed in August 1814. Early in July an American force of between 700 and 800 men sailed from Detroit under the command of Colonel George Croghan. On 4 August Croghan landed at the other end of Mackinac Island from the main fort, and McDouall met them soon after they landed with practically all his men supported by Indians. After a briskly fought engagement the Americans were forced to retreat and took to their boats, leaving thirteen dead and fifty-one wounded. The Americans now suffered further embarrassment when two schooners left to blockade the island were captured at anchor by British seamen and men of the Royal Newfoundland Regiment. On the evening of 3 September the British managed to row within a hundred yards of the American ships before being seen. Although fired on, they boarded and quickly captured the *Tigress*. On the following morning, pretending the *Tigress* was still American, the British managed to get within ten yards of the other American schooner, the *Scorpion*, before being discovered. They then quickly boarded her, and captured both vessels with only a handful of casualties.[10]

---

[9] Horsman, 'Wisconsin in the War of 1812', pp. 10–12.

[10] McDouall to Prevost, 14 Aug., to Drummond, 9 Sept., Lieut Bulger to McDouall, 7 Sept., Prevost to Bathurst, 4 Dec., 1814, CO 42/157, pp. 195–8, 244–8, 402–3; George Croghan to Armstrong, 19 Aug., 1814, WD, LR, Reg. Series; A. Sinclair to Jones, 9 Aug., 28 Oct., 1814, SN, CL, 1814, vol. 5, p. 78, vol. 7, p. 71.

The last effort of the Americans west of Lake Michigan came early in September 1814. In August Major Zachary Taylor led a force of some 330 men up the Mississippi to attack the Indians in the Rock River region. His task was a difficult one as there were a thousand Indians gathered around the mouth of the Rock River, and the British at Prairie du Chien sent a small force with a three-pounder to reinforce them. The unexpected gun proved too much for the American boats. The fire from the shore finally obliged Taylor to retreat on 5 September. For a time he stayed in a temporary fort at the mouth of the Des Moines, but in October he burnt the fort and retreated to St Louis. In 1814 this area west of Lake Michigan was one of the few in which the Americans attempted to take the offensive, but their efforts failed. American hopes of retaining the pre-war boundary in that area depended on events on battlefields further east.[11]

Bathurst's hopes that Prevost would be able to use his reinforcements to recapture Fort Malden and take Detroit were unrealistic for the campaigns of 1814. The new troops did not begin to arrive at Quebec until June, and Prevost felt that his reinforcements should first be used on fronts which presented greater danger. Moreover, because of the efforts expended on retaining a naval balance of power on Lakes Ontario and Champlain, there had been no opportunity to divert the resources necessary to regain the naval control of Lake Erie. Without that there seemed little chance of winning control of the whole Michigan country. In the winter of 1813–14 and the following spring, there was a stalemate in the area north of Lake Erie. The Americans used their base at Detroit, and their naval control of the lake, to send marauding expeditions as far as the Long Point region, but neither side made a decisive move with major forces. Prevost for a time had hopes of an expedition westwards in the winter, but this was never viewed with great optimism by the commanders on the spot, and the plan was abandoned.[12] In the summer of 1814 only Bathurst in London, thinking more of the conference table than the actual military and naval situation, had

---

[11] Horsman, 'Wisconsin in the War of 1812', p. 13.
[12] See Brannan, *Official Letters*, pp. 313–17; CO 42/156, pp. 77–85.

hopes of decisive British action against Detroit. Far more important in the United States and Canada was the situation on Lake Ontario, along the Niagara River, and on Lake Champlain.

Even before Bathurst emphasized it in his orders to Prevost, the British in Canada were thinking of offensive operations on Lake Ontario. The commander in Upper Canada, Lieutenant-General Drummond, was hopeful of destroying Sackett's Harbor, and suggested to Prevost late in April that he could accomplish this with a total of 4,000 men; he needed only a reinforcement of 800 to 1,000 regulars from Lower Canada to attain this strength. Prevost, still without reinforcements from England, felt that he could not spare the necessary troops from Lower Canada. Moreover, Prevost at that time was against any extensive offensive operations as he had agreed to discuss a proposal from Madison for a possible armistice. Nothing ever came of this proposal, and as soon as the British government heard of it they ordered Prevost to prosecute the war with vigour.[13]

In spite of Prevost's usual caution Drummond was in an excellent position for offensive operations at the beginning of May. The British naval force on Lake Ontario had been increased by two recently launched frigates, the *Prince Regent*, which carried 58 guns, and the *Princess Charlotte* which carried 44. American ships to meet this challenge would not be completed until July, and the lake was temporarily in British control. Thwarted in his hopes of an attack on Sackett's Harbor, Drummond decided to move against Oswego, a post of lesser importance, but one through which American naval stores and provisions passed on their way from the Hudson River to Sackett's Harbor.

On 4 May the British naval squadron sailed from Kingston with over 900 troops on board. They arrived off Oswego on the afternoon of the 5th, and launched their attack on the following day. The Americans were in no position to put up an effective resistance, as their total force amounted to only some 300 men. They resisted the British landing, but retreated within ten minutes after the British were ashore. The barracks were burned, stores destroyed, and several heavy guns carried away. The British lost 18 killed and 74

---

[13] Drummond to Prevost, 27, 28 April, to Bathurst, 3 July, Prevost to Drummond, 30 April, 1814, CO 42/355, pp. 91–2, 95–102; also CO 42/157, p. 43.

wounded, and the Americans 6 killed, 38 wounded, and 25 missing. Yet, in spite of General Drummond's reports of victory the attack was hardly a complete success; most of the American stores were at Oswego Falls, some ten to twelve miles above Oswego, and these were untouched by the British attack.[14]

The British failure to use their temporary naval supremacy to prevent the enlargement of the American fleet was compounded at the end of May in another attempt to prevent the shipment of American naval stores and armaments on Lake Ontario. In spite of the British control of the Lake, Commodore Chauncey was determined to transport naval guns from the Oswego region to Sackett's Harbor. As it was difficult to move them overland, he decided to risk taking them on boats close in along the shore of the lake. On 28 May the boats set out with guns, cables, and shot for the use of the American squadron. They were guarded by 130 riflemen, and the same number of pro-American Indians who followed the boats along the shore. The boats proceeded serenely on the first stage of their journey, and at noon on the 29th sheltered in Sandy Creek. While there they were attacked by the British. Captain Stephen Popham led 200 seamen and marines in the boats of the blockading squadron. They landed near the mouth of the creek, and as they advanced to the attack were surprised by the American riflemen and Indians. The British soon lost eighteen killed and fifty wounded, and Popham surrendered. It was a costly defeat. The British could ill-afford to lose seamen, and the Americans were able to equip the new vessel by which they would regain a balance of power on Lake Ontario. Soon after the Sandy Creek affair Yeo relinquished the blockade of Oswego and Sackett's Harbor.[15]

---

[14] British accounts of the attack are in Drummond to Prevost, 7 May, 1814, CO 42/156, pp. 299–303; also *ibid.*, 307, 309, and Adm 1/506, pp. 160–62. American reports are in Brown to Armstrong, 14 May, 1814, and report of Lt-Colonel Mitchell, Brannan, *Official Letters*, pp. 333–4. British naval force on Lake Ontario is listed in Prevost to Cochrane, 11 May, 1814, Adm 1/506, pp. 171–2.

[15] Popham to Yeo, 1 June, Prevost to Bathurst, 8 June, 12 July, 1814, CO 42/156, pp. 327–9, 331–2; 42/157, pp. 19–20; Chauncey to Jones, 2 June, 1814, and enclosure, SN, CL, 1814, vol. 4, p. 3.

For the Americans time was running out for any attempts at offensive operations on the Canadian frontier. It was quite apparent that reinforcements from Europe would soon be arriving in Canada, and the Americans simply did not have the military strength for any decisive operations against Lower Canada or Kingston before they arrived. Late in February Secretary of War Armstrong had revived his oft-repeated desire for an attack on Kingston, but Major-General Jacob Brown, the commander at Sackett's Harbor, and Commodore Chauncey had decided that the task was too difficult. Instead, they wanted a major effort on the Niagara frontier, and Armstrong had to acquiesce in his commanders' suggestion. On the recommendation of Armstrong the Cabinet decided that General Brown should cross the Niagara River and, flanked by Chauncey on the lake, advance on Burlington and ultimately to York. Armstrong wanted to bring troops eastward from Detroit to reinforce Brown, but was overruled by the Cabinet who sent them on the useless expedition to Michilimackinac. While waiting for Chauncey's new vessel, which would not be ready until July, Armstrong suggested that to keep up the spirit of the troops General Brown should cross and take Fort Erie at the southern end of the Niagara River, and then advance northwards to Chippawa, or even farther if the opportunity presented itself.[16]

Although this was to be the major American effort in the region General Brown had less than 3,400 effectives, together with about 600 friendly Indians to undertake the attack. The regular infantry, consisting of some 2,400 men, was mostly composed of New Englanders, and the two brigades into which they were divided were commanded by Brigadier-Generals Winfield Scott and Eleazar Ripley. There was also a battalion of over 300 artillerymen, and 600 Pennsylvania volunteers commanded by Brigadier-General Peter B. Porter. Although the force was comparatively small, its task was by no means hopeless as the British, still waiting for the promised reinforcements, had less than 2,500 men in the garrisons along the

---

[16] Armstrong to Brown, 20 March, 10 June, 1814, SW, LS, MA, vol. 7, pp. 146, 257–9; Armstrong to Madison, 30 April, 1814, War Department, Letters to President, vol. 1, pp. 266–7; Adams, *History*, VIII, 27–34; Lossing, *Pictorial Field Book*, pp. 792–3.

Niagara River from Lake Ontario to Lake Erie, and most of these were not in the vicinity of Fort Erie but were at Forts George and Niagara near the entrance to Lake Ontario.

The Americans crossed the river above and below Fort Erie on the morning of 3 July, and quickly secured the capitulation of its garrison of 137 men. Casualties were slight. On the morning of 4 July Brigadier-General Scott's brigade and a corps of artillery were ordered to advance northwards towards Chippawa. They hardly seemed likely to carry out the hopes of the American prisoners far away in Dartmoor who that morning hung out a flag with the motto 'All Canada or Dartmoor for Life'. Scott reached the Chippawa River that night, saw that the British were assembled beyond it, and retreated two miles to make camp with his right resting on the Niagara. At 11.00 p.m. he was joined by General Brown with Ripley's brigade and more artillery, and on the following morning by some of the Pennsylvania volunteers and Indians.

The British commander, Major-General Phineas Riall, heard of the American landings early on the morning of 3 July, and immediately ordered five companies of the Royal Scots to advance to reinforce the Chippawa garrison. Riall wanted to attack the Americans as soon as possible, but had to wait for the 8th Regiment which was returning from York. It joined him on the morning of the 5th at Chippawa, and that afternoon Riall decided to attack with 1,500 regulars and some 300 militia and Indians. He was attacking a superior force, but in view of the disorganized efforts of previous American armies on this frontier, he could well expect that any sudden, determined attack was likely to rout the enemy forces.

On the afternoon of the 5th General Porter was sent forward with his Pennsylvania volunteers and Indians to drive off the British who had been raiding the American pickets. Porter's force broke and fled when it became apparent that the whole British force was advancing across the bridge over the Chippawa River to attack the American position. Riall quickly discovered that this American army was no disorganized rabble, for Scott's brigade left the comparative security of its position behind a narrow creek to meet the British on the open ground. For the moment the British were in superior strength but the Royal Scots and the 100th Regiment were cut down as they advanced directly against the American front, and Riall was forced to retreat. He had lost 148 killed, 321 wounded, and 46 missing. The total American casualties were some 300, including 60 killed. At the time of the actual engagement Riall's regulars had outnumbered Scott's brigade, but had been unable to break the American line. Had the American army shown such effectiveness on the Canadian frontier in 1812 and 1813 then the threat to Canada would have been infinitely greater.[17]

Two days after the battle of Chippawa the Americans advanced to outflank Riall, and he was obliged to retreat north to Fort George. When Prevost reported the news of this setback to Bathurst on 12 July, he also stated he would have to confine himself to defensive operations until the British achieved complete naval ascendancy on Lakes Ontario and Champlain, which would not be until September. In reality his superiority on Lake Ontario in the early summer of 1814 was the best he could expect in the whole campaigning season. This was made apparent by Brown's advance along the Niagara. By 10 July the American force was established at Queenston, and Brown hoped that Chauncey would sail from Sackett's Harbor to supply him and support the American advance. He also wanted Chauncey to bring heavy guns to be used against Forts George and Niagara. None of this proved possible. Chauncey himself was in bed with a fever, his new ship was not yet ready, and the American fleet dared not leave port. General Brown's position was becoming increasingly insecure, for British reinforcements were hurrying to the aid of Riall, while Brown had received no additional support. On 24 July he withdrew his army to Chippawa; by this time there were only some 2,600 American effectives.[18]

As soon as General Riall heard of the American retreat, he sent Lieutenant-Colonel Thomas Pearson south from Fort George with 1,000 men. This force halted on the morning of 25 July at Lundy's

---

[17] Brown to Armstrong, 6, 7, July, 1814, WD, LR, Reg. Series; Riall to Drummond, 6 July, 1814, CO 42/157, pp. 37–41; Edgar, ed., *Ten Years of Upper Canada*, pp. 288–9; Andrew, *Prisoners' Memoirs*, p. 96 (Dartmoor quotation).

[18] Prevost to Bathurst, 12 July, 1814, CO 42/157, pp. 21–2; Brown to Armstrong, 22, 25 July, 1814, Brannan, *Official Letters*, p. 379; Brown to Chauncey, 6 Sept., 1814, Edgar, ed., *Ten Years of Upper Canada*, pp. 299–300.

Lane about one mile from Niagara Falls. For the moment the British were outnumbered by the Americans to the south, but as the morning advanced the situation rapidly changed. Riall quickly advanced south to reinforce his advance, and while he was on the march the commander-in-chief in Upper Canada, Lieutenant-General Drummond, arrived at Fort George from York with reinforcements. Drummond sent more troops to follow Riall, and also sent 500 regulars and a party of Indians across the Niagara River to advance southwards towards Lewiston while armed seamen in boats gave support on the river. When General Brown at Chippawa heard of British troops advancing south on the American side of the river, he feared they would menace his stores at Fort Schlosser on the American shore, and decided that the best way to bring the British back to the Canadian side was to advance north towards Queenston.

Late in the afternoon of 25 July General Scott's brigade of about 1,000 men marched north and came up to the British at Lundy's Lane. Riall first gave the order to retreat, but shortly afterwards General Drummond arrived and countermanded the order. The British now had between 1,600 and 1,700 men at Lundy's Lane, another 1,200 men were marching rapidly from Burlington under Colonel Hercules Scott, and the troops on the American side of the river had been recalled. General Scott's American brigade showed their usual confidence and flair. At 6.00 p.m. they moved into a frontal attack on the British who were drawn up on a low hill, their left on the main road which ran parallel and close to the Niagara River. The British troops were supported by two 24-pounders as well as some smaller guns and rockets.

The American attack was executed with bravery and determination against superior numbers. The main success was against the British left. Here the British line was forced back, and General Riall wounded and captured. In spite of determined efforts the Americans achieved no real success against the rest of the line. Scott's brigade repeatedly advanced against the British centre in an effort to take the guns, but though the Americans came close enough to bayonet British artillerymen they were driven off. By 9.00 p.m. the fight was continuing in increasing darkness, and there was a temporary lull while the rest of the American force came up to support Scott and his troops. The attack was now renewed, but the British position was soon greatly strengthened by the arrival of Colonel Hercules Scott with 1,200 troops. Still the Americans continued to attack, but by midnight, with Generals Brown and Scott both wounded, General Ripley finally withdrew his exhausted troops. As at the battle of Chippawa the fighting had been carried on with determination and bravery by both sides, and the American troops had shown the steadiness they had so often lacked in the first two years of the war. The Americans had lost 172 killed, 572 wounded, and 110 missing. Drummond reported 84 killed, 559 wounded, 197 missing, and 42 prisoners.[19]

On the following day the Americans retreated to Fort Erie. They had not been routed in battle, but their advance into Upper Canada had been stopped by the British. Although the American army had fought far more effectively than in its previous battles in the war, the actual result had been no better than before. In fact, the result could have been disastrous if the British had now acted promptly. Fort Erie was weak defensively, but General Drummond had a new respect for the American troops, and was reluctant to follow up the indecisive engagement at Lundy's Lane with a direct attack on the Americans. He knew more British regulars were on their way, and he decided to wait for these reinforcements.

This American effort of July 1814 had once again been a case of too little and too late. The American army had been too small to overwhelm the British defenders, even though they had not yet been reinforced by the major arrivals from Europe. Moreover, the failure to win naval control of Lake Ontario in the early summer had meant that, after the victory at Chippawa, Brown had neither the guns nor the naval support he felt he needed for an attack on Fort George. Not until August was the American fleet on Lake Ontario ready to sail and dominate the lake, and then Chauncey tried to prevent supplies and troops reaching the British on the Niagara River. Typical of the War of 1812 was the manner in which naval control

---

[19] Brown to Armstrong, endorsed 7 Aug., 1814, WD, LR, Reg. Series; Drummond to Prevost, 27 July, 1814, CO 42/157, pp. 107–13; Prevost to Cochrane, 3 Aug., 1814, Adm 1/507, pp. 208–9.

was held by both sides at the wrong time for offensive warfare.[20] When General Brown needed it the American fleet was in Sackett's Harbor, and in August when General Drummond turned to the attack the British fleet was in Kingston.

At the beginning of August Drummond laid siege to Fort Erie. Fort Erie was situated close to the lake, and the Americans had been strengthening it since its capture early in July. Apart from the original fort, the Americans had constructed a line of defensive works roughly parallel to the lake to enclose an area south of the fort. They had also fortified the short distance eastwards from the fort itself to the lake, and placed a battery near the shore. The south-western corner of the American works – well to the south of the fort itself – was defended by another battery, situated on a mound called Snake Hill.[21]

By August the British army consisted of over 3,000 men, and Drummond hoped to draw the Americans out of the fort. In an attempt to accomplish this he sent 600 men to destroy the supply depots at Buffalo and Black Rock; if they were successful then he hoped the Fort Erie garrison would come out and fight because of lack of provisions. The British, under the command of Lieutenant-Colonel J. Tucker, crossed the river in the night of 2–3 August. Although they landed unopposed, they never reached their objectives. As they advanced to cross a minor creek, the British troops skirmished with Americans who had come out from Black Rock. Casualties were not heavy – the British lost 12 killed, 17 wounded, and 4 missing, and the Americans 2 killed and 8 wounded – but, according to their commander, the British troops 'displayed an unpardonable degree of unsteadiness'. The British were thrown into confusion by the American resistance, and Colonel Tucker had to retreat without securing the object of his mission.[22]

On 4 August American Brigadier-General Edmund P. Gaines arrived at Fort Erie from Sackett's Harbor to assume the command

---

[20] Chauncey to Jones, 10 Aug., 1814, SN, CL, 1814, vol. 5, p. 84.

[21] Lossing, *Pictorial Field Book*, pp. 829–30, 839.

[22] Drummond to Prevost, 4 Aug., 1814, and enclosure, CO 42/157, pp. 134–7; Major L. Morgan to Brown, 5 Aug., 1814, Brannan, *Official Letters*, pp. 383–4.

in place of the wounded Brown. At this time the British were encamped in the woods some two miles north of the fort. Drummond had decided not to risk an attack on the American fortifications until he had weakened them with his guns, and had sent for more to Fort George. Until the completion of the main battery on 13 August little action took place, although the British succeeded in taking two of the three American schooners that were anchored off the fort in a position to harass the British left flank. This *coup* was accomplished by 70 seamen and marines in batteaux.[23]

On 13 August the British battery opened on the American fort, but it was quickly discovered that the range was too great. One British participant later remarked that he doubted if one shot in ten even reached the American ramparts, and the ones that did rebounded like tennis balls.[24] After two days of this ineffectual bombardment General Drummond determined to assault Fort Erie on the night of 14-15 August. His plan was to attack in three columns; one heavy column would move against the battery on Snake Hill at the south-west corner of the whole line of American fortifications, while two columns would advance from the British guns and assault the north side of the fort itself and the fortifications connecting it to the lake. The attack began at 2.00 a.m. on 15 August. The Snake Hill column had marched at 4.00 the previous afternoon to get into position while the others had assembled at midnight.

The largest column, consisting of 1,300 men under Lieutenant-Colonel Victor Fischer, began their assault with fixed bayonets on the Snake Hill battery at 2.00 a.m. General Ripley, who was responsible for that portion of the American defences, was expecting an attack, and had called out his brigade before it began. The main hope of the British was to breach the *abbatis* between the hill and the lake, but they fell back in confusion before the American fire; some who attempted to flank the fortifications by wading in the shallow waters of the lake were captured. Fischer's column was obliged to withdraw without penetrating the American lines.

The columns attacking the north side of the American position

---

[23] Gaines to Armstrong, 7, 11 Aug., 1814, WD, LR, Reg. Series; Drummond to Prevost, 13 Aug., 1814, CO 42/157, p. 146.
[24] Dunlop, *Recollections*, pp. 64-7.

met with great initial success. The two columns marched to the attack as soon as they heard the firing of Fischer's troops. The centre column, which was to attack Fort Erie itself, numbered less than 200 men, commanded by Lieutenant-Colonel William Drummond, and the left column which was to attack the brief line of fortifications between the fort and the lake consisted of 650 men under Colonel Hercules Scott. Scott's attack on the fortifications and the shore battery was repulsed, but the two columns managed to get into the north-east bastion of the fort. They held their position there until dawn, unable to advance any farther, and unaided by General Drummond's reserve. The end came as a result of the accidental explosion of ammunition stored in the bastion. Some of the British were killed by the explosion, and the Americans drove out the demoralized remainder. Colonels Drummond and Scott were killed in the action, and in the whole attack on the fort the British stated they lost 57 killed, 309 wounded, and 539 missing. The American commander, however, reported 222 British found dead on the field. Total American casualties numbered only 84. It had been a severe reverse for the British, and Drummond was fortunate that the reinforcing of Canada in 1814 allowed him to bring up over 1,000 men from Burlington and York to replace his losses.[25]

In spite of the reinforcements General Drummond's position was becoming increasingly uncomfortable early in September. The American naval blockade prevented his troops receiving enough supplies, they were depressed by incessant rain, and there was a shortage of ammunition. Sickness among the troops threatened the whole British position. On the other hand the Americans in Fort Erie were in good spirits after the repulse of the British attack. General Gaines had been wounded by a British shell late in August, but General Brown, although not completely recovered from his wounds, returned to command the American defences. His main problem was that the British were completing their third battery, and they were now within 500 or 600 yards of the fort. Brown decided

---

[25] Drummond to Prevost, 15 Aug., 1814, and enclosures, CO 42/157, pp. 148–155; Dunlop, *Recollections*, pp. 81–7; Gaines to Armstrong, 15, 23 Aug., 1814, WD, LR, Reg. Series; Ripley to Gaines, 17 Aug., 1814, Brannan, *Official Letters*, pp. 390–92; Lossing; *Pictorial Field Book*, pp. 832–5.

to attack the batteries, destroy the guns, and withdraw before the British reserve could come up from their camp. The British were using one brigade to defend their batteries. In all General Brown committed 2,000 men to the sortie. It was launched in a very heavy rain on the afternoon of 17 September. General Peter B. Porter led a column of 1,600 regulars and militia through the woods from Snake Hill to no. 3 battery on the extreme right of the British line. The British, whose attention was diverted by heavy artillery fire from Fort Erie, were caught unprepared. The battery was captured almost immediately, the guns spiked, and the magazine blown up, and the column moved on to attack the second battery, aided by 400 regulars who advanced in a separate column from Fort Erie. The second battery fell after heavier fighting. By this time British reserves had moved up, the American reserve had also been committed, and after fierce fighting around the last of the British batteries the Americans retreated to the fort. They had lost 79 killed, including three of Porter's senior officers, and 432 wounded and missing, while the British lost 115 killed, 178 wounded, and 316 missing. Again Drummond had been checked, and with increasing sickness among his troops he decided to abandon the siege of Fort Erie.[26]

On 21 September the British fell back towards the Chippawa, and the summer campaigns drew to a close. Early in October American reinforcements arrived on the Niagara frontier under the command of Major-General George Izard, and after a brief encounter in the middle of the month, Drummond's forces retreated to Fort George, parts of his army going to Burlington and York for the winter. Izard saw no opportunity of advancing so late in the season, and on 5 November blew up Fort Erie. His army completely withdrew from the Canadian side of the river.[27]

---

[26] CO 42/157, pp. 164-7, 219-26; Brown to Armstrong, 18, 29 Sept., Porter to Brown, 22 Sept., 1814, WD, LR, Reg. Series; Lossing, *Pictorial Field Book*, pp. 837-40.
[27] Prevost to Bathurst, 30 Sept., 16 Nov., Drummond to Prevost, 24 Sept., Drummond to Bathurst, 20 Nov., 1814, CO 42/157, pp. 217, 239-40, 341-3; 42/355, pp. 124-30; Izard to Sec. of War, 7, 16, 23 Oct., 2, 8, 17 Nov., WD, LR, Reg. Series.

The 1814 campaigns on the Niagara frontier had, as usual, been indecisive. Drummond blamed insufficient reinforcements and lack of supplies and ammunition for his failure to destroy General Brown's army. More important had been the ability of the Americans to put an effective and well led army into the field, and the British difficulties had been compounded by a lack of dynamic leadership on the part of General Drummond. He tended to blame his troops for setbacks, but his own failure to advance rapidly on Fort Erie after the battle of Lundy's Lane, and the manner in which his batteries were surprised by the American sortie, showed that his own leadership left something to be desired.

In this summer of 1814 Prevost showed little enthusiasm for Bathurst's orders to take the offensive. He was bedevilled by the lack of naval force on Lakes Ontario and Champlain, and by his own innate caution, and he argued that it would be September before he had the naval strength necessary for an attack on Sackett's Harbor and Plattsburg. He indicated to Bathurst that his attack along Lake Champlain would confine itself to the west side of the lake, as Vermont on the east shore was such a valuable source of supplies for the British armies. Even at this stage of the war the American trade with the British continued. On 27 August Prevost asserted that 'two thirds of the Army in Canada are, at this Moment, eating Beef provided by American Contractors drawn principally from the States of Vermont and New York.' At the same time at Cornwall on the St Lawrence the brigade of artillery which had recently arrived from southern France was feeding its horses on hay provided by the Americans.[28]

By the time Prevost again held a naval advantage on Lake Ontario it was too late in the season, Drummond and his troops were too sick and wearied, and the supply situation too uncertain for an attack on Sackett's Harbor. It was not until October that the British ship of the line *St Lawrence*, which carried 102 guns, was finally ready to sail from Kingston. With this new development Chauncey relinquished his blockade and went back into port, and Yeo took to the

---

[28] Prevost to Bathurst, 5, 27 Aug., CO 42/157, pp. 120–21, 157–8; Edgar, ed., *Ten Years of Upper Canada*, p. 319.

THE ATTACK FROM CANADA

lake for the first time since the end of July. In the middle of October he sailed to the Niagara River with provisions and stores for the British army.[29] Both Yeo and Chauncey were excessively cautious commanders, but for most of the war this had been more damaging to the Americans than to the British. Only in 1814 were the British anxious for decisive offensive operations, yet, even had Yeo been able to come out earlier, it seems doubtful whether the British had the strength needed to take Sackett's Harbor.

With this inability to strike at Sackett's Harbor in 1814, Prevost's main effort to carry out his orders for offensive operations had to be on the Lake Champlain front. The British had command of American territory west of Lake Michigan and in northern Maine, but for a dominant position at the peace conference they needed more striking territorial conquests. To attack along Lake Champlain seemed Prevost's main chance to secure these.

During this campaigning season of 1814 the Americans had never attained the strength for a serious advance on the Lake Champlain front. In March, before the snow melted, General Wilkinson had tentatively advanced towards the Canadian border with some 4,000 men, but he had retired on meeting British resistance. At the beginning of May Major-General George Izard of South Carolina assumed command on the Lake Champlain front. Izard had received a military education in England, Germany, and France, had served at Chateauguay, and had been promoted to Major-General early in 1814. It was quite apparent from early in his command that his main task was defensive.[30]

Control of Lake Champlain was basic to any British advance to the South, for in this way the British flank would be protected and a solid supply line secured. The opposing naval forces on the lake had remained small throughout the war, but in 1814 Prevost hoped to swing the balance by the construction of a frigate, the *Confiance* (36). He insisted throughout the summer that his armies could not move

---

[29] Drummond to Bathurst, 20 Nov., 1814, CO 42/355, p. 127; Chauncey to Jones, 2, 8, 17 Oct., SN, CL, 1814, vol. 7, pp. 3, 15, 46; Roosevelt, *Naval War of 1812*, II, 102–7.

[30] Brannan, *Official Letters*, pp. 325–6; Prevost to Bathurst, 31 March, 1814, CO 42/156, pp. 165–9; Adams, *History*, VII, 407–8.

south until this frigate was completed to augment his naval force. With it he hoped to win control of the lake, for efforts at gaining an advantage earlier in the year had proved unsuccessful. In May Captain Daniel Pring, British naval commander on the lake, had sailed from the Isle aux Noix in the hope of destroying the American vessels which were being made ready to sail at Vergennes in Vermont. The British found them so well defended that they had to retire without inflicting any damage.[31]

There was little action on Lake Champlain throughout the spring and summer. General Izard had control of the area from Plattsburg north to the Canadian border, while Prevost waited for his reinforcements from Europe to be gathered for the invasion, and the completion of his new frigate. The *Confiance* was finally launched on 26 August at Isle aux Noix. Prevost's joy at this event was limited by the news that the Americans had just launched the *Eagle* (20) to increase their naval force on the lake.[32]

Although it was now quite obvious that the British were about to use their European reinforcements to invade along Lake Champlain, American Secretary of State Armstrong chose this moment to transfer the American defensive forces. Late in July Armstrong had suggested to General Izard that he should advance to the St Lawrence to threaten British communications with Kingston. Izard had replied that he expected to be attacked along Lake Champlain by a large British force, and a movement to the St Lawrence would be too dangerous. Armstrong's remarkable reply to this was to order Izard and a large body of his troops westward to Sackett's Harbor; from there the Americans were, in theory, to be used to attack Kingston or to go to the aid of the Americans on the Niagara frontier. On 29 August, three days after the launching of the *Confiance*, General Izard obeyed his orders, and set out for Sackett's Harbor with 4,000 men.

This incredible decision of Armstrong's left Brigadier-General

---

[31] Prevost to Cochrane, 11 May, 1814, Adm 1/506, pp. 171–2; Prevost to Bathurst, 18 May, 1814, CO 42/156, pp. 293–7; Macdonough to Jones, 13, 14, 18 May, 1814, SN, MCL, 1814, vol. 1, pp. 126, 128, 129.

[32] Prevost to Bathurst, 27 Aug., 1814, CO 42/157, p. 156; Macdonough to Jones, 1, 16, 27 Aug., 1814, SN, MCL, 1814, vol. 2, pp. 12, 18, 25.

THE ATTACK FROM CANADA 187

Alexander Macomb in command of the American forces along Lake Champlain. He now made every effort to defend the fortifications which had been erected at Plattsburg. The total forces left to him numbered little over 3,000 men, and of these Macomb reported that only 1,500 were effectives. It seemed quite possible that the whole north-east was ready to fall into British hands. The New England leaders still would not commit their militia to federal control, and even Governor Chittenden of Vermont did not consider the invasion of the neighbouring state of New York justified him ordering his militia to its aid; it was agreed, however, that they could go as volunteers to serve in the defence of Plattsburg.[33]

General Izard had hardly marched out of sight when the British began to cross the border on their way to Plattsburg. The army consisted of over 10,000 men, nearly all of them veterans of the Peninsula campaigns, and it was undoubtedly the strongest army yet to take the field in the War of 1812. The only real weakness appeared to be in its command. Sir George Prevost had decided to take the field himself with Major-General Francis de Rottenburg as his second-in-command. Prevost was a cautious leader who had demonstrated no real ability as a military commander, and he soon found himself clashing with the commanders of the three brigades that made up his division. These three Major-Generals – Frederick P. Robinson, Thomas Brisbane, and Manley Power – were all veterans of the Peninsula, and were described by the Duke of Wellington as 'the best of their rank in the army'. When Wellington heard that Prevost had clashed with the general officers he had sent from France, he commented that Prevost should be removed.[34] Prevost, of course, had no easy task in coping with the officers and men who had fought their way into France. Many of them resented their quick departure for another battlefield, and these veterans were

---

[33] Armstrong to Izard, 10 Aug., 1814, SW, LS, MA, vol. 7, p. 280; Izard to Armstrong, 11, 23 Aug., to Macomb, 23 Aug., Macomb to Sec. of War, 31 Aug., 2 Sept., 1814, WD, LR, Reg. Series; Adams, *History*, VIII, 98 101, 221; J. T. Adams, *New England in the Republic*, p. 286.

[34] Wellington to Bathurst, 30 Oct., 1814, Francis Bickley, ed., *Report on the Manuscripts of Earl Bathurst preserved at Cirencester Park* (H.M.C., London, 1923), p. 302.

certainly in no mood to accept Prevost's rather rigid edicts. As fighting officers they resented an administrator telling them that even while campaigning they should follow the strict details of military discipline, even to the wearing of a uniform correct in all particulars. It would have been far better if one of Wellington's officers had been given command of the expedition.

The British army crossed into the United States on 1 September, and camped within eight miles of Plattsburg on the 5th. Prevost had advanced slowly on the bad roads, and while he was advancing General Macomb's troops worked day and night in Plattsburg to prepare the defences. Most of the inhabitants fled, although some stayed to take part in the struggle. General Benjamin Mooers of the New York militia managed to raise 700 men in the region, and on the 4th moved towards the British force, skirmished with the advance, and cut down the trees and destroyed bridges to impede the progress of the army.

Early on the morning of 6 September the British army was advancing on two parallel roads. The right column on the Beekman Town Road was farthest from the lake, and was commanded by Major-General Power. The left advanced along the Lake Road under the command of Major-General Brisbane. The column under Power advanced rapidly against an American force composed mostly of militia, and strengthened by 250 regulars. The militia fled in confusion, and the regulars had no choice but to retreat. This rapid advance of the right column effectively turned the stronger position held by the Americans on the lake road. At Deer Creek bridge Macomb had posted 200 regulars with two field pieces; they had orders to place *abbatis* in the woods, obstruct the road, and fortify their own position. Ahead of them were over 100 riflemen scouting the British advance. Yet, as the British right column advanced rapidly to within a mile of Plattsburg, Macomb was obliged to withdraw his men from the Deer Creek bridge, leaving his riflemen to harass the British flank. The total American resistance was slight, and the British never even deployed to meet the enemy, but continued to advance rapidly in columns.

Plattsburg was split by the Saranac River, and the Americans had erected three strong redoubts to the south of the Saranac, across the neck of the small peninsula formed by the Saranac and Lake Champlain. The American advance retreated across the two bridges over the river, removed the planks, and used them to form breastworks for the troops waiting to resist the British crossing. A further difficulty for the British was added by the presence of the American fleet anchored offshore. Prevost first asked General Robinson if he could attack immediately, but Robinson pointed out that his troops had been marching most of the day without eating, and that none of Prevost's staff was able to identify the fords by which the British troops would cross the river. Robinson also wanted the co-operation of the British fleet in attacking the American fortifications.[35]

Prevost, of course, had always thought that naval command of the lake was essential to any advance, and he decided to ask the British naval commander, Captain George Downie, for his co-operation. To help the troops on land Downie would first have to engage the American fleet positioned in Plattsburg Bay. The American squadron consisted of the ship *Saratoga* (26), the brig *Eagle* (20), the schooner *Ticonderoga* (17), the sloop *Preble* (7), and ten gunboats, with a total complement of nearly 900 men. They were commanded by Captain Thomas Macdonough, who had gained experience in the war against Tripoli.

The British force consisted of the frigate *Confiance* (36), the brig *Linnet* (16), the sloops *Chubb* (11) and *Finch* (10), and twelve gunboats. They had a total complement of between 900 and 1,000 men. In the weight of metal that could be delivered the two fleets were about equal, although the British had an advantage in long guns and in the possession of the largest ship in the engagement. To offset this the *Confiance* had only just been launched, and it soon became apparent that she was by no means ready for action.

On the morning of 7 September Prevost wrote to Captain Downie, who was with his fleet about fifteen miles from Plattsburg. He described the American fleet, asked if Downie felt strong enough to engage it, and stated that his movements would depend upon Downie's decision. Downie replied the same day that he knew of the

---

[35] Prevost to Bathurst, 11 Sept., 1814, CO 42/157, pp. 187-8; Macomb to Sec. of War, 8, 15 Sept., 1814, WD, LR, Reg. Series; Lossing *Pictorial Field Book*, pp. 859-64.

comparative strength of the two squadrons, and that he would engage the enemy as soon as he had the *Confiance* ready for action; it would take at least a day or two to accomplish this. Prevost's reply was to write even more urgently of the need for the co-operation of the fleet. He argued that he was waiting for Downie's arrival to attack, and that Downie's share in the operation would be to destroy or capture the American squadron, and then co-operate with the British army. From the 8th to the 10th more letters passed between them – Downie emphasizing that it was his duty not to commit his ships until they were ready for battle, while Prevost pointed out the dangers of delay, and argued that he had heard from deserters that the American fleet was inefficiently manned. This was small consolation to Downie, for he pointed out that he was so short-handed that he hoped to use a company of the 39th Regiment to supplement his sailors.

While Prevost waited for Downie his men erected batteries and prepared to attack, and the Americans continued the frantic strengthening of their defences which had begun over a week before when Prevost had crossed the American border. General Macomb later wrote of the New York militia and Vermont volunteers 'pouring in from all quarters'. On the night of the 9th Captain Downie wrote that he expected to round into Plattsburg Bay on the following morning, but though Prevost held his troops in readiness, an unfavourable wind caused a further delay. It was not until the morning of the 11th that Downie's fleet sailed into the Bay, after first warning Prevost that they were on their way. Prevost's intention was to begin his land attack simultaneously with the commencement of the naval battle.

Captain Downie had the task of engaging an American fleet anchored in a position of its own choosing, and the British commander on the lakes, Sir James Yeo, later argued that because of Prevost's urging, the British fleet had engaged at a decided disadvantage. If Prevost had first stormed the American works then the American squadron would have come out to meet the British in open water outside the bay. Captain Downie, however, sailed straight into the bay to engage the American ships, trying to place the *Confiance* (36) as close alongside the *Saratoga* as possible. The wind was light and shifting, and he eventually anchored about three hundred yards from the American vessel. The brig *Linnet* (16) anchored to engage the *Eagle* (20), and was aided by the *Chubb* (11). The *Finch* (10) and most of the British gunboats engaged the *Ticonderoga* (17) and the *Preble* (7), and most of the American gunboats. The remainder of the gunboats were engaged at the other end of the line.

The *Confiance* waited until she was anchored before returning the American fire, and then poured a destructive broadside into the *Saratoga*. Yet, soon after the engagement began the British chances were severely hindered by the death of Captain Downie, and by the loss of the two British sloops. The *Finch* was disabled by the *Ticonderoga*, drifted aground on Crab Island, and struck her colours after coming under fire from a battery manned by some of the American sick. The *Chubb* also drifted out of control after engaging the *Eagle*, and was taken possession of by a midshipman from the *Saratoga*; she was, however, in no condition to continue the engagement. The American *Preble* came under severe fire from the British gunboats, and had to drift inshore and anchor out of the engagement, but the *Ticonderoga* successfully resisted their attacks.

From the British point of view all depended on the *Confiance*; she was the biggest ship in the battle, and if she could overcome the *Saratoga* without being disabled then she could have swept up the rest of the American line. By 10.30 a.m. it seemed that the British might be carrying the day. The *Eagle*, which had been under fire from the British *Linnet* and *Confiance* had the springs of her cable shot away, and was unable to bring her guns to bear on the *Linnet*. Her captain cut her cable, and anchored between the *Confiance* and the *Ticonderoga*. This enabled her to fire on the former ship, but also left the *Saratoga* exposed to the fire of the *Linnet*. Both the *Saratoga* and the *Confiance* had suffered severely, and Captain Macdonough's starboard battery was in no condition to reply to the British. At this decisive moment Macdonough's seamanship prevailed. He managed to wind the ship around by means of an anchor and hawsers, and brought his port battery to bear on the *Confiance*. The *Confiance* tried the same manœuvre without success, and received so much damage from the fresh American broadside that she struck her colours. The *Saratoga* was then sprung around to bear on the *Linnet*, and the latter struck in fifteen minutes. The British gunboats fled, and Macdonough had won a vital victory. The Americans had lost 52 killed and 58 wounded, the British over 80 killed and 100 wounded.[36]

When the British ships had first appeared on the horizon, Prevost had ordered his troops into the attack on land. Covered by the fire of the British batteries, Major-General Robinson was ordered to lead part of his own brigade and that of General Power to a ford a little farther up the Saranac. He was there to cross the river and using scaling ladders assail the American works. While this main attack unfolded, Brisbane's brigade diverted attention by attacks against the two stripped plank bridges. The Quartermaster-General's Department provided the guides for Robinson's column, but they took the wrong road, causing one hour's delay. Even with this setback the British troops rushed across the shallow ford under fire from the American volunteers and militia; the American regulars were defending the crossing at the two bridges. Within a short time Robinson had four battalions across, and his advance was within range of the redoubts, when the order came to retire. As soon as Prevost realized that the British naval squadron had been defeated he ordered his troops to withdraw; this they did to the sound of the American troops cheering the naval victory.

In retreat Prevost attained a speed he never achieved in attack. That same evening the baggage was sent to the rear, and the batteries dismantled. The following morning before daylight the troops began their march back to Canada, and large quantities of excess ammunition and stores were destroyed. This fine army of Wellington's veterans had seen little action. The official casualties from 6 to 14 September were 37 killed, 150 wounded, and 55 missing, although in reality many more had taken the opportunity to

---

[36] Prevost's correspondence with Downie before the battle is contained in *Some Account of the Public Life of the Late Lieutenant-General Sir George Prevost, Bart.* (London, 1823), Appendix, pp. 78–83. For the battle see Macdonough to Jones, 11, 13 Sept., 1814, and enclosures, SN, CL, 1814, vol. 6, pp. 38, 51, 52, 55; CO 42/157, pp. 203–6 (British account); also *Bathurst Mss*, p. 285; Edgar, ed., *Ten Years of Upper Canada*, p. 325. The comparative naval strengths are discussed in Roosevelt, *Naval War of 1812*, II, 114–26.

THE ATTACK FROM CANADA   193

desert while on American soil. General Macomb reported on 15 September that over 300 deserters had already come in, and more were still arriving. Between 6 and 11 September the Americans lost 38 killed, 64 wounded, and 20 missing. The great threat to New York had ended. Well might General Robinson write that 'I am sick at heart'. Robinson, like Yeo, thought that the storming of the defences did not have to await the issue of the naval battle.[37]

Prevost placed the blame for the withdrawal squarely on the loss of naval power on Lake Champlain. Indeed, once the British naval squadron had been defeated there was good reason for the British to retreat. In this situation Prevost would have had to depend exclusively on a tenuous land line for his supplies, and his line of communication would have been exposed to any harassment that the Americans might attempt from their naval control of the lake. Yet, had Prevost been a more confident and dashing general he might well have flung his troops into the attack on Plattsburg as soon as they were rested from their march, without waiting for his naval squadron to come up. Given the experience of his officers and troops, there seems good reason to believe that they could have stormed the American fortifications and overwhelmed Macomb's small force of regulars and hastily gathered militia and volunteers. With Plattsburg taken the American fleet might even have taken refuge without engaging the British squadron; they certainly would not have remained anchored in Plattsburg Bay. Yet, Prevost had been told throughout the war that he should take no risks, and the arrival of troops from Europe did not suddenly transform him into a resourceful, attacking general.[38]

---

[37] Prevost to Bathurst, 11 Sept., 1814, CO 42/157, pp. 188–9, also *ibid.*, 191–2 (casualties); General Robinson to Merry, 22 Sept., 1814, *Bathurst Mss*, pp. 290–94; Macomb to Sec. of War, 15 Sept., 1814, WD, LR, Reg. Series; Adams, *History*, VIII, 101–13.

[38] Prevost gave his reasons for retreat in a private letter to Bathurst, 22 Sept., 1814, CO 42/157, pp. 209–11.

8

The Burning of Washington

The advance of Prevost into New York was only part of the crisis which threatened the United States in August and September 1814. Throughout the summer the British had also been reinforcing Admiral Cochrane for his operations against the southern coasts of the United States. A thousand marines had arrived at Bermuda early in June, another battalion in the middle of July, and on 24 July 3,000 troops from the Gironde under the command of Major-General Robert Ross. Ross had seen considerable experience under Wellington, and he was ordered to effect a diversion on the American coast to help the British armies in Canada. Admiral Cochrane, in consultation with Ross, was to decide the best point for the attack. At Bermuda no time was lost in forwarding the objects of the expedition. Cochrane sailed for the Chesapeake on 1 August, leaving Rear-Admiral Charles Malcolm to transport Ross's force after the ships from Europe had taken on water. Fortunately for the British their troops were in excellent health after the voyage, and Malcolm and Ross sailed from Bermuda on 4 August.[1]

On arriving in the Chesapeake Admiral Cochrane consulted with Cockburn who had spent the early summer marauding in the region. The initial decision was to use the strong force of troops to attack the American flotilla of gunboats which had taken refuge in the Patuxent River. If, after ascending the river, the way should seem clear, then it was hoped to attack the city of Washington. The British entered the Patuxent, and anchored off Benedict. From that village there were two possible roads to Washington. That which was of interest to the British ran parallel to the Patuxent to Nottingham and Upper Marlborough (some twenty-five miles away), and from there it was

---

[1] Croker to Cochrane, 19 May, 1814, Adm 2/1380, pp. 142–6; Cochrane to Croker, 23 July, 11 Aug., Malcolm to Croker, 24 July, 1814, Adm 1/506, pp. 490–93, 496, 550.

9a. Believed to be Tecumseh

9b. Battle of the Thames, 1813
(Lithograph of 1833)

10a. British woodcut of the Burning of Washington, 1814

10b. The Burning of Washington: British troops enter the city in August 1814

only fifteen miles through Bladensburg to the capital. While the army marched north, Admiral Cockburn was to take a flotilla of launches, pinnaces, barges, and other boats up the Patuxent. This force could supply the British troops with provisions, and if necessary transport them to the other side of the river to retreat to the fleet. Cochrane also detached a small force of ships and gun vessels to sail up the Potomac and bombard Fort Washington, some ten miles below the city. This it was hoped would provide an alternative route of retreat from Washington should the Bladensburg route be blocked by the gathering of troops from the surrounding country. A few other vessels were sent up the Chesapeake above Baltimore to divert the attention of the Americans.[2]

Although all this appeared to provide adequately for retreat in the event of danger, the prospect of marching an army of some 4,000 men on the very outskirts of the American capital might well have seemed to be inviting disaster had it not been for the ineptness of American defensive preparations in this region. The British had raided along the shores of the Chesapeake for much of the war, and had complete naval control of the area, and it was of course well-known to the American government that reinforcements were on their way from Europe in this summer of 1814. What was remarkable in view of all this was that Secretary of War Armstrong had failed to fortify the city. He had decided that as Baltimore not Washington was the most important city militarily, the capital was safe. He apparently ignored the psychological attraction of marching into the enemy's capital.

In the spring of 1814 other members of the government began to discuss the question of defence in the Washington area, and in spite of Armstrong's nonchalance eventually persuaded him to take some action. The main stimulus for this came in June when reports made it quite clear that troops were being sent from France to operate against the United States. At the beginning of July the Cabinet decided to form a new military district, the Tenth, from Maryland, the District of Columbia, and parts of eastern Virginia. Brigadier-General William H. Winder, a native of Maryland, was given the command. He had

---

[2] Cochrane to Croker, 2 Sept., 1814, Adm 1/506, pp. 598–9.

served in the army since 1812, had been captured at Stoney Creek on the Niagara frontier, and exchanged in the spring of 1814. Armstrong had not wanted to appoint Winder, but was overruled by the President.

In theory General Winder could call on 15,000 militia for the defence of Washington. These were to be obtained from the District of Columbia, Maryland, Pennsylvania, and Virginia, but in practice the requisitions remained unfilled. All through July Winder rode through the area attempting to obtain a good knowledge of the terrain, but on 1 August he had to report that his total force of regulars amounted to 1,000 men, and although on paper he had 4,000 militia in reality only a few hundred were ready and available. Moreover, no lines of defence nor fortifications had been prepared to defend the possible approaches to Washington. Armstrong, resentful of the interference of President Madison and Secretary of State Monroe, made no effort to stimulate Winder or the militia of the adjoining states.[3]

The British army of some 4,000 men landed at Benedict on 19 August. They met no resistance. On the following day the army began its march, Admiral Cockburn and the boats accompanying them on the Patuxent. No American troops were to be seen, and although the British army lacked cavalry, reconnoitring was carried out by artillery drivers mounted on any horses that could be seized and brought in. The army reached Nottingham by the evening of 21 August and a few shots were fired on the British boats, but the army marched on unopposed.

The next morning the force moved on to Upper Marlborough. Cockburn landed marines across the river on Pig Point to attack the village there and to attract the attention of any American troops who were in the vicinity. The flotilla of American gunboats could be seen beyond Pig Point in the Patuxent. At the approach of the British boats Captain Joshua Barney destroyed his sloop and fifteen gunboats to avoid their capture by the British. Another gunboat on which the fire had gone out was captured. The British also burnt or

---

[3] Material relating to the defence and burning of Washington is printed in *ASP, MA*, I, 524–99, see espec. 543–7; also Lossing *Pictorial Field Book*, pp. 916–20; Adams, *History*, VIII, 120–24.

seized another thirteen merchant schooners. Only a few shots were fired at the British, and the village of Pig Point was taken without resistance. On the morning of 23 August Cockburn went to Upper Marlborough to confer with Ross. The sailor was keen to attack Washington, and Ross agreed to undertake the expedition. It was also decided that Admiral Cockburn would accompany the army with the marine artillery and some of the seamen while the marines would garrison Upper Marlborough. That night the troops camped about five miles along the road from Upper Marlborough to Washington.[4]

While the British army was making its remarkably trouble-free march through the American countryside, the American government was desperately trying to organize the defence of the capital and gather all possible militia from the region. At the time of the landing at Benedict on 18 August General Winder had some 1,600 or 1,700 militia in the field. There were 250 of these at Bladensburg, and the rest, under militia General Tobias Stansbury, were near Baltimore. From 18 August Winder made desperate attempts to increase this force. As he had no organized army his chances of effectively resisting the British depended on the swift raising of militia, and a prompt decision on where to engage the enemy. Instead the confusion reached comic-opera proportions with senior members of the government assuming all manner of unfamiliar roles in this moment of crisis. On 19 August Secretary of State Monroe rode with a small party of horsemen to reconnoitre the situation along the Patuxent, and although he was able to report to Madison that a formidable British force was in the field, his summaries were of no help in the military situation. Armstrong was still reluctant to believe that the British were aiming at Washington not Baltimore, and General Winder in his effort to raise troops seemed to forget that his main responsibility was to use whatever force he had to impede the enemy in its march on the capital. Although the British were marching on narrow roads through well-wooded country, they had to contend with no *abbatis* or even simple trees felled across the road. Against

---

[4] Cockburn to Cochrane, 22 Aug., 1814, Adm 1/506, pp. 602–5; *A Narrative of the Campaigns of the British Army at Washington and New Orleans under Generals Ross, Pakenham, and Lambert in the Years 1814 and 1815* (London, 1821), p. 109; Adams, *History*, VIII, 127–30.

determined and organized men, the British would have suffered heavy losses on what became merely a peaceful march.

On 21 August General Winder managed to establish himself at the Woodyard, about twelve miles from Washington, and less than five miles south-west of Upper Marlborough. He had with him some 2,000 men, most of them militia but stiffened with 300 regulars. At the Woodyard these troops were only a few miles from the left flank of the British in their line of march from Nottingham to Upper Marlborough, but General Winder did nothing about it. Although he was hoping to gather an army for a major battle with the British, there seemed no good reason not to send skirmishers to harass the British from the woods along their line of march. This was not done, and Monroe warned the President that he should have the government records removed from the capital. On Monday, 22 August there was a general exodus out of Washington. By Tuesday evening very few women and children remained, and all possible movable property was being sent out of the city.[5]

With the British marching to Upper Marlborough it seemed quite obvious on 22 August that they were next likely to advance along the Bladensburg road to Washington, but Winder was uncertain. He still appeared worried that the British might yet make a major move against Fort Washington, and attack the city by the Potomac route. He also appeared most reluctant, perhaps understandably, to commit his ill-trained and disorganized men to battle at all. On the 22nd he withdrew to the Old Fields, about eight miles from Washington and eight from Bladensburg. That night General Winder's worries were compounded when the President and members of his cabinet came to view the army, which by this time had gained the reinforcement of Captain Barney and 400 sailors.

On 23 August, as the British marched from Upper Marlborough to Bladensburg, part of the American force came in sight of the British column and quickly withdrew. Even now, instead of marching to Bladensburg where militia from Baltimore had established themselves and crude entrenchments had been dug, Winder decided to withdraw to Washington itself, apparently still concerned that the British might be preparing to attack by way of Fort Washington and

---

[5] *ASP, MA*, I, 536–42, 560–75; Hunt, ed., *Forty Years*, pp. 98–9.

the Potomac. The demoralized American forces marched back to the Navy Yard bridge over the East Branch, which curved around Washington to the east. This retreat was a hasty, disorganized affair, and on the night of 23 August, while the British were encamped about eight miles from Bladensburg and only ten from Washington, Winder and his defenders were assembled on the outskirts of Washington about five miles from Bladensburg.[6]

On the morning of 24 August the President and his Cabinet went to the Navy Yard to confer with Winder, who had heard that the British had broken camp at daylight and were marching on Bladensburg. In the middle of the morning Winder at last set off to meet the British. Secretary of State Monroe went on ahead to help General Stansbury, who commanded the Baltimore militia, and the President and Cabinet followed Winder. Bladensburg was a small village at the head of navigation of the East Branch. The bridge there was on the main Baltimore–Washington road, and above the bridge the river was easily fordable. General Stansbury had endeavoured to form defensive positions on rising ground on the Washington side of the stream; the British would have to cross it to meet his forces. Soon after Monroe arrived on the field he changed the positions of the American troops without consulting Stansbury. There was no real chance for establishing firm defensive positions, as most of Winder's force arrived on the field when the British were already in sight. By the time the action actually began there were nearly 7,000 Americans present, but less than 1,000 of them were regulars, and of these 400 were sailors from the destroyed gunboat flotilla. The force had twenty-six guns, but twenty of these were only six-pounders. General Winder arrived to take overall command of the battle just before the British attacked, and most of the American troops were merely drawn up in three rather confused defensive lines.

As the British marched rapidly into Bladensburg they could see the Americans drawn up on the high ground on the opposite side of the river, with American artillery covering the bridge over which the British troops would have to cross. The British troops were confident and well-commanded. The light brigade of some 1,300 men under

---

[6] Winder's account of his proceedings is in *ASP, MA*, I, 552–60; Adams, *History*, VIII, 131–7.

the command of Colonel William Thornton dashed across the bridge or forded the stream in the face of American fire. The American troops were disorganized, confused, and lacking in experience, and though they temporarily checked the first British brigade, many panicked as more British troops advanced to the attack and rockets fell into the American lines. The first American line soon gave way, and after that most of the Americans fled in confusion from the field. In the American rear were Captain Barney and his sailors. Although they had marched with all possible speed from Washington, the battle was already under way when they arrived, exhausted from the heat and crippled from the unaccustomed marching. There were 400 sailors protecting the battery of eighteen-pounders covering the main road, and helping to defend a battery of twelve-pounders on their right which was served by the marines. Although the American militia were fleeing by in retreat, the sailors held firm, effectively preventing the British advancing along the main road. They retreated only when the British flanked them; Captain Barney was left wounded on the field. The British had lost 64 killed and 185 wounded, the Americans 26 killed and 51 wounded. Both Ross and Cockburn commented in their official reports that few prisoners were taken owing to the speed with which the Americans left the field.[7]

After the battle General Ross gave his men two hours' rest. There was now no army to protect Washington. President Madison was not on the field during the battle, but was informed by General Winder that the Americans had been defeated. In the late afternoon the President arrived at the White House; his wife Dolley had already left with the plate and the most valuable movables. Within a few hours the President also fled westwards to seek refuge with his Cabinet in the surrounding countryside.[8]

After his troops were rested Ross quickly pushed on for Washington. When the British entered the capital at 8.00 p.m. it was already dark. Most of the troops encamped on the outskirts of the town, but

---

[7] Winder to Armstrong, 27 Aug., Barney to Jones, 29 Aug., 1814, *ASP, MA*, I, 548, 579–80; Ross to Bathurst, 30 Aug., 1814, WO 1/141, pp. 31–4, 45 (casualties); *Narrative of the Campaigns*, pp. 115–21; Irving Brant, *James Madison: Commander-in-Chief, 1812–1836* (Indianapolis, 1961), pp. 298–301.

[8] Brant, *Madison: Commander-in-Chief*, pp. 301–4.

as Ross, Cockburn, and a group of officers rode past the first houses they were fired on. Cockburn asserted the fire also came from the Capitol. The houses were taken and set on fire, and there was no further resistance. The British now set about the task of burning public property.

On the night of 24 August and the following morning the British set fire to the Capitol, the President's house, the Treasury, the War Office, and the office of the *National Intelligencer*. At the President's house they found a table set for dinner. The Navy Yard was destroyed by the Americans. Secretary of the Navy Jones had left orders that this should be done if the British triumphed at Bladensburg. The officials waited until the last moment before they carried out their orders, and as they left Washington they could see the Capitol in flames. In the Dock Yard a newly completed frigate and a sloop burnt with the rest. The two bridges over the East Branch had already been destroyed by the Americans, and the British wrecked the main bridge over the Potomac. All military stores that could be found were destroyed, including two hundred pieces of artillery, and two rope walks were burnt. The British were unimpeded in all this, but suffered casualties in an accidental explosion in the Navy Yard. At 9.00 p.m. on 25 August the British marched out of Washington. They had reached Upper Marlborough by the evening of the 26th, and were back in Benedict by the evening of 29 August. Apart from the losses at Bladensburg, the only other major casualties had been in the explosion in Washington; 44 wounded had to be left there when the British retreated, and another 87 had to be left with medical attendants at Bladensburg. Another 111 men were missing, most of whom had fallen out on the rapid marches and had not rejoined.[9]

In later years, and to some extent at the time, British destruction in Washington caused considerable recriminations and accusations of barbarism. Yet, well before this time in the war, the destruction or

---

[9] For destruction in Washington see Ross to Bathurst, 30 Aug., 1 Sept., 1814, WO 1/141, pp. 34–7, 51–2, 57; Cockburn to Cochrane, 27 Aug., 1814, Adm 1/506, pp. 609–12; *Narrative of the Campaigns*, pp. 124–31; G. C. Moore Smith, ed., *The Autobiography of Lieutenant-General Sir Harry Smith* (2 vols., London, 1901), I, 200; Thomas Tingey to Jones, 27 Aug., 1814, *ASP, MA*, I, 578–9.

carrying away of public property had become routine by both sides. On 18 July, 1814, Admiral Cochrane had even authorized extending the onslaught to private property as retaliation for American marauding north of Lake Erie. The particular criticism regarding Washington came because it involved public legislative buildings and the like rather than merely barracks and military stores, yet even this type of destruction was certainly not unique. The only other capital occupied in the war was York (now Toronto), in Upper Canada, and in April 1813 the Americans in their temporary occupation burned the Parliament buildings and the house of the lieutenant-governor, and destroyed the printing press of the *York Gazette*. Criticism of the Washington episode appears to have been much exaggerated. The town was not pillaged. One prominent female resident, Margaret Bayard Smith, wrote after her return to the capital that Cockburn, and all his officers and soldiers, had been perfectly polite to the citizens, and all provisions were paid for. The later exaggerated descriptions of Cockburn's ferocity hardly accord with the statement that he 'deserves praise and commendation for his own good conduct and the discipline of his sailors and Marines, for these were the destroying agents'. She was less charitable to Secretary of War Armstrong, of whom she said he was followed by 'universal execration', and would have been torn to pieces had he passed through the city on the day after the engagement. Armstrong was finished as Secretary of War. On 28 August, when President Madison and Monroe had returned to Washington, the President gave Monroe acting powers over the War Department, and when Armstrong arrived in the capital on the 29th Madison suggested a temporary retirement from the city. At Baltimore Armstrong resigned, and Monroe held the positions of both Secretary of State and Secretary of War.[10]

While the main British force carried out its marauding raid on Washington, the other smaller forces detached by Cochrane carried out diversionary activities. The squadron under Captain James A. Gordon moved more slowly than expected up the Potomac to Fort Washington. They frequently grounded, and did not reach the fort

---

[10] Adm 1/506, pp. 460–61, 466–9 (18 July orders); see above pp. 92–93 for destruction at York; Hunt, ed., *Forty Years*, pp. 109–16; Adams, *History*, VIII, 155–63.

until the evening of 27 August. This force consisted of two frigates – the *Seahorse* (38) and the *Euryalus* (36) – two rocket ships, two bomb ships, and a dispatch vessel. Secretary of War Armstrong had ignored requests to strengthen Fort Washington, which was only twelve miles below the capital. Its garrison consisted of only some 80 men. The officer in charge, Captain Samuel T. Dyson, was in a weak situation to resist any land attack. He was ordered by General Winder to blow up the fort and retreat if the enemy moved against him on the land. Dyson apparently was confused, or believed the naval attack was part of a larger operation, for as soon as he came under fire from Captain Gordon's squadron he blew up the inner buildings of the fort and retreated.

On the morning of 28 August Gordon's force took possession of the fort, and he was then able to advance unmolested to Alexandria, Virginia, just below the capital. The citizens of Alexandria were helpless, most of their men and guns having gone to defend Washington. The town had to sue for terms, and Captain Gordon agreed that the town would not be destroyed, except for the public works, on condition that all naval and ordnance stores and shipping (both public and private), together with all merchandise, was given up. Twenty-one small vessels, and a quantity of flour, tobacco, and cotton were taken from the town, and the squadron was able to drop down the river on 1 September. The return proved far more difficult than the sail up the Potomac, for Captain Rodgers at Baltimore was ordered to proceed overland to the Potomac to harass the British as they withdrew. Rodgers took with him Captains Perry and Porter, and these distinguished seamen led a party of sailors to erect batteries along the Potomac. They were joined by militia, and as Captain Gordon's squadron moved down the Potomac it came under severe fire from the guns and small arms along the river. It was 6 September before Gordon managed to get past the Americans, and by then he had lost 7 killed and 35 wounded.[11]

---

[11] Gordon to Cochrane, 9 Sept., 1814, and enclosures, Adm 1/507, pp. 153–160; John P. Hungerford to Monroe, 6 Sept., 1814, Brannan, *Official Letters*, pp. 409–10; Captain S. T. Dyson to Armstrong, 29 Aug., 1814, *ASP, MA*, I, 591, also *ibid.*, 533–4, 591–6; Porter to Jones, 7 Sept., Rodgers to Jones, 9 Sept., Perry to Jones, 9 Sept., 1814, SN, CL, 1814, vol. 6, pp. 27, 33, 34.

Captain Gordon's squadron had a difficult retreat, but they fared better than the other diversionary British force, which was sent into the Upper Chesapeake in August. The main vessel on this service was the *Menelaus* (38) under the command of Sir Peter Parker, a distinguished sailor and a cousin of Lord Byron. At the end of the month Captain Parker learned from a Negro that there were some 200 militia encamped about half a mile inland. At 11.00 a.m. on the night of 30 August Captain Parker landed with 124 men, armed with bayonets and pikes. They discovered that the Americans had moved their camp, and the sailors marched four or five miles before coming up with them. The Americans were drawn up in line, and were charged by Parker and his sailors. The British were repulsed, with Parker and 13 others killed and 27 wounded.[12]

The capture of Washington, and the burning of its public buildings, was a profound shock to the American public, but it at least warned the citizens of Baltimore what to expect, and gave them time to organize their defences. Whatever the psychological advantage of taking Washington, there was no doubt that Baltimore was the richest commercial and military prize in the region. On 28 August, two days before Ross's troops had again embarked on the ships at Benedict, Cochrane had expressed the opinion in a letter to Bathurst that the present British force was inadequate, without excessive risk, for an attempt against Baltimore. On the return of the victorious Ross and Cockburn to the Patuxent this view was somewhat modified, and it was decided to make a demonstration against Baltimore, which might be converted into an actual attack if justified by circumstances.[13]

Baltimore, the third largest city in the United States, presented considerable difficulties to any attacker. It was situated on the Patapsco River, about twelve miles from Chesapeake Bay by water, and the very narrow entrance to its harbour was dominated by Fort McHenry. Some preparations for its defence had been made since 1813, and during the extensive British raids along the Chesapeake in

---

[12] Crease to Cochrane, 1 Sept., 1814, Adm 1/507, pp. 12-14, 9-10 (casualties); Lossing, *Pictorial Field Book*, pp. 945-6.
[13] Cochrane to Bathurst, 28 Aug., 1814, WO 1/141, pp. 27-30, Cochrane to Croker, 17 Sept, 1814, Adm 1/507, p. 171.

the spring and summer of 1814 more extensive preparations were made to provide for the safety of the city. News of the capture of Washington led to an immediate organization of working parties of citizens to dig trenches and erect fortifications around the city and scatter batteries along the lines of defence. Moreover, by the time the British approached the city nearly 14,000 men had gathered to man the works. Most of these were militia, but they were stiffened considerably by over 1,000 sailors under the command of Commodore Rodgers. Even small Fort McHenry was garrisoned by 1,000 sailors, regulars, and volunteers. The overall commander at Baltimore was militia Major-General Samuel Smith. Smith was a veteran of the Revolution, but in the years before the war as Senator from Maryland had been deeply involved in political intrigue. When General Winder arrived in Baltimore after the Bladensburg disaster, he attempted to assume command, but Smith would not yield it.[14]

The British fleet under Admiral Cochrane anchored off the mouth of the Patapsco River on 11 September. From there it was less than fifteen miles to Baltimore by land, and twelve by water. The troops under Ross, consisting of some 3,500 men, disembarked on the morning of 12 September. These were augmented by a brigade of 600 seamen, and several hundred colonial marines (mainly escaped slaves) and regular marines gathered together from the various ships of the squadron. In all, the force amounted to no more than 4,500 men. The British marched rapidly towards Baltimore along the peninsula formed by the Patapsco and Back rivers. Though generally two to three miles across, in places it was narrowed by inlets to less than half a mile. As in the march on Washington, Admiral Cockburn accompanied the land forces, while Admiral Cochrane sailed up the Patapsco towards Fort McHenry with the frigates, bomb and rocket ships, and sloops.

On Sunday, 11 September, General Smith had ordered Brigadier-General John Stricker to advance along the peninsula with 3,200 men and six four-pounders, and on that evening Stricker travelled about seven miles along the main road from Baltimore. The Americans then camped for the night, covered by an advance of 140 cavalry

---

[14] Winder to Monroe, 4, 5, 7 Sept., 1814, WD, LR, Reg. Series; Lossing, *Pictorial Field Book*, pp. 947–9; Adams, *History*, VIII, 166–8.

who had been sent forward three miles, and 150 riflemen who were positioned a mile behind the cavalry.

The news of the British landing was brought to General Stricker on the morning of the 12th, and he drew up his troops in three main lines three hundred yards apart. They had no defensive entrenchments. The British advanced in three brigades, led by the light brigade and the Negro troops. As the British approached, the American advance withdrew, but when Stricker realized that the British were nearly upon him, he sent forward several hundred men to harass them from the woods along the road. At this time General Ross was up with the British advance, and in a flurry of firing received a musket ball in his chest, and died soon after. The command of the British troops was now assumed by Colonel Arthur Brooke of the 44th Regiment. On observing the American line posted in dense order and supported by artillery, Brooke brought up his troops and formed in battle order. The American resistance to the British attack was somewhat stiffer than at Bladensburg, but part of the American line broke when hardpressed, and Stricker was obliged to retreat. The British lost 46 killed (including General Ross), and 295 wounded, the Americans 24 killed, 139 wounded, and 50 prisoners. General Stricker now retreated towards Baltimore, and took up a position about half a mile in advance of the Baltimore entrenchments. The British camped for the night on the battlefield.[15]

On the next morning, 13 September, the British continued their advance. By 10.00 a.m. the army halted about one and a half miles from Baltimore, and Colonel Brooke reconnoitred the defences of the town. He decided that with the co-operation of the fleet he would attempt to storm the entrenchments in a night attack. The British ships had moved up the Patapsco on the 12th, and were ready to attack Fort McHenry on the morning of the 13th. Admiral Cochrane was impressed by the strength of the American position. Apart from Fort McHenry itself, the Americans had sunk twenty-four vessels across the harbour between the fort and Lazaretto Point, and on the

---

[15] Cockburn to Cochrane, 15 Sept., 1814, Brooke to Bathurst, 17 Sept., 1814, WO 1/141, pp. 75–84, 95–8, 91–4 (casualties); John Stricker to Samuel Smith, 15 Sept., Smith to Monroe, 19 Sept., 1814. Brannan, *Official Letters*, pp. 420–24, 427–30.

latter there was a small battery. Within the harbour, beyond the sunken vessels, there were American gunboats.

In all the British had sixteen vessels, including five bomb and rocket ships, for the assault on Fort McHenry. In the fort were 1,000 men under the command of Major George Armistead. These included 600 regular troops and a detachment of Captain Barney's sailors, as well as local militiamen and volunteers. The British bombardment began at sunrise on the 13th from the bomb ships, at a range too long for the American defenders to return the fire, but when later in the day the British attempted to come closer they were driven back by the American guns. The British bombardment continued with only short intermissions until 1.00 a.m. on the morning of the 14th. At that time it was discovered by the Americans that the British had sent ships up the wide channel to the right of the fort. This channel was the main course of the Patapsco River, and from it the British could hope to land on the peninsula on which Fort McHenry was situated, and cross to the harbour and Baltimore behind the fort. That side of the peninsula was covered by Fort Covington and by a separate battery.

When the British opened fire on Fort Covington with their rockets, the defenders of Fort McHenry were able to use the blaze of the British rockets and the flashes of their guns to direct their fire, while Fort Covington and the other battery also put up a stout resistance. The British kept up their fire until 7.00 a.m. on the morning of the 14th, but long before that Admiral Cochrane had decided that he could not fight his way into Baltimore harbour. On the previous evening he had informed Colonel Brooke that naval co-operation in the attack on Baltimore was impracticable, and Cochrane and Brooke decided that to storm the defences by land alone would be too risky and too costly. It was agreed that a withdrawal would take place on the 14th.

The most famous account of the bombardment of Fort McHenry was that of lawyer Francis Scott Key, who having gone to Cochrane's fleet to arrange the release of a physician carried away by the British army in the Washington expedition, was able to watch the night's action from a ship off the fort, and a week later he published in a Baltimore newspaper what was to become America's national anthem. Its account of 'the Rocket's red glare, the Bombs bursting in air' has given it a surprising timelessness.

On the morning of 14 September the British rapidly marched back down the peninsula to the mouth of the Patapsco River, and the ships sailed away from the defences on which they had made so little impression; the Americans had suffered only 4 killed and 24 wounded from the naval bombardment. On the 15th the army was re-embarked at North Point. They stayed in Chesapeake Bay until the middle of October, when they sailed to Jamaica.[16]

Although the United States faced an acute crisis in the autumn of 1814, it could have been far worse. Since the early summer veteran British troops had been leaving for North America, but what should have been their most decisive blows against the United States had to this point been inconclusive. They had discovered what the Americans had learned on the Canadian border in 1812–13, and what the British themselves should have learned in the Revolution: offensive warfare in a vast, untamed country, with huge distances, poor roads, and great forests, was a task of incredible difficulty. Of most importance, not only for the United States, but also for the attitude of the British government, had been the failure of Prevost's proud expedition to Plattsburg. For all the veterans gathering in Canada, there seemed no immediate likelihood of Britain winning naval dominance on the Great Lakes, and without that there seemed little likelihood of any major invasion from Canada. Also, although Admiral Cochrane had always doubted that Baltimore could be successfully assailed with the force under his command, the British testing of its defences and withdrawal was viewed by the United States as an American victory. From the American point of view two armies of European veterans had been repulsed in major assaults on American soil, although in fact neither force had been defeated in battle. When this was added to the much improved showing of the American troops on the Niagara frontier, there was ample reason for amazement that the massive British naval superiority and experienced regular troops had not produced more striking

[16] For attack on Fort McHenry see Cochrane to Croker, 17 Sept, 1814, Adm 1/507, pp. 172–5; G. Armistead to Sec. of War, 24 Sept., 1814, WD, LR, Reg. Series; for retreat of army see WO 1/141, p. 84.

successes in the summer of 1814. Certainly, this had a powerful effect in Britain. The lack of dramatic victories in the summer of 1814 was a powerful inducement to the British to agree to a peace without victory.

Yet the degree to which the British had failed to achieve any dramatic change in the war in the summer of 1814 was not readily apparent to the Americans at the time. They were delighted that Prevost had turned back and that Baltimore was safe, and were proud that the American troops had acquitted themselves bravely on the Niagara frontier, but the accomplishments were overshadowed by the host of problems that beset the country. The talk was constantly of more British ships and more veterans of the European campaigns arriving on the American coasts and on the borders of the United States. The capital had been burned, part of Maine was occupied by the British, and the news from the American envoys who were already beginning negotiations for peace in Europe was that Britain was seeking sizeable advantages from any peace. A tight blockade entrapped the whole American coastline, trade in many parts of the country was at a standstill, the country was near bankruptcy, and there was ominous news of increased opposition to the war in New England.

The news of the capture of Washington which spread through the United States in late August and early September caused a shock of horror and near panic. Ross's army was now expected to turn against Baltimore, and at the same time the country awaited the news of Prevost's thrust into New York. Both Philadelphia and New York city made desperate attempts to provide for their own defence as it was obvious that the central government was in no position to help them. At Philadelphia militia gathered from the surrounding country, and the citizens went en masse to build fortifications, but the greatest effort was in New York. The fear of attack grew strong even at the beginning of August, and for the next three months Herculean efforts were engaged in by the local population to build fortifications all around the city. The news from Washington set the citizens to digging with a renewed zeal, and by the middle of September 15,000 militia were stationed in the vicinity of New York – on Staten and Barn Island, in Brooklyn, on Haarlem Heights (then farm country), and in the city itself. By the end of the month there were over 17,000 New York militia around the city, and these were augmented by United States naval personnel and New Jersey militia.[17]

The military situation could have been worse, but when Congress assembled in special session in September 1814 it would have been hard to imagine a more serious financial and political crisis. It had been obvious throughout the first part of 1814 that the government could no longer depend on loans to finance the war effort, and Secretary of the Treasury Campbell had little idea of how to cope with the situation. Confidence in the financial stability of the government reached a new low with the capture of Washington. The banks of Philadelphia and Baltimore suspended specie payments, and very soon all the banks outside of New England were obliged to follow suit. New England itself had been draining specie from the rest of the country throughout the war, and in 1814 a considerable quantity of this specie was helping the British more than the Americans. The New Englanders were buying British government bills at a discount, and they were also sending specie to Canada to pay for smuggled goods.

The special session of Congress convened in Washington on 19 September, 1814. Ignominiously the members had to gather in the Post and Patent Office, the only government building that had not been burned by the British. Their immediate and pressing problem was the financial situation, and Secretary of the Treasury Campbell was obliged to report that he needed $50,000,000, but had no real suggestion of how to raise it. The first step was to obtain a new Secretary of the Treasury. Alexander J. Dallas of Philadelphia, who previously had been politically unacceptable, was quickly confirmed on 6 October. He was an able man, but he could not hope to solve the financial chaos in the near future. Indeed, he had to announce in November that the government could no longer pay the interest on its debt. The Democratic-Republicans had also to hear other unpalatable facts: a second United States Bank was needed, and

---

[17] *Public Papers of Tompkins*, III, 497–8, 528–9, 543–4, 553–5; Lossing, *Pictorial Field Book*, pp. 965–70.

11a. Jackson at New Orleans

11b. The Battle of New Orleans: on a white horse, Andrew Jackson watches the British attempt to break the American lines

12a. Pakenham leading the attack on New Orleans (woodcut)

12b. Defeat of the British Army . . .
The Battle of New Orleans (Louis-Philibert Debucourt after H. Laclotte)
(*Yale University Art Gallery, Mabel Brady Garvan Collection*)

taxes would have to be increased. Throughout the winter, Congress attempted to cope with the financial crisis, and even after the successful defence of Plattsburg and Baltimore the country could well wonder how the war could be fought for many more months.[18]

The financial problems were compounded by an acute political crisis in the autumn of 1814. At last it seemed that the opposition of New England to the war might produce actual disunion. In Massachusetts many thought that the country was collapsing, and when Governor Caleb Strong called the Massachusetts legislature into a special session for October 1814 he strongly implied that the time for some independent action had come. Within a few days a committee of the legislature had recommended calling a convention of states 'the affinity of whose interests is closest' to discuss defence, and to provide for a future convention to revise the federal constitution. The legislature agreed to these suggestions, and on 19 October elected twelve representatives to meet on 15 December with representatives from other New England states. Connecticut agreed to send seven delegates, and Rhode Island four. The convention was to meet at Hartford, Connecticut. To the disappointment of the extremists, the other New England states did not agree to send official delegates. New Hampshire was split on the issue, and Vermont declined, being now convinced that the United States was fighting a defensive war. Two unofficial delegates came from counties in New Hampshire, and one from Vermont.[19]

The bitterness of New England was increased in October when Secretary of War Monroe recommended conscription to raise an army to fight the increasing number of British troops in North America. Such was the opposition in Congress, even among those who supported the war, that in spite of all the dangers to the United States the bill could not pass.[20] As the time came for the Hartford Convention in the middle of December many in the country feared

---

[18] Adams, *History*, VIII, 213–15, 240–55; Lossing, *Pictorial Field Book*, p. 1010; Dewey, *Financial History*, pp. 132, 139.

[19] Morison, *Life and Letters of Otis*, II, 95–108; Henry Adams, ed., *Documents Relating to New England Federalism, 1800–1815* (Boston, 1877), pp. 398, 400–402, 404–6; Adams, *History*, VIII, 225 (quotation).

[20] Adams, *History*, VIII, 264–80.

that the New England states were moving towards secession from the Union.

The convention met at Hartford from 15 December, 1814, to 5 January, 1815, and was more cautious than expected in many other parts of the country. The extremists did not win control, although the fact the convention met in secret encouraged its opponents to believe that traitorous discussions were taking place. In spite of these fears the report of the convention did not argue for immediate disunion. It recommended that individual states should be responsible for their own defence, and that for this they should receive a portion of the federal taxes collected within the state. Apart from this critical issue of defence, and the desire of these states not to relinquish their military powers to the central government, the convention suggested seven amendments to the constitution. These were more a listing of grievances than a practical programme, as there was no chance of gaining the support necessary to enact them. The suggested amendments reflected disgust at the political and commercial situation since 1800, a distrust of Virginia and the new western states, and a dislike of Jefferson, Madison, and their cabinet ministers. The convention suggested apportioning representation to the national legislature without regard to the number of slaves (also necessarily apportioning taxes the same way), asked for a two-thirds vote of both houses for the admission of new states, for the passing of non-intercourse acts, and for a declaration of war, wanted embargoes to be limited to sixty days, Presidents to serve for only one term (aimed at Jefferson and Madison), and no two Presidents in succession from the same state (aimed at Virginia), and recommended that no naturalized citizen should be eligible for elective or appointive federal office (aimed at Albert Gallatin).[21]

All in all, the Hartford Convention was more petulant than revolutionary; the members disagreed with the policies of the national government, and wanted to make it quite clear that they were not prepared to support them. It could have been far worse, but throughout the last months of 1814 the threat of New England

---

[21] Morison, *Life and Letters of Otis*, II, 130–55; J. T. Adams, *New England in the Republic*, pp. 290–99; Timothy Dwight, *History of the Hartford Convention* (Boston, 1833).

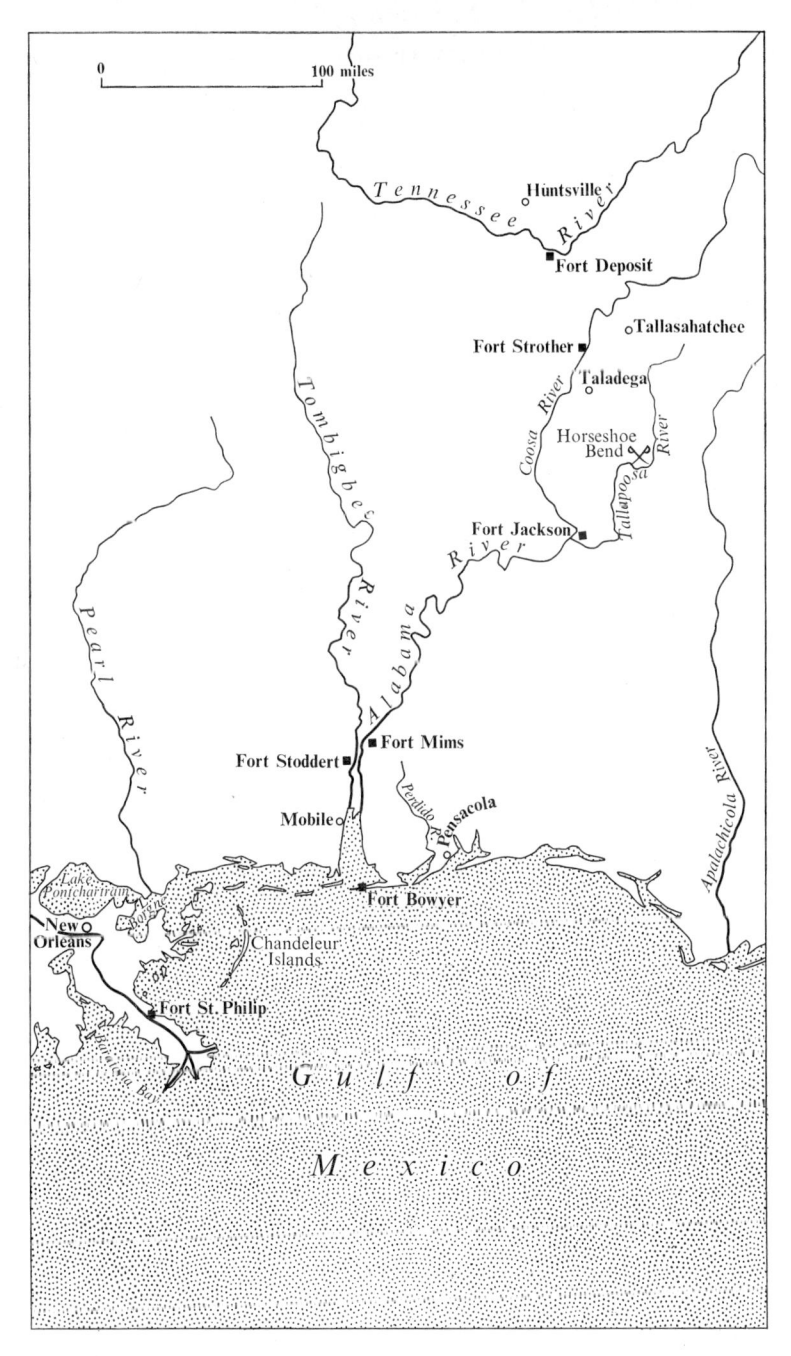

MAP 4 New Orleans and the Gulf Theatre of the War

separatism hung over the nation, along with fears of financial catastrophe, interminable war, and new and powerful invasions by British forces. At the end of January 1815 Governor Strong of Massachusetts appointed commissioners to go to Washington with the resolutions of the Hartford convention, but before they got there their cause assumed an air of utter futility.[22] Major events in the South and in Europe had completely transformed the situation of the United States.

---

[22] Morison, *Life and Letters of Otis*, II, 160–64.

9

The War in the South

At the beginning of the War of 1812 much of the lower half of the Mississippi Valley was still a wilderness. Tennessee had a population of over 260,000 by 1810, but to the south in what is now Alabama and Mississippi (then combined into Mississippi Territory) there was only a scattering of population. Most people in that area were gathered on the Mississippi River in the region of Natchez. The whole of western Georgia was still in the hands of the Creek Indians, and there were only the most tenuous land connections between the eastern seaboard and the settlers on the Mississippi. Most of the people on the lower Mississippi were in the state of Louisiana, which had entered the Union in April 1812. Its population was still largely French and Spanish, but increasing numbers of American settlers had moved into the area since the Louisiana Purchase in 1803.

The key to the whole region was the city of New Orleans near the mouth of the Mississippi. With a population of over 10,000 it was the largest city west of the Appalachians, but more important it controlled the trade of most of the settlers in the Mississippi Valley. In the years since the American Revolution settlers had been advancing in ever increasing numbers across the Appalachians; Kentucky had become a state in 1792, Tennessee in 1796, and Ohio in 1803. Other pioneers had opened up the land in western Pennsylvania and what is now West Virginia, and had pushed farther down the Ohio Valley to Indiana and Illinois, and across the Mississippi into Missouri. All of these settlers depended upon the Mississippi River for the export of their produce. Eastwards there were only atrocious roads and a mountain barrier that made the shipment of produce prohibitive in cost. It was far simpler and more economical to ship down the Ohio and Mississippi to New Orleans and the Gulf. Along the wharves of New Orleans were boats with flour from western Pennsylvania, pork from Ohio, lead from Missouri, hemp from Kentucky, cotton from Tennessee and Mississippi Territory, and a mass of other products. New Orleans controlled the whole valley, and in the 1780s and 1790s when Spain possessed it there seemed a chance that even that troubled country would be able to win away the western settlements from their American allegiance.

Spain had transferred New Orleans and her lands west of the Mississippi to France in 1800, but had retained control of East and West Florida. These territories consisted of the modern state of Florida with the addition of a strip of land south of the 31st parallel westward along the Gulf to the Mississippi. In the years after the Louisiana Purchase the United States had exerted great pressure on the Floridas, arguing that West Florida had been bought along with New Orleans and the great area west of the Mississippi. The pressure had culminated in October 1810 when, after an insurrection at Baton Rouge, President Madison annexed West Florida as far east as the Pearl River. This territory had become part of the state of Louisiana in 1812.[1]

Although the United States did not go to war against Spain in 1812, many in the south were quite ready to use the opportunity presented by the struggle against Britain to advance the American possession of the Floridas. President Madison also thought this would be possible, and in the fall of 1812 took the first steps to bring it about. Secretary of War Eustis asked the governor of Tennessee, Willie Blount, to provide 1,500 militia for the defence of New Orleans and the lower Mississippi. It was also hoped that this force could be used for the invasion of the Floridas. Tennessee was enthusiastic about the war against Britain, and with more than enough volunteers the Tennesseans quickly raised 2,000 rather than 1,500 men. Their commander was Major-General Andrew Jackson of the Tennessee militia. Jackson had come into Tennessee from the Carolinas in 1788, at a time when the area was under general Indian attack, had risen to prominence as a lawyer and politician and was

---

[1] Isaac J. Cox, *The West Florida Controversy, 1798–1813; A Study in American Diplomacy* (Baltimore, 1918), pp. 312–436; *Historical Statistics of the United States*, p. 13.

longing for a chance to fight the Indians, the British, or the Spanish. Jackson and his infantry left Nashville by water on 10 January, 1813, and reached Natchez in the middle of February. The mounted troops rode to Natchez overland by way of the Natchez Trace.[2]

All was now ready for the invasion of the Floridas, but even before Jackson had reached Natchez, Madison had discovered that Congress was not prepared to accept an overt invasion of Spanish territory. The bill to occupy the Floridas, which was introduced into Congress in January 1813, was amended to authorize the invasion of only what was left of Spanish West Florida. This was embarrassing to the President on two counts. First, as Jackson's force was not needed to take possession of Mobile, the only major post left in West Florida, the Secretary of War ordered Jackson to disband his militia force. The second problem was that from the time of an American-inspired insurrection in East Florida in 1812, Madison had kept American troops on Amelia Island and the St Mary's River. In March 1813 these were ordered to withdraw. Jackson's instructions presented great difficulties as he had been ordered to disband his troops hundreds of miles from home across a wilderness. Jackson refused to do this, and marched them back to Tennessee before mustering them out. By this long, futile journey to and from Natchez the government had wasted the services of some of the most enthusiastic militia in the nation.

The President had, however, received the authority to occupy Mobile, and in the middle of February 1813 General James Wilkinson, who commanded at New Orleans, was ordered to invade West Florida. There was no resistance. Fort Charlotte at Mobile was weak and short of supplies, and the commandant surrendered when the American force appeared before it. The Spanish garrison withdrew to Pensacola. Although there had been no declaration of war against Spain, that country was never to regain possession of West Florida.[3]

The major warfare in the lower Mississippi Valley through most

---

[2] John Spencer Bassett, ed., *The Correspondence of Andrew Jackson* (7 vols., Washington, 1926–35), I, 242–3, 252–3, 256–68; James Parton, *Life of Andrew Jackson* (3 vols., Boston, 1887), I, 360–73.

[3] *Annals of Congress*, 12th Cong., 2nd Sess., pp. 130, 133; Bassett, ed., *Correspondence of Jackson*, I, 275–6, 291; Pratt, *Expansionists of 1812*, pp. 217–37.

of 1813 and 1814 was only indirectly connected to the main Anglo-American struggle. Since the Revolution the Creek Indians had been under constant pressure from the state of Georgia, and in spite of all their protests, and at times open warfare, had gradually been losing their lands. The War of 1812 gave the Creeks the opportunity to strike at the Americans, and in this they were encouraged by visits from Tecumseh in 1811–12. In the summer of 1813 the Upper Creeks, those living on the Coosa and Tallapoosa rivers in what is now central Alabama, decided on war against the Americans. The Lower Creeks, living on the Chattahoochee River on the Georgia-Alabama border, kept the peace, or even gave aid to the Americans.

In July 1813 Peter McQueen, a Creek half-breed, visited Spanish Pensacola with over 300 warriors to obtain supplies, and it was quite obvious to settlers on the Tombigby and Tensaw north of Mobile that war was likely. When McQueen and his followers returned from Pensacola they clashed with a party of Americans, and by the end of August the war flared into horrifying violence. On 30 August, 1813, 1,000 Creeks led by William Weatherford, who was only one quarter Indian, attacked Fort Mims, forty-five miles north of Mobile on the Alabama River. Frontiersmen and their families had gathered in the fort for protection; crowded together were 100 Mississippi volunteers and some 400 settlers, including women, children, Negro slaves, and even friendly Indians. On 29 August a Negro slave who reported seeing hostile Indians near the fort was flogged for lying, but on the 30th at noon the Creeks, who had crept up to the fort, rushed in before the gate could be closed. All afternoon a desperate fight raged around the buildings within the fort, until at last the Indians took possession of the blazing structure. A few Americans escaped, and many of the Negroes were taken as slaves, but when ten days later troops arrived at the fort to bury the dead, they found a mass of mutilated, scalped bodies. They counted and buried 247, but the toll was certainly higher. Settlers throughout the region were now in terror for their lives, and fled into the stockades or down the river to Mobile. The main hope for immediate help lay to the north in Tennessee.[4]

---

[4] Ferdinand L. Claiborne to General Flournoy, 3 Sept., 1813, Brannan, *Official Letters*, pp. 202–5; Lossing, *Pictorial Field Book*, pp. 745–58.

Even before the Fort Mims massacre, Governor Blount had warned Jackson in the middle of August that the hostility of part of the Creek nation was likely to require action from Tennessee. Typical of the Tennesseans was that although the Secretary of War had suggested that 1,500 men might be raised in the state, the governor suggested that 5,000 might be more appropriate. When in September news of Fort Mims arrived, a special session of the Tennessee legislature agreed that the larger number should be raised. The need for troops was very great, for even at the beginning of October, a month after the Fort Mims massacre, there were only some 1,400 troops available in eastern Mississippi Territory to defend the exposed settlers of that region, a force which included only one regiment of regulars.

Andrew Jackson was again given the command of the 2,500 troops to be sent from the western part of the state, while General John Cocke was to bring the other half of the men from East Tennessee. By the beginning of October the armies were gathering at Fayetteville, on the border of the Mississippi Territory, and at Knoxville in eastern Tennessee. Jackson had sent Major-General John Coffee with his cavalry and mounted riflemen in advance to Huntsville, in what is now northern Alabama, and there were scouts still farther forward in the Creek country. Jackson himself was delayed as he was convalescing from a wound received in a duel, but before the middle of October he had advanced south with his troops across the Tennessee border and encamped on the Tennessee River. His main problem was lack of supplies, which arrived irregularly and there were not enough. South of him stretched only a wilderness leading to the Creek villages, but by the end of October he had advanced to the Coosa River, and there built Fort Strother.[5]

From his camp on the Coosa Jackson was within easy striking distance of some of the Creek villages, and early in November General Coffee was sent with 900 cavalry and mounted infantry to attack Tallassahatche (near modern Jacksonville, Alabama). It was a massacre. The American force fell upon the Indian village one hour after sunrise on 3 November. No one escaped. Coffee's force

[5] Bassett, ed., *Correspondence of Jackson*, I, 315–16, 319–20, 326–8, 331, 336–7; Brannan, *Official Letters*, p. 215.

counted 186 Indian dead, including all the warriors and a number of Indian women and children killed in the heat of the battle; 84 women and children were taken prisoner. The Americans lost only 5 killed and 41 wounded. The discrepancy in casualties was not surprising in that the Indian warriors had been taken unawares and hopelessly outnumbered. Ironically, fighting on the American side in the action were a party of friendly Cherokees.[6]

A few days later Jackson received the news that 160 friendly Creeks were surrounded by hostiles at Talladega, thirty miles south of his camp on the Coosa. Jackson immediately marched south with 2,000 men. He left only a small guard with his sick and baggage because General James White was hourly expected with the advance of General Cocke's army of East Tennesseans. On the night of 8 November Jackson encamped only six miles from Talladega, and received the disquieting news that White had been recalled by General Cocke, and was not marching to Fort Strother. Jackson decided to attack Talladega, and then retreat to protect his base. He marched at 4.00 a.m., with cavalry on his wings to encircle the enemy, his militia and volunteers in the centre, and an advance to lure the enemy into an attack against the middle of the American line. When the Indians attacked, the advance retreated as planned. For a moment there was great danger when some of the militia broke and ran, but the Indians, about 1,000 strong, were held by the rest of the American infantry, encircled by the cavalry, and quickly forced to flee. There were 299 Creeks found dead on the field. Jackson lost 17 killed and over 80 wounded. Although Jackson had not yet penetrated into the heart of the Creek nation, the tribe was suffering such losses as few Indians ever suffered in battle with the United States.[7]

With the battle won, Jackson quickly returned to Fort Strother. He was now in dire straits for supplies, for he had been hoping for help from Cocke's East Tennesseans. East and West Tennessee had long developed in their separate ways (for many years linked by only a tenuous road through the wilderness), and General Cocke had no

---

[6] Coffee to Jackson, 4 Nov., 1813, Brannan, *Official Letters*, pp. 255–6; Jackson to Blount, 4 Nov., 1813, Bassett, ed., *Correspondence of Jackson*, I, 341.

[7] Jackson to Blount, 15 Nov., 1813, Bassett, ed., *Correspondence of Jackson*, I, 348–50; Jackson to Armstrong, 20 Nov., 1813, WD, LR, Reg. Series.

intention of rushing to place his troops under the command of General Jackson. Like Jackson, he was short of supplies, and he could not see how a union of the armies would improve the position. Moreover, he was anxious that the East Tennesseans should win an equal share of the military glory. Accordingly, Cocke stayed in Fort Armstrong, which he built on the Coosa seventy miles above Fort Strother, and after recalling General White, sent him to attack the Creeks at the Hillibee Town on the upper reaches of the Tallapoosa River. The Creeks there had already sent a messenger to make their submission to Jackson, but they were dealing with the wrong general. On 18 November General White fell on the Hillibee Town, killed over 60 warriors, and captured over 250 Indians. There was no resistance, and the Americans suffered no casualties in what was a simple massacre. The rest of the Creeks in the vicinity of the Hillibee Town not unnaturally believed they had been betrayed, and joined the war against the Americans with a desperate mood of vengeance.[8]

While the Tennesseans entered the outskirts of the Creek country in their two columns from the north, 950 Georgia militia under the command of Brigadier General John Floyd approached from the east. The Georgians marched for the village of Auttose, which was on the Tallapoosa only twenty miles from where it joined the Coosa. On the night of 28 November Floyd's force camped within a few miles of the village, and during the night he marched his force to be in position for a dawn attack. He could not execute this sudden attack in the way he had hoped, having discovered there was a second Indian village, which he had not known about, near to the first, but at dawn he attacked both villages. The Indians put up a fierce resistance, but were overpowered. Floyd estimated 200 Indian dead. The Georgians had 11 killed and 54 wounded, and the friendly Indians also suffered some casualties.[9]

In the month of November some 750 Creek warriors were killed out of a total fighting force of at the most 3,500 to 4,000, but the

---

[8] White to Cocke, 24 Nov., 1813, WD, LR, Reg. Series; Parton, *Life of Jackson*, I, 446–53; Cocke to Jackson, 27 Nov., 1813, Jackson to Armstrong, 30 Nov., 1813, Bassett, ed., *Correspondence of Jackson*, I, 355 7, 361.
[9] Floyd to Major-General Pinckney, 4 Dec., 1813, Brannan, *Official Letters*, pp. 283–5.

main resistance of the nation was yet to be broken. The Tennesseans had the largest army in the field, but in late November they found themselves unable to follow up their earlier successes because of lack of supplies. Although General Cocke's force at last joined Jackson at Fort Strother on 12 December, Jackson had by this time far more to contend with than his commissariat. His troops had originally enlisted for one year in December 1812, and now wanted to go home. Jackson at first tried to resist this, but soon decided he would have to allow his militia to return to West Tennessee. Cocke's force could be of no major assistance, as their term of enlistment was also nearly over. Although Jackson immediately sent to Tennessee for more troops, he could not act until the New Year.[10]

In December the Creeks were thus given some time to recover, but were harassed farther to the south by a combination of regulars and Mississippians led by Brigadier-General Ferdinand L. Claiborne. His original base was Fort Stoddert on the Alabama River, but in November he advanced north some eighty-five miles and built Fort Claiborne. On 13 December he left the fort, marched north over a hundred miles more, and on the 23rd attacked the village of Econochaca where Chief Weatherford and some of the hostile Creeks were gathered. Claiborne had about 1,000 men, including regulars, militia, and volunteers, and there was even a party of Choctaw Indians. The Americans destroyed the town, killed thirty Indians, drove off the rest, and retreated to Fort Claiborne. American casualties were only 1 killed and 6 wounded. General Claiborne now, however, faced the same difficulties as Jackson. The terms of enlistment of his volunteers expired, and most of his men disappeared.[11]

The campaign against the Creeks was hardly proceeding in any organized and logical manner, although the Indians were having to contend with raids and expedition from north, south, and east. As one volunteer force disintegrated, another obtained fresh recruits, and the attacks continued. In January 1814 both Jackson's Tennesseans and Floyd's Georgians were again in action against the Indians.

---

[10] Bassett, ed., *Correspondence of Jackson*, I, 345–6, 354–5, 387, 396, 400.
[11] Claiborne to Armstrong, 1 Jan., 1814, WD, LR, Reg. Series; Lossing, *Pictorial Field Book*, pp. 771–3.

By the middle of January another 800 volunteers from Tennessee had joined Jackson at Fort Strother. With his usual eagerness for action, he marched again on 17 January with a total force of 930 men and one six-pounder. On his march he was joined by 200 to 300 friendly Creeks and Cherokees. His intention was to attack hostile Creeks who had established themselves near the mouth of Emuckfaw Creek on the Tallapoosa River. The Creeks were ready for him, and attacked him on 22 January when he had nearly reached his objective. This assault was beaten off, and Jackson continued his advance, but was again attacked by the Indians. Once more the Creeks were driven off, but Jackson, fearing that he would be overwhelmed, decided to retreat. On the 24th he was again fallen upon by the Creeks, and on this occasion the troops, who were raw recruits and had been under considerable strain for several days, almost brought disaster. Most of the rearguard quickly broke when attacked, but a few held firm and rallied the rest of the army, who again drove the Indians from the field. Jackson stated in an official letter that in all these engagements 189 Indians were found dead on the field, although in a letter to his wife he wrote of 72 found dead, and gave 200 as his estimate of those probably killed. In all the Americans lost 24 killed and 71 wounded. Jackson had not reached his objective, and had been forced to retreat, but had shown his qualities as a general by the efficiency with which he had extricated his beleaguered army from the heart of the Indian country.[12]

The Creeks also showed remarkable tenacity in their resistance to the Georgians in January 1814. On 18 January General Floyd marched from Fort Mitchell on the Chattahoochee with the intention of attacking Tuckaubatchee on the Tallapoosa, less than fifty miles from the object of Jackson's expedition in the same month. Floyd had over 1,200 volunteers, and 400 friendly Creeks. Early on the morning of 27 January, when encamped within ten miles of his objective (nearly fifty miles west of Fort Mitchell) he was attacked by the Creeks. It was a bitterly fought engagement, and though the Indians were driven off, leaving 37 dead, the Americans suffered losses of 17 killed and 132 wounded, and the friendly Creeks 5 killed

---

[12] Jackson to Pinckney, 29 Jan., to Mrs Jackson, 28 Jan., 1814, Bassett, ed., *Correspondence of Jackson*, I, 444–54.

and 15 wounded. Like Jackson, Floyd decided to retreat after the battle, taking his army back to Fort Mitchell.[13]

Creek resistance in January 1814 was remarkable when one considers that in the previous two months they had lost about one-fifth of their warriors in battle, in addition to an undetermined but undoubtedly large number of wounded. Yet, their hopes of successful future resistance were slight, for in Jackson they faced a ruthless general who was determined to exact more than full revenge for Fort Mims. The troops he needed were gradually being provided: in January 4,000 Tennessee militia were called out, and in February he was reinforced by the United States 39th Regiment. Jackson was able to use the regulars to instil military discipline into the militia.

The Creeks had decided to fortify themselves in a small peninsula of 80 to 100 acres, formed by a bend of the Tallapoosa River. Here at Horseshoe Bend gathered some 1,200 Creek warriors. Across the neck of the peninsula the Indians had constructed a log breastwork, and at the far end away from the breastwork many canoes were kept to allow the Indians to escape across the river if hard pressed. Jackson decided to march against this entrenched Creek position. He took with him about 3,000 men, including friendly Cherokees and Creeks.

The American force reached the Horseshoe Bend on the morning of 27 March. Jackson decided to attack immediately. He sent General Coffee with his mounted men and the friendly Indians across the river to take up a position opposite the bend. There they could prevent any escape by means of the waiting canoes. His six and his three-pounder he placed in front of the fortifications, and they bombarded the breastwork with no apparent effect. Meanwhile, some of the Cherokees had swum across the river, taken canoes, and carried some of Coffee's men and friendly Indians into the Horseshoe itself. When Jackson realized this, he ordered his infantry to make a frontal attack on the breastwork. The assault was led by the 39th Regiment of regulars, well-supported by the militia.

The Creeks fought desperately at the breastworks, but the

---

[13] Pinckney to Jackson, 5 Feb., 1814, *ibid.*, I, 458–9; Floyd to Pinckney, 27 Jan., 1814, Brannan, *Official Letters*, pp. 296–7.

Americans took it by storm. Once they were into the horseshoe it was more a massacre than a battle; even Jackson commented that 'the *carnage* was *dreadfull*'. Many tried to escape across the river, but were drowned or shot while in the water by Coffee's force. Not until nightfall was the slaughter over. The Americans counted 557 dead Creeks on the peninsula. Jackson thought another 300 had died in the river, and there were 350 prisoners, only three warriors among them. The Americans lost 26 killed and 106 wounded, the friendly Cherokees 18 killed and 36 wounded, and the friendly Creeks 5 killed and 11 wounded. Jackson's Creek allies had taken part in the destruction of their tribe.[14]

In April Jackson was able to move forward to the junction of the Coosa and Tallapoosa Rivers without resistance. Fort Jackson was built there, and in May 1814 Jackson himself was appointed Brigadier-General in the United States army, given the brevet rank of Major-General, and appointed commander of the 7th Military District based on Mobile. At Fort Jackson in August the Creeks were forced to cede over half their lands to the United States. The friendly Creeks who had fought with Jackson fared no better than the hostiles; they were regarded as one and their lands forfeited.[15]

It was as well for the United States government that an efficient general had made his mark and had been placed in command of the Gulf coast in the spring of 1814, for Britain was preparing a major effort in the region. Since the beginning of the war the British cabinet had well realized the vital importance of New Orleans and the mouth of the Mississippi to the whole Mississippi Valley. The power that dominated New Orleans controlled the huge areas to the north, and could ruin the trade of America's rapidly expanding trans-Appalachian settlements. Until 1814 no major effort could be made

---

[14] Jackson to Armstrong, 2 April, 1814, WD, LR, Reg. Series; Jackson to Pinckney, 28 March, to Blount, 31 March, to Mrs Jackson, 1 April ('carnage' quotation), 1814, Bassett, ed., *Correspondence of Jackson*, I, 489–94; Lossing, *Pictorial Field Book*, pp. 777–81; Adams, *History*, VII, 251–7.
[15] Jackson to Blount, 18 April, 1814, Brannan, *Official Letters*, pp. 327–8; Armstrong to Jackson, 22 May, 1814, Jackson to Blount, 9 Aug., 1814, Bassett, ed., *Correspondence of Jackson*, II, 4, 24; Jackson to Armstrong, 10 Aug., 1814, WD, LR, Reg. Series; Parton, *Life of Jackson*, I, 549–60.

in that region because the troops could not be spared from Europe, but once the European war was over, New Orleans and the control of the Mississippi was an obvious point of attack.

In the early summer of 1814 the British government was considering the project of sending a large force from the south of France under the command of Lord Hill to undertake the invasion of Louisiana. This original idea was abandoned because of the difficulties of establishing peace in Europe and because of tension with the Russians, but a modified plan of invasion was adopted as a result of the receipt of optimistic information from Admiral Cochrane on the North American station.[16]

Early in the spring of 1814 Admiral Cochrane had ordered Captain Hugh Pigot of the frigate *Orpheus* to proceed with the *Shelburne* to the Gulf to open communication with the Creeks and supply them with arms. On 10 May the British ships anchored near the mouth of the Apalachicola River, and a landing party scoured the country. By the 20th ten chiefs, an interpreter, and other Indians were brought on board the *Orpheus* to confer with Captain Pigot. In the meantime the British disembarked with arms, and put on shore a British agent and two marines to help organize the Indians. Pigot in his report to Cochrane estimated that there were 2,800 Creek warriors ready to help the British, that another 1,000 in the swamps near Pensacola could be recruited, and that the Negroes of Georgia would be likely to join the Creeks if they knew arms were available. Mobile, Pigot argued, could easily be conquered with the co-operation of the Indians on land. Then, with the assistance of the Choctaws, 'a handful' of British troops and a few gunboats could take possession of Baton Rouge, and from there New Orleans would be an easy conquest. The British, stated Pigot, could also expect assistance from the pirates at Barataria (about 800 of them), if they were promised future protection.[17]

Pigot's report ignored the crushing effects of the American

---

[16] From early in the war even amateur private strategists had written to the Prime Minister suggesting an expedition against Louisiana, see Liverpool Papers, Add. Mss, 38249, pp. 194–8, 38251, pp. 330–35, British Museum. See also WO 1/142, pp. 1–3, and Wrottesley, *Life and Letters of Burgoyne*, I, 298.

[17] Pigot to Cochrane, 8 June, 1814, Adm 1/506, pp. 394–7.

THE WAR IN THE SOUTH 227

victories over the Creeks, and was remarkably optimistic regarding the difficult task of collecting and combining operations with a large force of Indians. He also underestimated the American efforts that would be made to defend Mobile and New Orleans. In spite of all this, Cochrane on 20 June urged the British government to undertake an expedition, and stated that 'three thousand British Troops landed at Mobile where they would be joined by all the Indians, with the disaffected French and Spaniards, would drive the Americans entirely out of Louisiana and the Floridas.' It was later said that his eagerness for the rich prize money that would be obtained from the capture of New Orleans blurred his judgement. Cochrane said he would lead such an expedition himself, and that the best season for it would be October or November. Pigot's suggestions were, however, modified in one important respect. Cochrane requested shallow draft boats suitable for use along the coast from Mobile westward to Lake Pontchartrain. From Lake Pontchartrain Cochrane could attack New Orleans.[18]

With the usual slowness of communications it took until August for the British to respond to Cochrane's suggestions, and in the meantime the Admiral attempted to ensure Indian support for any expedition. Early in July he instructed brevet Major Edward Nicholls of the Royal Marines to take a party of over 100 marines to the Gulf coast to organize the Indians and train them in the use of firearms; they were to take with them two howitzers, a field piece, and a thousand stands of arms. Nicholls was also to enlist any Negroes who could be persuaded to flee from the United States, and was given printed proclamations to distribute among the slave population. In order to facilitate the conquest of New Orleans, Nicholls was to find out as much as he could about the country westwards from the Apalachicola River. In a message to the Indians Cochrane urged them to use every means to encourage slaves to flee from Georgia and the Carolinas, and told them that as the British had beaten the French great fleets and armies were crossing the Atlantic 'to chastise Mr Madison and his worthless associates'.

---

[18] Cochrane to Croker, 20 June, 1814, *ibid.*, pp. 390–93; Wrottesley, *Life and Letters of Burgoyne*, I, 304–5.

16

Captain William Percy of the *Hermes*, and the sloop *Carron*, were to transport Nicholls and the arms. Percy was to assume command of the small British squadron in the Gulf, keep up communication with Nicholls at the mouth of the Apalachicola, and maintain a blockade of the mouth of the Mississippi.[19]

Cochrane was confident of success, and even a letter from Bathurst stating that slaves should not be encouraged to rise against their masters did not embarrass him. He told the Secretary for War in the middle of July that he was simply giving protection to those slaves who chose to join the British standard. To Bathurst he was even more sanguine regarding the number of troops needed for his operation, arguing that 2,000 men would give Britain command of the Gulf country and New Orleans. Cochrane did not like the Americans. 'I have it much at heart to give them a complete drubbing before Peace is made,' he wrote, 'when I trust their Northern limits will be circumscribed and the Command of the Mississippi wrested from them.'[20]

Nicholls did not reach the Gulf until the middle of August, and by that time the British government had decided to implement Cochrane's suggestions. The Admiralty informed him on 10 August that in this endeavour he would have the troops under the command of Major-General Ross, and these would be reinforced by 2,130 men from Europe. These troops should arrive at Jamaica by the middle of November, and that was to be the point of general rendezvous. The Admiralty had been more careful than Cochrane in deciding the best time to strike at New Orleans, and had judged that the troops should not reach New Orleans before December because of the climate. At Jamaica the force was to be increased by the 5th West Indian Regiment and 200 Negro pioneers.[21]

---

[19] Cochrane to Croker, 23 July, Instructions to Nicholls, 4 July, Instructions to Percy, 5 July, 1814, Adm 1/506, pp. 478–88; Cochrane to Indian Chiefs, 29 June, [1814], *ibid.*, 1/505, pp. 163–4. Cochrane gave Nicholls the local rank of lieutenant-colonel to impress the Indians, but the Admiralty would not confirm this, *ibid.*, 1/505, p. 75.

[20] Cochrane to Bathurst, 14, 15 July, 1814, WO 1/141, pp. 7–14.

[21] Croker to Cochrane, 10 Aug, 1814, *ibid.*, 1/141, pp. 15–25; also WO 1/142, pp. 523–9 (decision regarding best time of arrival).

On 6 September, less than a week before Ross's death near Baltimore, Bathurst sent him instructions for the campaign against New Orleans; he was never to read them. Bathurst pointed out that the 3,400 men of Ross's existing force were already more than Admiral Cochrane had said was necessary for the expedition. To be quite safe, however, the government was sending reinforcements that would bring his army up to some 6,000 men, without the seamen and marines. He could also, wrote Bathurst, expect support from the Indians, and arms were being sent out for them. The objects of the expedition were, first, to obtain command of the mouth of the Mississippi and deprive the American backcountry settlements of their outlet to the sea, and, second, to obtain some important possession by whose restoration the conditions of peace could be improved, or whose cession could be exacted as a price of peace. It was left to Cochrane and Ross to decide whether to proceed directly to New Orleans, or first to proceed to the back parts of Georgia and the country of the friendly Indians.[22]

In the middle of September the reinforcements for Ross sailed from Plymouth under the command of Major-General John Keane. There were also 600 supernumary seamen, boys, and marines to help Cochrane, and arms for the Indians. Soon after, it was decided to send the 40th Regiment as an additional reinforcement, but an accident to one of the transports caused the fleet to put back into Cork, and it did not finally sail until 2 November. By that time the expedition had become more elaborate as a result of the news of the capture of Washington which reached London on 27 September.

The general optimism produced by this news encouraged the government to throw in more troops in the hope of producing a decisive result. The original idea was to send 2,220 men under Major-General John Lambert to Bermuda because of the idea that after his success Ross might want to continue operations in the same area. From Bermuda they could either reinforce Ross, or be directed to the Gulf if operations in that region had been decided upon. Yet again there had to be changes, for on 17 October there arrived the

---

[22] There is a summary of Bathurst to Ross, 6 Sept., 1814, in *ibid.*, 1/142, pp. 495–501.

news of the death of Ross, and of Cochrane's intention to sail to the Gulf. Lambert was then ordered to proceed directly to Jamaica, and Major-General Sir Edward Pakenham, Wellington's brother-in-law, was ordered to sail to take command of the expedition. It seemed inevitable that the troops would already be on their way to the Gulf before Pakenham reached Jamaica. Pakenham was to follow Ross's instructions, but it was now clear that the basic military decisions would be taken by Admiral Cochrane.[23]

This launching of an expedition against New Orleans was a very piecemeal affair. The original plan to send a large, organized army from Europe to undertake the expedition had been abandoned, and the government had then agreed to the suggestion of two naval officers, Captain Pigot and Admiral Cochrane, who grossly overestimated the degree of Indian assistance that could be expected, and grossly underestimated the amount of American resistance that might be encountered. Cochrane had originally argued that only 3,000 troops would be needed, and at one point had even said 2,000 would be enough. Captain Pigot's original report had envisaged the taking of Mobile, an expedition across country to take Baton Rouge, and the isolation of New Orleans. Cochrane's had modified this so that the taking of Mobile would be followed by the transportation of the troops by shallow draft boats along the island-studded coast of the Gulf into Lake Pontchartrain. The military details of the plan were vague, and it would appear that Cochrane had concocted it without discussion with General Ross. The death of Ross meant that the senior army officers involved in the Gulf expedition were all fresh from Europe, and had to accept a military situation already created by Admiral Cochrane, who was to change the plans yet again in the autumn of 1814.

In September and October, while the British government arranged to send Admiral Cochrane more troops than he had asked for, Cochrane himself was beginning to realize that the expedition was not likely to be the rather simple affair he had depicted to the British government in June. The ships bearing Major Nicholls and his marines had finally sailed from Havana early in August, and arrived

---

[23] For sailing of reinforcements see WO 1/142, pp. 503-5, 511-14.

at the mouth of the Apalachicola on the 13th. They landed, but discovered that the British Indian agent had gone to Pensacola to work with the Creeks who had taken refuge in that vicinity. The British ships now sailed there with Nicholls and his force, and finding that the Spanish feared American attack, the British marines occupied the local fort. On 29 August Major Nicholls issued a high-flown proclamation to the inhabitants of Louisiana, asking them to help 'in liberating from a faithless imbecile government, your paternal soil'. He even asked the inhabitants of Kentucky to rise against the Americans on behalf of the British.[24]

Early in June Captain Pigot had reported that Mobile would be an easy conquest for a few troops assisted by small armed vessels and Indian co-operation. He had been too sanguine even then, and by September Andrew Jackson had infused a new vitality into the attitudes of the defenders. Jackson's main task in the early summer had been to complete the subjugation of the Creeks, and to accomplish the treaty for the cession of their lands, but as soon as the treaty of Fort Jackson had been signed, Jackson on 11 August left to descend the Coosa and Alabama Rivers to Mobile. By 22 August he was there, over four hundred miles below Fort Jackson.

At Mobile Jackson quickly began his arrangements for the defence of the Gulf coast. He heard on 27 August that the British were at Pensacola, and immediately sent out a flurry of letters to the governors of the region asking for militia, and asserting in one letter that 25,000 British troops had arrived at Bermuda, and that Russia had offered 50,000 troops to conquer Louisiana. He had no doubts about British intentions, although in theory British plans were strictly secret, and stated that the British intended to attack Mobile and New Orleans. He told the commander at the latter city to put it into the best possible state of defence. The British were hoping that by December they would capture a weakly-defended and ill-organized Gulf coast, but allowed neither for the fact that their general intentions were obvious to the Americans, nor for Jackson's enthusiasm.

---

[24] Percy to Cochrane, 9 Sept., 1814, Adm 1/505, pp. 152–3; Nicholl's proclamation is printed in Major A. Lacarrière Latour, *Historical Memoir of the War in West Florida and Louisiana in 1814–15* (Philadelphia, 1816), Appendix, pp. vii–viii.

At Mobile itself Jackson also infused new energy into the defences. The village of Mobile had a population of less than 1,000, and its defence depended upon Fort Bowyer, thirty miles away from the town at the entrance to Mobile Bay. Jackson garrisoned the fort with 160 United States regulars commanded by Major William Lawrence. It was not a particularly strong fort, having mostly twelve and nine-pounders, supported by only two larger guns, but Lawrence immediately put it into the best possible state of defence.[25]

Captain Percy sailed from Pensacola on 11 September to attack Fort Bowyer. His total naval force consisted of the *Hermes* (22), *Carron* (20), *Sophie* (18), and *Childers* (18), along with a land force of Major Nicholls and 60 marines, 12 marine artillery, and 130 Indians. The British vessels reached the vicinity of Mobile Bay on 12 September, and landed Nicholls and his force nine miles east of Fort Bowyer. Because of contrary winds the British ships could not pass the Mobile bar until the 15th, but that afternoon the Americans in Fort Bowyer saw the British vessels standing directly for the fort under full sail. The action began at about 4.00 p.m. The *Hermes* and *Sophie* sailed to within pistol shot, anchored, and fired broadsides, but as the wind failed the other two British ships were unable to manœuvre into position. After heavy firing by both sides, the *Hermes* had her bow-spring shot away, swung around with her bows to the fort, and grounded. She then suffered heavily from the American fire, although eventually Percy managed to swing her around and bring the port broadside to bear. At 6.10 the *Hermes* tried to get out of range of the fort, but her sails were cut to pieces, her rigging shot away, and she again grounded. This time her crew was taken off by the boats of the squadron, and at 7.20 p.m. the British set fire to the ship. She blew up later in the evening. The British land forces did not attempt to take the fort. Nicholls, who had been on board the *Hermes* because of illness, assisted on deck in the action and lost an

---

[25] John S. Bassett, ed., *Major Howell Tatum's Journal While Acting Topographical Engineer (1814) to General Jackson Commanding the Seventh Military District* (Smith College Studies in History, vol. VII, nos. 1, 2, and 3, 1921–22, Northampton, Mass.), pp. 10–52; Bassett, ed., *Correspondence of Jackson*, II, 31–4, 40–41, 50–51; Latour, *Historical Memoir*, p. 34 (says garrison was 130 men).

eye. In all, the *Hermes* had 22 killed and 20 wounded, the *Sophie* 9 killed and 13 wounded, and the *Carron* 1 killed and 4 wounded. The American defenders lost only 4 killed and 5 wounded.[26] The Americans at Fort Bowyer had given a severe shock to the British. Admiral Cochrane's original plan of taking Mobile, winning control of the region, and from there taking New Orleans, was in jeopardy. After Jackson's victories over the Creeks earlier in the year, the British hopes of recruiting thousands of Indians had always seemed unrealistic, and they were doomed by the failure to take Fort Bowyer. Moreover, even in lesser endeavours the British met disappointment early in September as they attempted to prepare the way for an easy conquest of New Orleans.

Under orders from Captain Percy of the *Hermes*, Captain Nicholas Lockyer of the sloop *Sophie* had sailed from Pensacola on 1 September to seek the support of the pirates and smugglers at Barataria, some sixty miles south-west of New Orleans. In return for their co-operation and armed vessels the British were prepared to consider them as British subjects and assign them lands in the British colonies. The pirates at Barataria had long waxed rich on the profits of privateering and smuggling, and had benefited from the connivance of some of the most prominent citizens of the region. Their leader was the colourful Jean Laffite, who with his brothers Pierre and Dominique held sway in this bay, protected by a battery of heavy guns. Laffite apparently feared American less than British rule, and told the Americans of the British offers. This did not prevent the break-up of the settlement, for the Americans had already planned it. On 11 September an American expedition from New Orleans took possession of the Baratarian fleet. In spite of this attack Laffite was to give his support to the Americans in the defence of New Orleans.[27]

---

[26] Percy to Cochrane, 16 Sept., 1814, Adm 1/505, pp. 156-9, and 161-2 (casualties); Wm Lawrence to Jackson, 15 Sept, 1814, Brannan, *Official Letters*, pp. 424-6; Jackson to Sec. of War, 16, 17 Sept., 1814, WD, LR, Reg. Series; memorial of Major Nicholls, WO 1/144, pp. 420-21.

[27] The British letters to the Baratarians are printed in Latour, *Historical Memoir*, Appendix, pp. ix-xi; see also *ibid.*, pp. 17-22, Appendix, pp. xi-xiv For a full discussion of the Baratarians see Jane Lucas de Grummond, *The Baratarians and the Battle of New Orleans* (Baton Rouge, 1961).

In the weeks following the successful defence of Fort Bowyer Jackson continued to prepare for a British attack. Later in September he issued a proclamation to both the general population and the free Negroes of Louisiana asking them to resist the British, and, still fearing for Mobile, sent to New Orleans for heavier guns to protect it. In October Secretary of War Monroe wrote to warn him that the news from Europe was that the British were massing men for an attack on New Orleans, but Jackson was not placidly sitting waiting for the British to move. Before undertaking the defence of New Orleans he had determined to ensure the safety of Mobile by an attack on Spanish Pensacola; he would undertake the expedition as soon as reinforcements arrived. Jackson kept more of the Revolutionary spirit than many who fought in this War of 1812. He wrote to his wife in October that he hoped she was reconciled to their separation – 'the situation of our country require it for who could brook a British tyranny, who would not prefer dying free, struggling for our liberty and religion, than live a British slave.'[28]

In view of Captain Pigot's and Admiral Cochrane's view of the best way to take New Orleans, Jackson's decision to attack Pensacola was a shrewd estimate of the situation. Such an attack, if successful, would ensure that there would be no flocking of the Indians to join the British standard. That Pensacola was in Spanish territory held no terrors for Jackson. Monroe wrote from Washington that nothing should be done which might provoke war with Spain, but Jackson had already acted. On 23 October he left Mobile, and travelled northeast to meet some of his reinforcements. Two days later on the Tombigby he met General Coffee who had brought over 2,000 Tennesseans. Jackson also had with him three regiments of regulars, some Mississippi dragoons, and a large party of Choctaws, in all some 3,000 to 4,000 men.

Jackson knew quite well that he was invading Spanish territory without (and in fact against) the orders of the government, and he informed Monroe on 26 October that he was doing it to put an end

---

[28] Bassett, ed., *Correspondence of Jackson*, II, 42, 56–9, 70, 72–4; Monroe to Jackson, 10 Oct., Jackson to Mrs Jackson, 21 Oct., 1814, *ibid.*, II, 71, 78–9; Adams, *History*, VIII, 324–5.

to the Indian war in the South by cutting off all foreign influence, thus ensuring the safety of the region. Once this was done he could leave for New Orleans. Even while on his way to Pensacola he ordered a total of 5,500 Kentuckians and Tennesseans to proceed directly to New Orleans, and asked the militia of Mississippi Territory to be ready for action at any time.

The American force arrived in the neighbourhood of Pensacola on the evening of 6 November. Pensacola itself was only a village overlooked by a small fort; at the entrance to the bay was the stronger Fort Barrancas. After the British had returned to the Apalachicola River after the failure of the attack on Fort Bowyer, they received a letter from the Spanish Governor of Pensacola asking their assistance in repelling a threatened attack by the Americans. The British ships and Nicholls' force immediately sailed, and arrived there on 31 October. They found the fortifications in a ruinous state, but the Spanish military did not want to co-operate with the British in strengthening them. They also would allow no attack on the Americans until they were actually in sight from Pensacola.

Jackson's initial attempt to contact the Spanish defenders ended when an officer with a flag of truce was fired on, and on 7 November the Americans attacked the town. There was little resistance. The British, deciding the Spanish were lukewarm and Jackson's force too strong, embarked the friendly Indians and about 200 Spanish troops, and blew up Fort Barrancas. Again the British sailed for the mouth of the Apalachicola. Major Nicholls built a fort on that river, and until the end of the war detached parts of his force to harass the Georgia frontiers.[29]

By 19 November Jackson was back in Mobile, and three days later he left for New Orleans, travelling by land to view the places at which the British might effect a landing. Three regular regiments were left at Mobile, and Jackson estimated that in all a total of 8,000 men would be available for the protection of the eastern part of his district. Jackson was criticized for not going to New Orleans earlier

---

[29] Monroe to Jackson, 23 Oct., 1814, Bassett, ed., *Correspondence of Jackson*, II, 79–80, also 82–3, 86–7; Bassett, ed., *Tatum's Journal*, pp. 65 83; Brannan, *Official Letters*, pp. 451–3; Jackson to Monroe, 14 Nov., 1814, and enclosures, WD, LR, Reg. Series; Adm 1/505, pp. 167–70, 172–4; WO 1/144, p. 421.

with his whole force, but he appears to have gauged possible British lines of approach with remarkable accuracy. He arrived at New Orleans at the beginning of December, and immediately began to organize its defences.[30]

The British troops from the Chesapeake had arrived at the rendezvous at Negril Bay, Jamaica, at the beginning of November, and the force under Major-General Keane three weeks later. Keane, an Anglo-Irishman who had won a good reputation in the Peninsula, took over the general command of some 6,000 men. There was every sign in the following days that Admiral Cochrane now much regretted his far too optimistic statements of the early summer, and was exceedingly concerned about the dangers of the expedition. With the failure of the attack on Fort Bowyer and the lack of general Indian support, he had decided to proceed directly against New Orleans, but the rosy optimism had disappeared. He complained to the Admiralty in December that everyone in Jamaica knew about the secret expedition, and that there were far too few flatboats and vessels of shallow draft for negotiating the waters around New Orleans. Although some had been sent from England, the Admiralty had ordered the rest to be obtained in Jamaica; the transport officers there, however, had been unable to obtain enough. This was a serious handicap to the British in their movement of troops into position near New Orleans.

On 27 November Admiral Cochrane, accompanied by General Keane, sailed for the Gulf on the *Tonnant*. The fleet followed on the next day. On Cochrane and Keane depended the details of the operation, although Cochrane had already formulated its general outlines. Even yet Cochrane had dreams of enlisting hordes of Indians for the expedition, and had a proclamation printed at sea announcing that the British were coming in large numbers to defeat the Americans and restore the Indian lands. It was distributed at the mouth of the Apalachicola, but after Horseshoe Bend, the failure to take Fort Bowyer, and Jackson's capture of Pensacola, it had little effect. The *Tonnant* arrived at the Chandeleur Islands near the entrance to Lake

---

[30] Bassett, ed., *Tatum's Journal*, pp. 85–7; Bassett, ed., *Correspondence of Jackson*, II, 101–7.

Borgne on 8 December, and on the 11th was joined there by the rest of the fleet.[31]

New Orleans presented major difficulties for any attacker. The complications stemmed from the nature of the terrain in this delta region. Although New Orleans itself is situated a hundred miles from the actual mouth of the Mississippi, it is well-protected on all sides by water. To the north is Lake Pontchartrain, to the east Lake Borgne (to which there was direct access from the Gulf), and the intervening country was cut up by rivers, creeks, and bayous. New Orleans was obviously not a difficult city to defend, but when at the end of August Jackson had ordered all possible speed in the defensive preparation, much remained to be done. Best protected was the approach by way of the Mississippi River. Fort St Philip, some sixty or seventy miles below the city, was armed with some twenty-eight 24-pounders, and at English Town, eighteen miles below the city, there was supposed to be a battery of nine guns, though it was out of use. At New Orleans itself Fort St Charles was rundown, and as it was nearly in the centre of the city could not be used to protect it. Six miles north of the city Fort St John guarded the main bayou leading out of Lake Pontchartrain, but it was a small brick fort, and in a bad state of repair.

After his arrival at New Orleans at the beginning of December, less than two weeks ahead of the British, Jackson began to survey its defences. He was pleased with Fort St Philip, and ordered another battery to be built there to cover the river, 200 slaves being assigned to the task. It was obvious to Jackson and to the British that the British could not expect to take New Orleans by an attack up the Mississippi River. Jackson also visited the possible land route east of the city. This led from the narrow straits separating Lakes Borgne and Pontchartrain by way of the Gentilly Road, and Jackson decided that any attack from that direction would be the best possible for the defenders as the road ran narrowly between a bayou and

---

[31] Cochrane to Prevost, 5 Oct., to Croker, 7, 16 Dec., to Indians, 5 Dec., 1814, Adm 1/508, pp. 131-2, 357-9, 395-7; 1/505, pp. 150-51; WO 1/141, pp. 129-30, 249; Bourchier, ed., *Memoir of Codrington*, I, 328. For additional correspondence regarding vessels of shallow draft see Adm 1/508, p. 398; 2/933, pp. 215-16, 224, 234.

swamps. From the British point of view the numerous bayous, water courses, and swamps meant that any path of attack had to be on a limited front. It was difficult to overcome this by surprise and speed because of the great difficulty in finding any suitable spot for the swift disembarkation of troops. Jackson also hoped that any approach by way of Lake Borgne would be hindered by the American gunboats stationed there.[32]

Cochrane and Keane decided that the British troops would be disembarked at the Bayou Bienvenu at the west end of Lake Borgne. Once landed there the troops would be within fifteen miles of New Orleans. A basic disadvantage was that, owing to the shallowness of Lake Borgne, the fleet had to anchor over fifty miles away from the bayou, and the troops transported in boats of shallow draft; of these there were only enough to transport half the army, even without the supplies. The boats would have to make two trips across the lake, and even before this could be done, the American gunboats on the lake had to be engaged and defeated.

On the night of 12 December the launches, barges, and pinnaces of the fleet, manned by 1,000 seamen and marines, rowed into Lake Borgne in search of the American gunboats. Lieutenant Thomas Ap Catesby Jones, who commanded the American flotilla, sighted the British on the morning of the 13th, and at first thought the boats were engaged in disembarking the troops. Within a few hours he realized that they were coming to attack the American gunboats. The American vessels tried to sail away while the British boats patiently rowed after them. The chase lasted thirty-six hours, but as the wind had died the British closed with the anchored Americans on the morning of 14 December. About 10.00 a.m. the British stopped just out of range and had breakfast, but within fifty minutes rowed directly for the American vessels under a heavy fire of round and grape shot. By noon the British boarded the American flagship, took her, and turned her guns on the others. By 12.40 p.m. all five gunboats were captured; the British had earlier taken an armed sloop that had endeavoured to join in the action. The British lost 19

---

[32] Bassett, ed., *Correspondence of Jackson*, II, 46–7, 111–12; Bassett, ed., *Tatum's Journal*, pp. 96–101.

killed and 75 wounded, the Americans 6 killed and 35 wounded.[33]

News of the capture of the gunboats shocked New Orleans. Jackson, not yet reinforced by the expected troops from Kentucky and Tennessee, declared martial law, and called out all the Louisiana militia. The Americans were short of arms, the government having failed to supply them in time, but by 22 December Jackson was reinforced by General Coffee with 1,250 men, and by Major-General William Carroll with 2,500, as well as a squadron of Mississippi cavalry and some of the Baratarian pirates. Jackson also had parts of the 7th and 44th United States regular regiments, but he still did not know where the British intended to land, and he was still awaiting the arrival of 2,500 Kentuckians.[34]

Even after the defeat of the American gunboats, the British lack of boats of shallow draft delayed operations. In order to have quick support for the British troops who would land first, it was decided to transport all the army half-way across Lake Borgne to the Isle aux Poix, near the mouth of the Pearl River. The island was swampy and deserted, covered with little but reeds and scrubby bushes, and the men suffered from severe frosts and strong winds. While the troop movement was taking place, the British reconnoitred the Bayou Bienvenu to within six miles of New Orleans, helped by Spanish fishermen in a village at the mouth of the bayou. Jackson had ordered this area to be picketed after the loss of the gunboats, but the Louisiana militia did not arrive at the mouth of the bayou until after the British had finished their reconnoitring expedition.

Not until 21 December did the British have enough troops and supplies on the Isle aux Poix to continue with the invasion (most of the West India regiments and the dragoons were at this point left on the ships of the fleet). On the morning of the 22nd the advance of 1,600 men under Colonel Thornton set off in the boats of the fleet, accompanied by General Keane. They had trouble in the shallow

---

[33] Cochrane to Croker, 28 Dec., Captain Lockyer to Cochrane, 16 Dec., 1814, Adm 1/508, pp. 268–9, 364–7; Ap Catesby Jones to Captain Patterson, 12 March, 1815, Brannan, *Official Letters*, pp. 487–90.

[34] Jackson to Monroe, 16 Dec., 1814, Bassett, ed., *Correspondence of Jackson*, II, 115–16; Bassett, ed., *Tatum's Journal*, pp. 103–6.

water, but by the morning of the 23rd reached the bayou, captured the American picket, and landed about five miles inland in daylight, entirely unobserved by American troops. They were then about three miles from the Mississippi River, in flat, reed-covered country intersected by deep ditches. The engineers quickly built small, temporary bridges and cleared a path, and the troops advanced alongside a canal leading to the plantation of General Jacques Villeré of the Louisiana militia. There they captured Villeré's son and his militia company (though Villeré's son soon escaped). The British advance then took up its position across the main road to New Orleans. The road ran parallel to the river, and the British were positioned about seven miles from the city. Jackson had originally expected too much of the gunboats on Lake Borgne, and had then suffered from the failure of the Louisiana militia to be sufficiently enterprising in their watch for the British. Had the British pressed on immediately for New Orleans, they would have taken it before its defences could have been organized, but the troops were very tired, and the extent of American ignorance was unknown. The British troops encamped across the main road, with the Mississippi on their left and a cyprus swamp on their right.[35]

At noon on the 23rd Jackson received news of the British approach. With his usual decisiveness, he resolved to attack them immediately. Afraid of a two-pronged British assault, he left General Carroll's Tennesseans and the city militia to guard the Gentilly Road while he advanced to attack the British advance with a force of over 2,000 men, comprised of nearly 900 regulars, 550 of General Coffee's mounted riflemen, and over 650 Louisiana and Mississippi militiamen (including 200 free Negroes). He was also supported by the schooner *Carolina* in the river. Just before 8.00 p.m., with many of the British troops already asleep, they were suddenly awakened by a heavy flanking fire of grape and round shot from the *Carolina* in the

---

[35] Major Forrest, A. Q. M. General, 'Journal of the Operations against New Orleans in 1814 and 1815', *Louisiana Historical Quarterly*, XLIV (July–October, 1961), pp. 112–16; William Surtees, *Twenty-Five Years in the Rifle Brigade* (London, 1833), pp. 336–8; Lossing, *Pictorial Field Book*, pp. 1028–9; Cochrane to Croker, 18 Jan., 1815, Adm 1/508, pp. 376–8; Adams, *History*, VIII, 337–8.

Mississippi. Jackson launched a frontal attack with his regulars and Louisiana militia, while General Coffee took over 700 men to turn the British right by skirting the edge of the swamp.

The attack was a confused struggle on a night made darker by the smoke from the guns and a light fog. Much of the engagement was fought hand to hand in confused groups, and it was fortunate for the British that they had regular troops who did not panic under this sudden night attack. The Americans were not driven off until about midnight, when the first troops of the British second division began to arrive (the boats had gone back for them after landing the advance). The British lost 46 killed, 167 wounded, and 64 missing, and the Americans 24 killed, 115 wounded, and 74 missing.[36]

On the following morning (the 24th) Jackson retreated about two miles, and took up a position behind a canal which stretched from the river, at almost a right angle, over a thousand yards to the cypress swamp. The canal was about ten feet wide, but very shallow. Jackson immediately began to entrench himself behind the canal, and also made a number of minor breaks in the levee holding back the Mississippi to inundate the open ground in front of the American position. After about a week, however, the Mississippi fell, and the ground began to dry up, while the British attempted to repair all breaks in the levee. On the 24th as the Americans established their position they had no way of knowing that far away in Ghent their country's envoys were signing the treaty of peace.

On the next two days the British were occupied in the laborious task of moving all their troops from the Isle aux Poix to the Villeré plantation. Their morale was improved by the arrival on the field of Major-General Sir Edward Pakenham, who had been appointed to succeed General Ross. Pakenham's reputation rested on more than his status as Wellington's brother-in-law. He had fought with bravery in the Peninsula, and had been highly praised for his

---

[36] Jackson to Gov. Holmes, 25 Dec., 1814, Bassett, ed., *Correspondence of Jackson*, II, 124; Jackson to Monroe, 27 Dec., 1814, A. P. Hayne to Jackson, 10 Jan., 1815, Brannan, *Official Letters*, pp. 453-5, 457-8; Bassett, ed., *Tatum's Journal*, pp. 107-10; Keane to Pakenham, 26 Dec., 1814, WO 1/141, pp. 149-56, also 179-81 (casualties).

conduct in the battle of Salamanca. With him from England had come Alexander Dickson, the commander of Wellington's artillery.[37]

The British had determined to remove the *Carolina* which flanked them in the Mississippi, and on the morning of the 27th opened fire on her with a specially prepared battery. She was set on fire, and blew up. The *Louisiana*, which had come up to support the other American ship was withdrawn out of range, and at daylight on the 28th the British army advanced in two columns under the command of Major-Generals Keane and Gibbs. They drove in the American pickets, but Pakenham, who had been unable to reconnoitre close to the American position because of the flat, exposed terrain, was surprised to find the enemy so close. The British troops advanced under fire to within 700 or 800 yards of the American line. Since the 24th the Americans had worked with all possible energy at their entrenchments, which were studded with gun emplacements, and Pakenham decided that he could not risk an immediate attack. He withdrew his troops to a position less than two miles from the American line.[38]

Pakenham now decided to bring up additional guns to bombard the American position. Two eighteen-pounders had already been laboriously floated and dragged to the plantation, and Pakenham wanted eight more, along with the necessary ammunition and four 24-pound carronades. The precarious British line of supply now became fully apparent. In places along the Bayou Bienvenu the creek was so narrow that the boats could not be rowed for lack of room, and had to be pushed through the mud by oars shoved against the banks. With backbreaking labour the guns were brought up, but it was only possible to bring up a minimum amount of ammunition.

---

[37] Bassett, ed., *Tatum's Journal*, pp. 111–12; Bourchier, ed., *Memoir of Codrington*, I, 332; Carson I. A. Ritchie, 'The Louisiana Campaign', *Louisiana Historical Quarterly*, XLIV (Jan.–April, 1961), pp. 13–32.

[38] Alexander Dickson, 'Journal of Operations in Louisiana', *Louisiana Historical Quarterly*, XLIV, 6–23; Bassett, ed., *Tatum's Journal*, pp. 113–18; Jackson to Sec. of War, 29 Dec., 1814, WD, LR, Reg. Series.

The guns were up by 31 December, and it was decided to construct the batteries that night and bombard the American line early on the following morning; hopefully this would immediately precede a general attack. After dark the American pickets were pushed back to capture the ground on which the guns were to be placed, and throughout the night the construction of the batteries, the laying of the guns, and the bringing up of ammunition went on with feverish haste. The artillerymen who were to man the guns had to work all night, and the final result was unsatisfactory; the batteries were built of sugar casks filled with earth, the platforms uneven, and the gunners only half-protected from American fire. The morning of 1 January opened with a heavy fog, and it was not until 10.00 a.m. that it cleared sufficiently to allow the British to see the American works.

The Americans had been making use of the delay to strengthen their position, and within their fortifications had one 32-pounder, three 24-pounders, and one 18-pounder, together with smaller guns. Also they had threatened the British flank by establishing one 24-pounder and two 12-pounders on the opposite bank of the Mississippi. In contrast to the sugar casks of the British, the Americans had used cotton bales to strengthen their line. The British bombardment and the American response continued for three hours, at which time British ammunition was running short, and no appreciable damage to the American line had resulted. The British artillery commander, Colonel Dickson, blamed the hastily erected batteries and platforms for the failure, but his artillerymen had also been harassed by the accurate American fire, which penetrated the British batteries. The assault was abandoned, and that night in heavy rain the guns were dragged back through the mud.[39]

General Pakenham again decided to wait – this time for the arrival of the reinforcements under Major-General John Lambert. These were expected at any time, and had actually arrived at the anchorage of the fleet on 1 January in the dense fog. Lambert had brought the

---

[39] Dickson, 'Journal', pp. 24–40; Bourchier, ed., *Memoir of Codrington*, I, 334; Bassett, ed., *Tatum's Journal*, pp. 120–22; Jackson to Monroe, 2 Jan., 1815, Bassett, ed., *Correspondence of Jackson*, II, 130; Adams, *History*, VIII, 358–66.

élite 7th Fusiliers and the 43rd Regiment. As they prepared to come up, the main army was employed in improving the road to the Bayou Bienvenu, and in bringing up large quantities of ammunition and provisions. Pakenham also decided to dig through the levee to carry the Villeré canal from the Bayou Bienvenu right into the Mississippi. This would enable troops to be sent across the river in the boats of the fleet to capture the American batteries on the opposite bank of the river.

Lambert's force was finally brought up to the British position by 6 January, but the difficulty of digging the canal delayed the beginning of operations until the night of 7 January, and the actual frontal assault until 8 January. It was now nearly a month since the British fleet had arrived at the entrance to Lake Borgne, and over two weeks since Jackson had heard of the British advance by way of the Bayou Bienvenu. The Americans had been given two weeks to establish a position on a front 1,000 to 1,500 yards wide, flanked on the left by an impenetrable cyprus swamp, and on their right by the Mississippi River. To their front was a flat, muddy plain, allowing a perfectly clear line of fire on any advancing troops.

Jackson's main force was now entrenched in a particularly strong position. By 8 January his front line was protected by a parapet five feet high, and immediately below the parapet was a ditch or canal up to ten feet wide and four feet deep (although there was little water in it). At regular intervals along this line were batteries of heavy guns, and there was a redoubt alongside the river. Jackson had also used slaves to construct two more lines of defence between his front line and New Orleans. By the morning of 8 January there were some 3,500 men in the front line, and up to 1,000 more in reserve. The main line consisted of 1,300 men under Colonel George Ross on the right wing (including the regulars and Louisiana militia), 1,400 Tennesseans under General Carroll in the centre (closely supported by 1,000 Kentuckians), and on the left near the swamp 800 Tennesseans under General Coffee, with Choctaws scouting the swamp itself. Over 2,000 Kentuckians had at last arrived on 4 January, but many of them were without weapons.

The weakest point in the American defences was across the Mississippi. Although Jackson had established guns there to enfilade the British position, he did not foresee that the British might extend the Villeré canal through the levee, and use their boats on the Mississippi. The Americans had used the delay to mount more guns in their battery across the river, but these had been positioned to bear on the main battlefield across the river, and could not be effectively used in their own defence. Work had been begun on a line in advance of the batteries, but at first this was garrisoned by only 450 Louisiana militia under General David Morgan. Not until 7 January did Jackson receive the news that the British were extending the canal to the Mississippi. He immediately ordered 400 Kentuckians to reinforce his position across the river, but as there were no boats they had to march back to New Orleans, cross the river, and then march down the other bank. They had trouble finding weapons, and General Morgan ultimately had no more than 800 militia to defend his side of the river.

The British plan of attack combined a blow across the river with a main frontal attack on the American line. During the night of 7–8 January Colonel Thornton, who had led the light brigade at Bladensburg, was to take a force of some 1,200 to 1,300 men across the river by boat, attack the unfinished American line, and capture the batteries. To accomplish this task, boats had to be dragged out of the Villeré canal through the cut in the levee, and into the Mississippi. As the water was low this involved back-breaking work. The assault against Jackson's main line was planned to coincide with the assault across the river, and was to consist of two columns. The main thrust was to be against the Tennessee and Kentucky militia on the left of Jackson's line. It was to be undertaken by a strong column under the command of Major-General Gibbs, and was to consist of 2,200 men – the 4th, 21st, and 44th Regiments, and three companies of the 95th. Simultaneously, Jackson's right, resting on the river, was to be attacked by a column of 1,200 men under Major-General Keane. This column consisted of the 93rd, two companies of the 95th, and two companies of the 43rd and fusiliers. The 1st West Indian Regiment, consisting of 500 Negroes, was to skirmish in the swamp. The attack was to be supported by six 18-pounders, and Major-General Lambert was to hold the 7th Fusiliers and the remainder of the 43rd Regiment, consisting of 1,200 men, in reserve.

The reserve was comprised of newly arrived, élite troops. 'Those fellows would storm anything,' commented Pakenham, 'but, indeed, so will the others, and when we are in New Orleans, I can depend upon Lambert's Reserve.'[40]

These British regulars who were to advance on the morning of 8 January had fought with distinction in the Peninsula, but many of them had been shipped to America at the very moment they were due for their discharge after seven years service; some pointed this out to the officers on the night before the British attack. The night also presented other problems, for the passage of the boats out of the Villeré canal into the Mississippi proved far more difficult than expected. As a result even the first of the British troops were not across the river until daylight on the 8th, and as they moved to the attack they saw, by the flashes of the guns, that the main assault had already begun.

At daybreak on the 8th the flat fields in front of the American line were covered by a heavy mist. The artillery on both sides opened a rapid fire, and although the mist began to clear, it now mingled with the smoke of the guns. Into the mist and smoke marched the British columns, while the Americans waited safely behind their parapet; the drummers along the whole of their line beating 'Yankee Doodle'. Gibbs's main column advanced almost directly into the line of fire of an 18-pound battery, and was also raked by batteries on either side together with the fire of the American infantry. American grape and ball wrought great destruction, and twice the column was stopped, reformed, and renewed the attack; 'with a firmness,' wrote

---

[40] Lambert to Bathurst, 10 Jan., 1815, WO 1/141, pp. 137-40; Dickson, 'Journal', pp. 38-57; Captain John Henry Cooke, *A Narrative of Events in the South of France and the Attack on New Orleans in 1814 and 1815* (London, 1835), pp. 157 ff.; John Spencer Cooper, *Rough Notes of Seven Campaigns in Portugal, Spain, France, and America, During the Years 1809-10-11-12-13-14-15* (London, 1869), pp. 126-7; Surtees, *Twenty-Five Years*, pp. 370-71; Bassett, ed., *Tatum's Journal*, pp. 122-4; Jackson to Monroe, 13 Feb., 1815, Bassett, ed., *Correspondence of Jackson*, II, 164-70, also p. 132; Adams, *History*, VIII, 367-374; Stuart O. Landry, *Side Lights on the Battle of New Orleans* (New Orleans, 1965), pp. 44-6; Smith, *Autobiography of Sir Harry Smith*, I, 235 (quotation regarding 7th and 43rd).

Jackson, 'which reflects upon them the greatest credit.' Major-General Gibbs was mortally wounded when almost at the American line, and when General Pakenham rode up to rally the troops he also received a mortal wound. Those troops of Gibbs' column who actually reached the ditch and parapet found that the half of the 44th Regiment who were responsible for bringing the fascines and scaling ladders had not collected them in time. The troops wavered, and as General Lambert advanced to within 250 yards with the reserve the whole of Gibbs's column fell back on him in confusion. The reserve held their position flat on the ground, but did not renew the attack.

General Keane's smaller column advanced rapidly along the levee road to attack the right of the American position, and for a time achieved some success. They gained possession of the advanced demi-bastion on the river, but once in it were directly open to the fire of the right of the American line. Most of the column were driven back, although some were by this time actually in the ditch, and were eventually captured or shot when they tried to retreat. As in the other column, great devastation was caused by the American guns, some of them manned by the Baratarians, ably backed by the American infantry, and the British commander, Major-General Keane, had to be carried from the field with a severe wound.

The one successful aspect of the British attack was across the Mississippi. As soon as Colonel Thornton crossed the river with his first 600 men, he advanced to the attack. He quickly drove the Americans from their unfinished line, and the gunners had to spike their guns and run. Jackson, who had sent the British fleeing in confusion on his side of the river, feared that the British on the opposite bank could turn his whole position, and hurriedly arranged for troops to cross to the other side of the river via New Orleans. But General Lambert, with Pakenham dead, Gibbs dying, and Keane severely wounded, was in no mood to continue the attack. On the 8th the British had lost 291 dead, 1,262 wounded, and 484 missing; although the British had sent only 3,400 in direct assault against the main American line, along with 600 who attacked across the river and some skirmishers in the woods. Lambert felt he could not risk continuing the attack. He would have had even more reason to disengage had he known that the total American casualties had been 71 – 13 killed, 39 wounded, and 19 missing. What with the nearly 300 British casualties in the battle of 23 December, and almost 150 from the 23rd through 7 January, this had been a disastrous expedition.[41]

That night Colonel Dickson was sent to give his opinion of the position on the opposite side of the river. He reported back that 2,000 men would be needed there, and Lambert decided to withdraw from the captured American batteries. Given his lack of strength, and limited means of transport across the river, he could have done little else. In the following days a truce allowed the burial of the dead. General Lambert, newly arrived from the European fighting, commented on 10 January, after being on the scene less than two weeks, that the services of both the army and navy had been 'arduous beyond anything I have ever witnessed'. In the following week Lambert made careful preparations for his retreat, and on the night of 18 January quickly withdrew to the ships of the fleet.[42]

The failure had even extended to the ships sent by Admiral Cochrane to bombard Fort St Philip in the Mississippi and create a diversion. They bombarded from 9 to 17 January with little effect, in that whole time only killing two and wounding seven Americans. Jackson was now famous, and late in March a New Englander held prisoner in Dartmoor rejoiced at the news from New Orleans. 'We had heard of Generals Dearborn, Brown, Scott, Ripley, Gaines and Miller,' he wrote, 'but no one knew who *General Andrew Jackson* was; but we said that it was a New England name, and we had no

---

[41] Cooper, *Rough Notes*, pp. 121, 129–33; Dickson, 'Journal', pp. 57–70; Forrest, 'Journal', pp. 123–4; Cooke, *Narrative*, pp. 230–40; Surtees, *Twenty-Five Years*, pp. 374–6; George Laval Chesterton, *Peace, War and Adventure. An Autobiographical Memoir* (2 vols., London, 1853), I, 206–8; WO 1/141, pp. 137–46, 157–62, 165, 219–22; Adm 1/508, pp. 376–83; Bassett, ed., *Correspondence of Jackson*, II, 134, 136–8, 142–4, 162–3; Brannan, *Official Letters*, pp. 474–480; Bassett, ed., *Tatum's Journal*, pp. 125–37. A detailed treatment of the whole attack is given in Charles B. Brooks, *The Siege of New Orleans* (Seattle, 1961).

[42] Lambert to Bathurst, 10 Jan., 1815, WO 1/141, pp. 144–6; Dickson, 'Journal', pp. 66–82.

doubt but he was a full blooded Yankee.'[43] A year which had begun with the United States in the utmost danger had ended in triumph, and that all this fighting from 24 December had been after the signing of peace in no manner diminished the American rejoicing.

---

[43] Brannan, *Official Letters*, pp. 464-5; Waterhouse, *Journal of a Young Man*, p. 216.

10

The Peace of Ghent

There is no clearer indication of the inextricable links between the War of 1812 and the Napoleonic Wars than the manner in which the former was concluded. This war had been entered into with remarkable reluctance. The British had not wanted it, and the Americans had taken a variety of measures to try to avoid it. Desperation rather than any realistic set of objectives had impelled the United States into the War of 1812. Above all else she had desired to obtain a recognition of American rights at sea, in particular the end of impressment and the repeal of the Orders in Council. The withdrawal of the Orders at the very beginning of the war had ended one basic area of American complaint, and in some ways had left the United States fighting more out of resentment of past injustice than for the realization of any positive aims; only the ending of impressment was left as a tangible war aim.

In the first summer of the war the British hoped that as soon as the news of the repeal of the Orders in Council reached America the United States would end the war. When Admiral Sir John Borlase Warren was sent out to take command of the North American Station he was also authorized to offer peace feelers to Secretary of State James Monroe. It was, however, made quite clear to Warren by the Americans that nothing could be done without the British abandonment of the policy of impressment. Once the United States had so painfully declared war, it was too much to expect that the government would declare a false start, and call back its armies and ships.[1]

Yet, in spite of the failure of this rather forlorn British hope, steps were taken in the first few months of the war which eventually led to

---

[1] Bradford Perkins, *Castlereagh and Adams: England and the United States, 1812–1823* (Berkeley, 1964), pp. 11–19; Warren to Monroe, 30 Sept., Monroe to Warren, 27 Oct., 1812, *American State Papers, Foreign Relations*, I (Washington, 1832), pp. 595–7.

direct negotiations between the two countries. Within a few days of the American declaration of war Napoleon had crossed the Niemen and begun his campaign against Russia. While the United States tried to organize a few thousand men to cross the Canadian border, Napoleon advanced into the heart of Russia with half a million. News of the American war reached the Russian capital early in August, and although the policies of the Russian government were obviously dominated by Napoleon's advance on Moscow, there was concern that the United States, with whose pretensions as a commercial neutral Russia had sympathy, was now fighting Russia's new friend, Britain. Late in September 1812, the Russians approached the American Minister, John Quincy Adams, with the suggestion that Tsar Alexander would like to offer his mediation. The proposal was also submitted to the British government.

To the British the Russian offer was an embarrassment. The main point at issue with the United States was the question of neutral rights in time of war, and Britain was prepared to admit no interference from a third power which might in any way infringe on British naval strength, particularly as Russia was likely to lean towards the American point of view. Yet England did not want to offend her new ally, and delayed making any formal reply.

The Russian offer had finally been transmitted to the American government in Washington in March 1813, and resulted in a prompt acceptance. Two envoys were sent to join Adams in Russia. James A. Bayard, a Federalist, was sent as a concession to the opposition, and Albert Gallatin, the Secretary of the Treasury, requested that he should be the other envoy. He had served in the Treasury since 1801, and was weary of the opposition, the collapse of his economic policy, and the reluctance of Congress to pay for the war. Madison tried to retain his services at the Treasury by appointing an acting Secretary, but the Senate refused to confirm his appointment. By the time Gallatin knew this he was in Europe.[2]

Bayard and Gallatin sailed from America in May 1813, and arrived in St Petersburg in July. While the Americans were travelling, the British were endeavouring to extricate themselves from Tsar

---

[2] Adams, *History*, VII, 26–47; Charles Francis Adams, ed., *Memoirs of John Quincy Adams* (12 vols., Philadelphia, 1874–77), II, 401–4.

Alexander's apparent enthusiasm to mediate, with Castlereagh finally succeeding by suggesting that, though the British could not accept mediation, they would consider negotiating directly with the Americans. The British government was in no hurry – they were most concerned with avoiding mediation – and it was November 1813 before Castlereagh formally offered direct negotiations to the American government. With Napoleon approaching defeat, Madison had little choice but to accept. He named John Q. Adams, James A. Bayard, Henry Clay, Jonathan Russell, and Albert Gallatin as commissioners for the negotiation. Adams, Bayard, and Gallatin were already in Europe, although, in order to secure Senate approval for Gallatin, the government had to replace him as Secretary of the Treasury. Russell, who had been chargé in England at the beginning of the war, sailed for Europe with Henry Clay in late February. At first it was intended that the negotiations would take place at Gothenburg, but after further British delays it was agreed to meet at Ghent.[3]

In the spring of 1814 the British had reason to move slowly in actually carrying out any negotiations. The collapse of France was followed by the massing of troops for the American campaigns, and the British government confidently expected that large areas of the United States would be occupied before the close of the year. Although the American commissioners began to arrive at Ghent in June, the delay in the arrival of the British representatives meant that it was August before negotiations could begin.

The two commissions presented a strange contrast. In Clay, Adams, and Gallatin the Americans had three of their major political figures of the early nineteenth century, and Bayard and Russell were both men of considerable experience. The British were represented by comparative unknowns. Castlereagh himself was preparing to go to Vienna to settle the peace of Europe, and those chosen to go to Ghent were expected to exercise no independent judgement. The most prominent of the commission at the time was Admiral Lord

---

[3] Perkins, *Castlereagh and Adams*, pp. 21–3; Adams, *History*, VII, 339–63; Castlereagh to Monroe, 4 Nov., 1813, Department of State, Record of Negotiations Connected with the Treaty of Ghent, vol. 1, (vol. labelled 'Ghent &c'), National Archives.

Gambier. Although best known for his part in the bombardment of Copenhagen in 1807, he had served in the British navy in the American Revolution, had been commander-in-chief at Newfoundland, and had been one of the Lords of Admiralty. His presence at the negotiations confirmed to the British public that British naval rights would not be compromised. The importance of this aspect of the negotiations to the British was further demonstrated by the choice of William Adams, Ll.D., a well-known expert in maritime law, but otherwise of little note. The third member of the commission, Henry Goulburn, was eventually to have the most prominent political career, but was only a young man in 1814. Since the summer of 1812 he had served as Under-Secretary for War and the Colonies.

The discrepancy in the status of the two groups of negotiators was at first matched by a wide divergence in their positions. The Americans were governed at the start of the negotiations both by the instructions sent to Russia in 1813, and by those issued at the time of the appointment of Clay and Russell in early 1814. The only *sine qua non* was obviously enough to end any hope of success in the negotiations, for the British were to abandon the principle of impressment. For the rest, there was nothing insuperable, although Monroe's suggestion that the cession of part or even all of Canada would be best for both nations took on an air of absurdity in view of the military situation in the summer of 1814. Castlereagh's instructions to the British commissioners at the end of July also contained a completely unacceptable *sine qua non*: an American guarantee of the land of the Indians. The British were also hoping for boundary changes, and earlier in July Prevost had been told that the war should be pressed with all possible vigour up to the moment of peace.[4]

[4] Monroe to Gallatin, Adams, and Bayard, 15 April, 1813, to Adams, Bayard, Clay, and Russell, 28 Jan., 1814, Department of State, Diplomatic Instructions, vol. VII, National Archives. These basic instructions were amplified in other communications. Castlereagh to the British Commissioners, 28 July, 1814, Charles W. Vane, Third Marquess of Londonderry, ed., *Correspondence, Despatches, and other Papers of Viscount Castlereagh, Second Marquess of Londonderry* (12 vols., London, 1848–53), X, 67–72; Adams, *History*, IX, 1–17; Perkins, *Castlereagh and Adams*, pp. 39–50, 59–61; Bathurst to Prevost, 11 July, 1814, CO 43/23, pp. 157–9.

The question of impressment was at least partially solved soon after the negotiators first met, for the Americans received word from Monroe that the British abandonment of the principle of impressment was no longer a *sine qua non*. The ending of the war in Europe, and the gathering of troops for the attack on the United States, had convinced the American government that it could no longer insist on what the British obviously did not intend to grant.[5]

In spite of this concession the early discussions of the negotiators showed them to be far apart on any agreement. At the first meeting, on 8 August, Henry Goulburn declared the British would discuss impressment, the Indian lands, the Canadian boundary, and the American privilege of landing and drying fish on British shores which had been granted at the end of the Revolution. The Americans were disturbed that the fisheries question should be discussed at all, and felt that the War of 1812 had not reopened the issue of what they considered an established right. They also knew quite well that they could not agree to any guarantee of Indian lands. After more discussions on the following day, both sides decided to communicate with their governments.

This delay only increased the difficulties, for Castlereagh in his instructions of 14 August now suggested an Indian barrier state in the Old Northwest, based on the line established between the Americans and the Indians at the treaty of Greenville in 1795. He also wanted the Americans to yield Fort Niagara and Sackett's Harbor, the elimination of any American naval force on the lakes, and a cession of land in northern Maine to allow for easier communication between Halifax and Quebec. Castlereagh of course thought that this was within the bounds of possibility, as he had already ordered the occupation of parts of Maine, Sackett's Harbor, and Fort Niagara.[6]

---

[5] Monroe to American Commissioners, 27 June, 1814, Department of State, Instructions, vol. VII. For British discussion of impressment controversy see FO 5/104, pp. 123–5. Perkins, *Castlereagh and Adams*, pp. 72–3.

[6] *Memoirs of Adams*, III, 3–12; Adams, *History*, IX, 17–20; Protocol of Conference, 8 Aug., 1814, American Commissioners to Monroe, 12 Aug., 1814, Record of Ghent Negotiations, vol. 1; Castlereagh to British Commissioners, 14 Aug., 1814, Vane, ed., *Correspondence of Castlereagh*, X, 86–9.

The British effort to include the American Indians in the peace treaty stemmed from earlier British desertions of the Indians, and a persistent Canadian policy of interference in the Old Northwest. For over twenty years it had been feared that the American advance across the Ohio River would eventually threaten the British ownership of Upper Canada, and since the 1780s the Canadian authorities had attempted to use the Indians of the Old Northwest as a buffer. For over twenty years England had at different times brought up the idea of an Indian barrier state. The Indians themselves had learned to distrust the British. After fighting in the Revolution they had been ignored in the peace treaty, and after receiving British encouragement in the early 1790s they discovered that this encouragement fell short of any general military assistance against the American frontiersmen. Since early in the War of 1812 the British authorities in Canada had tried to convince the British government that on this occasion the Indians should not be deserted in any peace settlement, and the government felt that they would be accused of lack of faith if yet again they deserted the allies they had encouraged.

From the American point of view the British suggestions were completely unrealistic, and the idea of a settlement based on the Greenville line was an indication of the extent to which the British government was out of touch with the realities of the American situation. The Greenville line had begun to collapse within five years after it was established in 1795, and between 1802 and 1809 Governor William Henry Harrison of Indiana Territory had obtained huge cessions of Indian land between the Greenville line and the Mississippi River. American pioneers in their thousands had moved across the line into central and western Ohio, Indiana, and Illinois. Moreover, Tecumseh had been killed at the battle of the Thames, and the last efforts at Indian resistance crushed. If England wanted to retain possession of a large part of the Old Northwest she would have to occupy and defend it, for no Indian barrier state would halt the westward rush of the American settlers.

On 24 August the American commissioners replied firmly to the British demands, and prepared to leave Ghent, believing that the negotiations were over. Henry Goulburn, who was taking the major role in the British commission, was not perturbed by this, and was himself prepared to break off negotiations and return to Britain. The British government, however, had no desire to end all discussion, particularly as the Americans could point out that the breakdown was because of excessive British territorial demands. The British wanted all they could get out of the negotiations, but wanted it with the acquiescence of the Americans. They hoped this would be possible because they expected news from America of major victories. Thus at a time when it appeared that the negotiations would collapse, the British government demonstrated a flexibility that had not been evident in the statements of the commissioners in Ghent. If the negotiations continued, then it was hoped that the American commissioners would be overwhelmed by the news of disasters to American arms.[7]

Early in September the British commissioners delivered a new note, but the Americans again refused to compromise on the question of armaments on the lakes and the Indians. Even now the British government did not want to sever negotiations. Liverpool's comment to Bathurst on 14 September was that if any reasonable article in favour of the Indians could be included, he would settle for keeping possession of Fort Niagara and Michilimackinac in the peace. Liverpool also made it quite clear to Bathurst that he considered a 'reasonable article' was something less than full protection for the Indians. He thought the Americans would settle for a provision which restored to the Indians the rights and privileges they enjoyed at the beginning of the war, and asked 'are we honour bound to do more for them?' As for the Canadian border, Liverpool thought that if England asked for Fort Niagara, Michilimackinac, and Sackett's Harbor, the American commissioners would concentrate on resisting the claim to Sackett's Harbor, which was still in American possession. This would delay matters, and perhaps allow

---

[7] American to British Commissioners, 24 Aug., 1814, Record of Ghent Negotiations, vol. 1; Goulburn to Bathurst, 23, 24 Aug., to Castlereagh, 26 Aug., 1814, Liverpool to Wellington, 2 Sept., 1814, Arthur R. Wellesley, 2nd Duke of Wellington, ed., *Supplementary Despatches, Correspondence and Memoranda of Field Marshal Arthur Duke of Wellington, K.G.* (9 vols., London, 1858–72), IX, 189–91, 193–4, 211–13; Adams, *History*, IX, 21–5; Perkins, *Castlereagh and Adams*, pp. 81–5.

time for the arrival of favourable news from America. In any case the British government could then decide at a later date whether or not to insist on Sackett's Harbor. In the meantime it was to be made quite clear to the Americans that the British no longer insisted on exclusive military possession of the Great Lakes. Above all else the negotiations should continue. The boundary problem, thought Liverpool, would be decided by the military events in America.[8]

By the autumn of 1814 the British government was weary of the American war. There had been a great victory in Europe, but taxes had still to be maintained at a high level to pay for the American campaigns. It was also becoming apparent at the Congress in Vienna that there were sharp differences of opinion between the victorious powers. The British government was most suspicious of the aims of Alexander, and even feared a complete breakdown of relations. The American war was a sideshow, and Liverpool wanted it to end. Yet, negotiations were continued because there seemed a good possibility that there would be news of major military victories. When that happened, Britain hoped to obtain both peace and territorial gains.

The American commissioners at first rejected the suggestion that an article should be included restoring the pre-war rights of the Indians, even though the British proposal was accompanied by the abandonment of the demand for exclusive military possession of the Great Lakes, but the arrival of the news of the burning of Washington created a new situation. Liverpool now had no need to be perturbed by the uncompromising American answer. 'We need not, therefore, be in any great haste about our reply,' he wrote to Bathurst on 30 September, 'Let them feast in the mean time upon Washington.'[9]

In the first two weeks of October the American commissioners were confronted with the unpalatable fact that Washington had been taken, and that news might soon come of the fall of Baltimore and of a victory by Prevost in New York. Against this background, they agreed that they would include in any treaty an article restoring the

---

[8] Adams, *History*, IX, 26–27; Bickley, ed., *Bathurst Mss*, pp. 286–9.
[9] Bickley, ed., *Bathurst Mss*, pp. 294–5; Perkins, *Castlereagh and Adams*, pp. 87–9.

Indians to their situation in 1811. It was little enough to concede, as it meant nothing except an easing of the British conscience. The last real Indian resistance in the Old Northwest had been extinguished at the battle of the Thames, and nothing said at Ghent could restore the pre-war situation.

When all seemed blackest for the American commissioners, news arrived in the middle of October that Prevost had retreated to Canada, and that Ross had been killed before Baltimore. Although the two commissions were still to engage in considerable argument, the news made possible a settlement that would not involve a loss of American territory. At first this was not apparent, for on 18 October Bathurst suggested *uti possidetis* as a basis for peace. He argued that, allowing for exchanges, this would leave Britain in possession of Fort Niagara, Michilimackinac, and part of northern Maine. The American commissioners rejected this proposal, and argued for a mutual restoration of territory. On 3 November the British cabinet met to discuss the American situation, and decided both to ask the Duke of Wellington for his opinion of the military position, and to offer him the command in Canada.[10]

Wellington's answer was decisive. He thought his presence in Canada would be of little use without naval control of the Great Lakes, and even more bluntly he stated that with the present military position in America, Britain was not justified in asking for any territorial cessions.[11] When Britain's greatest general offered such little hope, the British government had little reason to expect any sudden change of fortune in America. With the British–Russian rift increasing in Vienna, and the public unenthusiastic about a distant war, Britain was prepared to settle for a peace without territorial gains.

---

[10] British to American Commissioners, 8, 21 Oct., American to British Commissioners, 13, 24 Oct., 1814, Record of Ghent Negotiations, vol. 1; Bathurst to British Commissioners, 18, 20 Oct., 1814, Vane, ed., *Correspondence of Castlereagh*, X, 168–73; Liverpool to Castlereagh, 2, 4 Nov., to Wellington, 4 Nov., 1814, Wellington, *Supplementary Despatches*, IX, 401–2, 404–7; *Memoirs of Adams*, III, 50–52; Perkins, *Castlereagh and Adams*, pp. 97–108; Adams, *History*, IX, 31–40.

[11] Wellington to Liverpool, 9 Nov., 1814, Wellington, *Supplementary Despatches*, IX, 424–6.

THE PEACE OF GHENT

Even now another month elapsed before agreement could be reached, for there was difficulty in regard to two legacies of the 1783 peace: the British right of navigation of the Mississippi, and the American right to land and dry fish in British possessions. At first Britain argued that the latter right had been forfeited by the War of 1812, and was a matter for negotiation, but this was a concept unacceptable to New Englander John Quincy Adams. Further complication was added by a rift in the American delegation. Westerner Henry Clay was not perturbed at the prospect of surrendering the fishing right, but did not want a continuance of the British right to navigate the Mississippi. Even a statement that these would be subject to future negotiation was unacceptable to the American commissioners, and finally the question was passed over by simply remaining completely silent on these issues in the final treaty.[12]

With these difficulties ignored there was little left to put into the treaty except an announcement of the end of the war. The United States had allowed impressment and the whole question of neutral rights to go unmentioned, and the British had given up any hope of territorial gains. The treaty was finally signed on 24 December, 1814, on the basis of the restoration of the *status quo ante bellum*. The only exception to this was the islands in Passamaquoddy Bay, which were claimed by the United States as part of Maine and by Britain as part of her colonies. The fate of these islands was to be decided by a commissioner from each country. If they disagreed their reports would be referred to a third power for decision. Commissioners were also to be appointed to settle boundary problems along the Canadian-American border which had arisen out of the inadequate geographical knowledge at the time of the treaty of Paris in 1783.[13]

It had been a strange peace conference. At first the British had made rather extravagant claims, hoping that before the discussions were over some of the demands would be substantiated by military

---

[12] Adams, *History*, IX, 42–52; Perkins, *Castlereagh and Adams*, pp. 117–27. There is also considerable information in Fred L. Engelman, *The Peace of Christmas Eve* (London, 1962).
[13] Frank A. Updyke, *The Diplomacy of the War of 1812* (Baltimore, 1915), pp. 358–478 discusses the aftermath and settlement of problems in the treaty.

victories. An added complication was the lack of any notable personalities in the British delegation. The British commissioners were cyphers, so much so that in the middle of December Goulburn asked Bathurst for an answer based on an informal communication rather than waiting for the formal American note 'as the Americans *entre nous* have rather hoaxed us for the number of our references home'.[14] The American commissioners were a capable group, but with the ending of the war in Europe, and a paucity of conquests, had few cards to play. Peace came when the seas were once again free of maritime disputes, and when both sides had shown their inability to carry out successful offensive warfare along the Canadian frontier.

Although the peace was signed, the war continued. Even the battle of New Orleans was not the end. In the middle of January Rear-Admiral Cockburn captured the town of St Mary's, Georgia, and at the end of the month Admiral Cochrane and General Lambert decided to use their New Orleans force to salvage something from their disastrous expedition by an attack on Fort Bowyer and Mobile. On the night of 7–8 February 600 troops were landed three miles east of Fort Bowyer. It was decided to avoid losses by erecting batteries in a position to bombard the fort. These were completed by the 11th, and the American garrison surrendered. The British had lost only 13 killed and 18 wounded in the operation. The American garrison consisted of less than 400 men, along with a small number of women and children. Before further operations could be carried out, Cochrane on 13 February received the news of the treaty of Ghent. Operations were now suspended in order to wait for the news of the ratification of the treaty.[15]

At sea sporadic warfare continued throughout the early months of 1815. The Admiralty had issued specific orders that hostilities should not cease until after the exchange of ratifications, and this did not come until the middle of February. Even then naval warfare continued until the news could reach distant vessels. In January the

---

[14] Goulburn to Bathurst, 13 Dec., 1814, Bickley, ed., *Bathurst Mss*, p. 316.
[15] Brannan, *Official Letters*, pp. 471–4; Lambert to Bathurst, 14 Feb., 1815, WO 1/141, pp. 259–63, also 267–8, 271; Cochrane to Croker, 14 Feb., 1815, Adm 1/508, pp. 527–9; W. Lawrence to Jackson, 12 Feb., Winchester to Monroe, 17 Feb., 1815, WD, LR, Reg. Series; Adams, *History*, IX, 62–3.

Americans, not knowing of the peace, tried as usual to take advantage of the difficult blockading conditions to put some of their remaining warships to sea. On the evening of 14 January Stephen Decatur attempted to sail from New York in the frigate *President* (44) at a time when the British blockading squadron had been blown off Sandy Hook. The manœuvre started badly when the *President* grounded on a bar, but that night she got off and ran along the shore of Long Island. The British squadron under Captain John Hayes on the razee *Majestic* quickly gave chase, and on the morning of the 15th Decatur sighted the British blockading squadron in pursuit. As the day went on the British fifty-gun frigate *Endymion* gradually gained on him.

Decatur did all he could to lighten his ship, throwing provisions, boats, cables, anchors, and everything possible overboard, but by 3.00 p.m. the *Endymion* was close enough to open fire, and by 5.00 p.m. was in position on the starboard quarter of the American ship. For two and a half hours the *President* fought the *Endymion* until the latter was obliged to break off the engagement because her sails had been cut away. The action had also caused considerable damage to the sails and rigging of the *President*, and had given the British frigates *Pamone* and *Tenedos* the opportunity to come up. The *President* had six feet of water in her hold, and had suffered casualties of 25 killed and 60 wounded. With the rest of the British squadron closing, the American captain could do little else but surrender. The *Endymion* had suffered 11 killed and 14 wounded in her successful action to prevent the escape of the American ship.[16]

The frigate *Constitution*, under Captain Charles Stewart, was more fortunate than the *President*. She managed to escape from Boston in December, and although the Admiralty put special forces to sea in an effort to take her, she managed to cruise successfully until the following March before returning to the United States. Her main success was in February when she fell in with the British sloops-of-war *Cyrene* and *Levant* about 60 leagues off Madeira. The

---

[16] Adm 2/1381, pp. 96–7, 101–2, 109–10 (re end of hostilities); Captain John Hayes to Hotham, 17 Jan., Captain H. Hope to Hayes, 15 Jan., 1815, Adm 1/508, pp. 387–92, also pp. 393–4; Decatur to Crowinshield, 18 Jan., 1815, Brannan, *Official Letters*, pp. 481–3.

Cyrene carried 33 and the *Levant* 21 guns, but they were nearly all carronades. As the *Constitution* carried thirty-two long 24-pounders, as well as other guns, the American ship had every possible advantage. The British ships, however, engaged the American in the hope of damaging her sufficiently to stop her cruise. The hope was a forlorn one, and after a forty-minute engagement both British ships were captured, the *Levant* being retaken later. In the engagement the *Constitution* lost 3 killed and 12 wounded, and the British 19 killed and 42 wounded.[17]

The last American warships still seeking action in this War of 1812 were the sloops *Hornet* (18) and *Peacock* (18). They managed to slip out of New York in January with the object of proceeding to the Indian Ocean and attacking British shipping in that region. They were to meet at Tristan da Cunha, and on 23 March, when the *Hornet*, under Captain James Biddle, was about to anchor off the north end of the island, a sail was sighted. It was the British sloop-of-war *Penguin* (18). The *Hornet* was slightly superior in force, the major difference being two extra 32-pound carronades. Both ships were anxious for action, and the British vessel came close up alongside. In twenty minutes the action was over, and the *Penguin* struck her colours. She was riddled by American shot, her foremast and bowsprit were shot away, and she was so badly damaged that the Americans scuttled her the next day. The *Hornet* suffered mainly in cut rigging and sails. The British lost 14 killed, including the captain, and 28 wounded, and the Americans 2 killed and 9 wounded.[18]

In the following weeks the two American sloops continued their cruise, still unaware that a peace treaty had been signed nearly four months before. On 27 and 28 April they chased a strange sail, but discovered that it was the British 74 *Cornwallis*. The British ship now gave chase to the *Hornet*, and everything movable was thrown overboard, with the exception of one long gun. Captain Biddle escaped into the harbour of San Salvador. The *Peacock* continued

---

[17] Stewart to Sec. of Navy, May 1815, Brannan, *Official Letters*, pp. 492–4; Roosevelt, *Naval War of 1812*, II, 164–9.

[18] Biddle to Sec. of Navy, 25 March, 1815, *American State Papers, Naval Affairs*, I, 377.

her cruise throughout June, capturing four more British ships, and not until the 30th did she hear of the peace. When told of this by a small British vessel, Captain Lewis Warrington of the *Peacock* asked her to haul down her colours. She refused, and the *Peacock* fired a broadside into her. On this ungallant note ended the naval war at sea, over three years after it had begun.[19]

Even at this late date American sailors were still under British restraint, for there had been inept and sad proceedings connected with the camp for American prisoners-of-war at Dartmoor. When possible in the War of 1812 the two powers exchanged their prisoners, and allowed them to fight again, but in the latter part of the war the British accumulated more prisoners than the Americans. American prisoners were held during the war at Halifax, Bermuda, and on prison hulks in various British ports, but by the end of 1814 most of them, over 5,000, had been gathered together at Dartmoor. This number increased to nearly 6,000 in early 1815, nearly all of them sailors. Among them were about 1,000 American Negroes, who formed an important element in the crews of the American privateers.[20]

Throughout the war this had been a miserable prison. It was always damp, with water running down the huge stone blocks, and much of the time it was shrouded in mist and drizzle. Over 250 prisoners had died of smallpox or pneumonia, and the news of peace was greeted with great joy. On 31 December the prisoners showed their naval origin by displaying a banner with the motto 'Free Trade and Sailors' Rights'. Their spirits were still high. 'This forenoon,' wrote one prisoner, 'some English officers came up to see the prisoners & the band of No. 4 [the Negro barracks] played up Yankee doodle dandy O It galls them.'[21]

Any hopes of swift repatriation faded in the following months. First came the wait for the ratification of the treaty, and when this arrived on 14 March smallpox was again raging in the prison. The

---

[19] Biddle to Decatur, 10 June, 1815, Brannan, *Official Letters*, pp. 494–8; Roosevelt, *Naval War of 1812*, II, 183–8.
[20] Andrew, *Prisoners' Memoirs*, pp. 139, 149, 162.
[21] *Ibid.*, pp. 261–80 (deaths), 21–4, 127–37; *The Diary of Benjamin Palmer, Privateersman* (The Acorn Club, 1914), pp. 126–7.

British were now willing to free the prisoners, but there was a further delay while the Americans slowly gathered together the vessels to take the prisoners home. The impatience of the prisoners could hardly be contained, and on 6 April, after they had expressed their displeasure at a shortage of bread, the prison commandant, Captain Thomas G. Shortland of the Royal Navy, thought there was going to be an attempt at a mass breakout, panicked, and ordered his troops to fire; 7 prisoners were killed and 54 wounded, over three months after the signing of the treaty of peace. With this tragedy the British Admiralty now agreed to share the expense of repatriating the American prisoners, and to provide sufficient ships to supplement those already supplied by the Americans. Yet until July prisoners were still detained at Dartmoor; some of the last to leave were many of the Negroes, who did not want to ship out in any vessels bound for a southern port in the United States. For the American prisoners at Dartmoor this had been no comic-opera war.[22]

In view of the ineptness of so many of the offensive operations in this War of 1812, perhaps its most surprising feature is the overconfidence of so many of its participants. The optimism with which in 1812 the United States began the invasion of Canada was most insecurely based. The Americans had no trained army, lacked a coherent direction of the war, and had failed to secure naval control of the Great Lakes. Strategically, they were hurt not only by the lack of efficient planning, but also by the New England opposition to the war. The lack of state co-operation in that region severely hampered any offensive along the Lake Champlain route towards the St Lawrence, and this was the decisive route for any successful attack against Canada.

At the beginning of the war the Canadians had the advantage of a small body of British regulars, and a naval force on the Great Lakes sufficient for defensive warfare. The regulars were able to form a nucleus around which the Canadian militia could rally. In some

---

[22] Andrew, *Prisoners' Memoirs*, pp. 144–51, 167–206, 222–35; Adm 98/228, pp. 195, 203; 98/123, pp. 193, 194; 98/291, pp. 236–7, 243; *Journal of Joseph Valpey, Jr. of Salem* (Detroit, 1922), p. 27; Basil Thomson, *The Story of Dartmoor Prison*, p. 191.

ways Canada was more prepared for war than the power which declared it. Since 1807 the British authorities had feared invasion, and had attempted to organize Canadian defence. Although Britain could offer little additional help in 1812, the core of professionals, the ineptness of the Americans, and the difficulty of offensive warfare on wild, undeveloped border regions all served to thwart American hopes.

The most surprising facet of the war on land was not the failure of the attack on Canada, but the inability of the British to inflict severe defeats on the Americans in 1814. This failure stemmed from the improvement of American forces after two years of war, the same difficulties of terrain and communications faced by the Americans in 1812, a degree of overconfidence, and a lack of able leadership. Prevost possessed few of the characteristics of a successful general, and wasted a fine army on the Lake Champlain front. Pakenham at New Orleans attacked in the nearly impossible situation created for him by Admiral Cochrane. Throughout the war neither power was able to solve the problems of offensive warfare on the North American continent, and defence predominated.

At sea the war was a disappointment to both powers, particularly to Britain where this aspect of the war had the most impact on public opinion. The land war was of little consequence to the British public – the feeble operations of tiny armies were dwarfed by the mighty clashes on the Continent – but any encounters at sea absorbed the British attention. The defeats inflicted on British frigates in the first year of the war were a profound shock, even though these victories were won by American ships of greater force. In the mind of the British public this discrepancy in force was not enough to account for the series of seeming disasters. The disappointment was compounded in Britain by the great success of the American privateers. The British public was not accustomed to reading about enemy ships sailing unscathed in the Channel and the Irish Sea. The Americans helped to reveal the extent to which trained seamen were spread so thinly over the British fleet, and an unevenness in the quality of leadership. The regular American navy had excellent ships, and was so small that the best officers could be appointed to command them. It was also a navy of volunteers, and as in the case of the officers the lack of ships meant that the best seamen could be selected to serve in those that were in commission.

Yet, for all the complaints of the public, the British navy achieved a dominance in the War. From the summer of 1813 a ring of British ships encircled the waters around the United States, ruining American commerce, and laying open the whole American coastline to British attack. The American navy was so small that it could not engage any British squadron of any size, and its operations were confined to seeking out single British frigates or smaller ships, and raiding British commerce. It could not challenge the British blockade, nor could it protect the American coastline.

The ineptness of American military operations and the vulnerability of the American coasts stemmed in large measure from the inconsistencies in the policies of the Democratic-Republicans in the years before the war. Jefferson and his party genuinely hoped that the United States could avoid war and separate herself from the turmoils of Europe, but this hope was allowed to obscure the realities of the situation. Such were the pressures of the Napoleonic wars that for the whole period from 1803 to 1812 it was likely that the United States would have to choose between submission to belligerent restrictions on her commerce and a declaration of war. Economic coercion was tried as an alternative to war, but in spite of Jefferson's optimism there was no certainty that it would succeed. War always seemed a possibility.

In this time of contant crisis due prudence demanded the establishment of an army and navy at least competent to protect the United States. Above all else it demanded a navy capable of protecting American maritime rights. With such a navy, an undeclared war at sea might better have served American interests than a declaration of war and the attempted invasion of Canada. Yet the Democratic-Republicans did not provide the military forces or make the financial preparations for a war that was a constant threat until actually declared in 1812. As a result, in 1814, the United States came perilously close to disaster. That this disaster was avoided, however luckily, turned the War of 1812 from a débâcle into a near success. A war that was begun to win respect for American maritime rights by the conquest of Canada was finally viewed as a success in the United

States because it resulted in the loss of no American territory, and did not bring about the collapse of the government.

The legacy of the War of 1812 in Britain was inevitably very slight. The manufacturers and exporters who engaged in the lucrative American trade were understandably delighted that the war was over, but general disquiet at the failures of 1814 was soon to be overwhelmed by the news of Waterloo. Unfortunate battles in America and surprising naval defeats were soon forgotten in the joy of the successful conclusion to over twenty years of war against France. The disaster at New Orleans and frigate defeats seemed little enough when measured against the world-shaking victories of Waterloo and Trafalgar. Time so erased the memory of the little war across the Atlantic that within a hundred years the well-educated Englishman had never heard of it.

In Canada the situation was much different. Here the war was of vital importance. Although the major role in the resistance to the American invasion fell to the British regulars, they were supported by numerous Canadian militia. To many Canadians this seemed a war for existence. Whatever the stated aims of the United States in invading Canada, there was no guarantee that if conquered it would ever be given up. The failure of the United States to conquer Canada both enhanced the sense of Canadian identity and helped to create a long-lasting suspicion of the United States. A hundred years later, when the British had forgotten the war, Canadians found in it the patriotic past they desired. Militia disturbances, martial law, and traitors were forgotten, and the militia of 1812 were enshrined as the saviours of their country. The Americans who later in the nineteenth century wanted to annex Canada found that the invasion of 1812 had made their task far more difficult.[23]

For the United States, as for Canada, the War of 1812 stimulated the development of national feeling. The bitter arguments and near disunion of the conflict were forgotten in the glorious sense of relief produced by the repulse of the British at Plattsburg, Baltimore, and, above all, New Orleans. The United States achieved none of her

---

[23] See C. P. Stacey, 'The War of 1812 in Canadian History', in Zaslow, ed., *Defended Border*, pp. 331–7, also *ibid.*, 315–30.

war aims in the peace treaty, but by 1814 the war begun to force a change in British policies had become a war for survival. The country was bankrupt, her coasts lay open to the attackers, New England spoke of disunion, and across the Atlantic streamed the conquerors of Napoleon. It seemed that nothing could save the United States from humiliating defeat and dismemberment. Could the ill-trained levies who had surrendered to Brock at Detroit and time and time again faltered along the Canadian border, hope to turn back the veterans of the Peninsula?

In August 1814 a pathetic mob of an army scattered before the British at Bladensburg, Madison and his cabinet fled into the countryside, and the capital was burned. It seemed a miracle had happened when news came that Prevost and 10,000 men were not marching into the Hudson Valley but were in retreat to Canada, and that Baltimore had held firm. Above all, in the new year came the incredible news that Jackson had lost only 70 men in completely defeating a veteran British army. The failure of the United States to achieve her aims in the peace treaty was passed over in the rejoicing that the war had ended with a complete American victory on land.

The glittering American enthusiasm and nationalism of the postwar years has to be viewed against the blackness of the summer of 1814. Although the war aims had not been gained, nothing had been lost. Commerce immediately flowed freely into its accustomed channels, and the protection of economic coercion and war had even given a stimulus to the infant American industries. Since the Revolution the questions of whether the United States could establish a unified national government and survive without dismemberment had been in doubt. The country had been buffeted and threatened throughout the Revolutionary and Napoleonic wars; her foreign policy had constantly been formulated in reaction to immediate outside pressures and dangers. From 1815 this changed. The United States henceforth acted rather than reacted, and herself posed a threat to all powers who held territory on the North American Continent. Her settlers poured west to create a nation whose strength would have amazed the disorganized troops of 1814. In declaring war without preparing for it the Democratic-Republicans had risked disaster. This disaster had been avoided as much by chance as by resolution, but once escaped from the war was seen as the successful conclusion to over twenty years of danger to American national sovereignty. The war that was so quickly forgotten in Britain marked the end of an era in the United States.

Bibliographical Note

In writing this book I have attempted to examine primary sources both in Britain and the United States. The details are given in the notes, and here I wish only to indicate the most important materials which I used.

In Britain I made most use of the primary material in the Public Record Office, particularly the Admiralty, Colonial Office, and War Office archives. The Admiralty records which proved most useful were Adm 1/502-8, letters from Admirals on the North American Station, and Adm 2/1374-81, secret orders and letters. I also made use of Adm 2/932-3, Secretary's letters to Commanders-in-Chief at Stations Abroad (North America), and Adm 98/123, 98/228, and 98/291-2 from which I obtained information regarding prisoners-of-war and impressment.

The archives of the Colonial Office are particularly important for the War of 1812 as they include a mass of information relating to the conduct of both civil and military affairs in Canada during the conflict. Of particular importance were CO 42/146-57, despatches from Lower Canada, CO 43/352-6, despatches from Upper Canada, and CO 43/23, letters of the Secretary of State to Lower Canada. I also made use of CO 43/40, letters of the Secretary of State to Upper Canada, CO 43/49-51, which contains mainly miscellaneous inter-departmental correspondence relating to North America, and CO 42/160, which contains mainly trade and maritime matters.

Among the most important collections in the War Office archives were WO 1/96, in-letters, WO 1/141-4, expedition to the southern coasts, 1814-15, WO 71/243 for the court martial of Procter, and WO 3/602-8, out-letters of the Commander-in-Chief (private). The War Office records regarding the American conflict are very scattered, and it is necessary to make use of the indices to locate additional materials. Although I also found some items of value in the

Liverpool Papers in the British Museum, by far the most important sources used for the British conduct of the war were from the Public Record Office.

For the American side of the war the manuscript materials contained in the National Archives proved the most valuable. Of basic importance are the Records of the Office of the Secretary of War. There is a great deal of information in Letters Received, both the Registered and Unregistered Series, and to a lesser extent in Letters Sent, Military Affairs. These are rather poorly arranged, however, and somewhat incomplete, and have to be supplemented by other materials. The records of the Department of the Navy are more convenient to use, and are also essential for a study of the war. The basic collections are Letters Sent by the Secretary of the Navy to Officers, Ships of War, and three collections of Letters Received by the Secretary of the Navy: from Captains, from Masters Commandant, and from Officers (below the rank of Master Commandant). Also relevant in the National Archives are the Department of State archives relating to the diplomacy of the war and the Peace of Ghent. Of most importance is the material gathered together under the general title of Record of Negotiations Connected with the Treaty of Ghent, and Diplomatic Instructions, All Countries. These basic materials from the National Archives are now available on microfilm.

My debt to a variety of printed collections of source materials, memoirs, and journals is made evident in my notes, but I would like here to mention works which proved particularly useful. A good survey of the whole war from the American point of view is provided by the letters in John Brannan, *Official Letters of the Military and Naval Officers of the United States during the War with Great Britain in the Years 1812, 13, 14 & 15* (Washington, 1823). From the Canadian point of view an excellent collection is William H. Wood, ed., *Select British Documents of the Canadian War of 1812* (3 vols., Toronto, 1920-28). The British have shown considerably less interest in the conflict, but there is material of interest in Arthur R. Wellesley, 2nd Duke of Wellington, ed., *Supplementary Despatches, Correspondence and Memoranda of Field Marshal Arthur Duke of Wellington, K.G.* (9 vols., London, 1858-72).

BIBLIOGRAPHICAL NOTE

In the twentieth century there has been little interest in the War of 1812 in Britain, and even in the United States far more detailed work has been written on the causes of the war than on the war itself. The most recent studies of the origins of the conflict are Bradford Perkins, *Prologue to War: England and the United States, 1805-1812* (Berkeley, 1961), Reginald Horsman, *The Causes of the War of 1812* (Philadelphia, 1962), and Roger Brown, *Republic in Peril* (New York, 1964). Although a number of histories of the war itself have been published in recent years, these have by no means superseded the classic account contained in Henry Adams, *History of the United States during the Administration of Jefferson and Madison* (9 vols., New York, 1889-91). This is still indispensable for a study of the whole period. Other older works are also still of great value: Alfred T. Mahan, *Sea Power in its Relations to the War of 1812* (2 vols., Boston, 1905) is essential reading for an understanding of this period, and Theodore Roosevelt's *Naval War of 1812* (2 vols., Boston, 1904) is particularly useful for its analysis of comparative strengths in the various naval engagements of the war. A still older work, of different type, but still very well worth consulting is Benson J. Lossing, *The Pictorial Field Book of the War of 1812* (New York, 1868). Although somewhat anecdotal in nature, this large work contains considerable information.

Of recent works the most balanced is Harry L. Coles, *The War of 1812* (Chicago, 1965). This is a clear narrative based essentially on printed source materials and secondary accounts. It also has a good bibliography. J. Mackay Hitsman, *The Incredible War of 1812* (Toronto, 1965) presents a modern Canadian view of the war, but there is a strong emphasis on the Canadian aspects of the war to the exclusion of other areas. The best modern account of the diplomatic aspects of the conflict is contained in Bradford Perkins, *Castlereagh and Adams: England and the United States, 1812-1823* (Berkeley, 1964).

My debt to other secondary accounts is indicated in the notes.

Index

Index

Acasta, 56
Adams, 163
Adams, John Quincy, 251, 252, 259
Adams, William, 253
Admiralty: impressment, 10; reinforcements, 67-8, 168-9; and single ship engagements, 69, 72, 152; Great Lakes, 87-8, 138-40; lack of faith in Warren, 140-41, 142; orders to Cochrane, 155; approves retaliation, 157; New Orleans attack, 228; peace, 260
Aeolus, 56
Africa, 56, 57, 59
Albany, N.Y., 50
Alert, 57, 66
Alexander I, Tsar, 251, 252, 257
Alexandria, Va., 203
Allen, Andrew, 58
Amherstburg, Can., 28, 35, 38, 110
Amiens, peace of, 5-6
Ancaster, Can., 122
Apalachicola River, 226, 227, 228, 231, 235, 236
Arbuthnot, Capt. James, 151
Argus, 56, 63, 74
Ariel, 106
Armistead, Major George, 207
Armstrong, John: Minister to France, 14; Secretary of War, 86; invasion of Canada, 89-90, 117-18, 130, 175; at Sackett's Harbor, 124-5; weakens Lake Champlain front, 186-7; fails to fortify Washington, 195, 196, 197, 203; resigns, 202
Army, British: condition in Canada, 26; 1st Regt. (Royal Scots), 57, 176-7; 4th Regt., 245; 7th Fusiliers, 244, 245; 8th Regt., 176-7; 21st Regt., 245; 40th Regt., 229; 41st Regt., 112-13; 43rd Regt., 244, 245; 44th Regt., 206, 245, 247; 49th Regt., 33; 70th Regt., 123; 95th Regt., 245; 100th Regt., 176-7; 102nd Regt., 159; 103rd Regt., 131; Canadian Fencibles, 26-7; Canadian Voltigeurs, 128; Glengarry Light Infantry Fencibles, 27, 121; Royal Newfoundland Fencibles, 171; 1st West Indian Regt., 245; 5th West Indian Regt., 228; Independent Foreigners (French), 77, 79, 80. *See also* Militia, Canadian
Army, U.S.: strength, 9, 19-20, 30, 89, 168; officers, 31-2; 4th Regt., 34; 7th Regt., 239; 39th Regt., 224; 44th Regt., 239. *See also* Militia, U.S.
Astor, John Jacob, 146
Auttose, Creek village, 221
Avon, 151

Bacchante, 162
Bacon, Ezekiel, 20
Bainbridge, Joseph, 148
Bainbridge, Capt. William, 65, 66
Baltimore, 153, 197, 198, 204-8, 209, 211, 257, 258, 267, 268
Bangor, Me., 163
Bank of the United States: First, 20; Second, 210
Baratarian pirates, 226, 233, 239, 247
Barbados, 59
Barclay, Capt. Robert Heriot, 104, 105, 106-7
Barney, Capt. Joshua, 154-5, 196, 200, 207
Bass Islands, 106
Bathurst, Henry, 3rd Earl, 78, 123, 136, 138, 140, 158-9, 169, 172-3, 177, 184, 228, 229, 256, 257, 258
Bayard, James A., 251, 252
Baynes, Col. Edward, 94, 121
Bay of Fundy, 59
Beaver Dam, battle of, 97
Beckwith, Col. Sir Thomas Sydney, 78-9, 79-80
Belfast, Me., 162, 163
Belvidera, 56, 57, 142
Benedict, Md., 194, 196, 201
Berkeley, Vice-Adm. George C., 11
Berlin Decree, 8, 11, 14
Bermuda, 58, 59, 78, 144, 194, 263
Biddle, Capt. James, 262
Bienvenu, Bayou, 238, 239, 240, 242, 244

INDEX

Birmingham, 22
Black Rock, N.Y., 47, 48, 103, 136, 156, 180
Bladensburg, Md., 195, 197, 198, 199–200, 201, 205, 206, 245, 268
Blakely, Capt. Johnston, 150
Blockade, 6–7, 7–8, 24, 57–8, 60, 68–9, 71, 74, 142–3, 144–5, 151–2, 153, 160, 167, 209, 228, 261, 266
Blount, Gov. Willie, 216, 219
Boerstler, Lieut.-Col. C. G., 97
Boston, 57, 58, 60, 63, 65, 69, 71, 72, 73, 142, 148, 261
Boxer, 74
Boyd, Brig.-Gen. John P., 128–9
Brazil, 12, 65
Brisbane, Maj.-Gen. Thomas, 187, 188
Brock, Maj.-Gen. Sir Isaac: energy, 25–6, 102, 268; American immigrants, 27; plans for war, 28–9, 33; and Fort Malden, 35, 38; Upper Canadian Legislature, 38; Detroit, 39–41; arrives Fort George, 43; battle of Queenston Heights, 46; killed, 46
Broke, Capt. Philip Bowes Vere, 57, 72, 73
Brooke, Col. Arthur, 206, 207
Brougham, Henry, x, 22
Brown, Maj.-Gen. Jacob, 94, 128, 175, 176–7, 180, 182, 183, 248
Brownstown, battle of, 37
Buffalo, N.Y., 89, 115, 133, 136, 156, 180
Bulwark, 144, 158, 162
Burlington, 95, 134, 175, 182, 183. *See also* Lake Ontario, head of
Burr, Aaron, 117
Byron, Lord, 204

Caledonia, 45, 103
Calhoun, John C., 17
Campbell, George Washington, 166, 210
Campbell, Col. John B., 156
Canning, George, 12, 13
Carden, Capt. John Surman, 64, 65
Carolina, 240, 242
Carroll, Maj.-Gen. William, 239, 240, 244
Carron, 232, 233
Castine, Me., 162
Castlereagh, Robert Stewart, Viscount, 12, 22, 253, 254
Chambly, Can., 49
Champlain, N.Y., 50
Chandeleur Islands, 236, 237

Chandler, Brig.-Gen. John, 96
Charleston, S. C., 69
Chateauguay, battle of, 126
Chauncey, Commodore Isaac: commander on lakes, 86; attacks on York, 91, 97; bombards British, 95; caution, 98, 177, 185; captures troopships, 124; plans for Niagara frontier, 175; relinquishes blockade, 184
Cherokee Indians, 220, 223, 224, 225
Cherub, 146, 147, 148
Chesapeake, 16, 73, 74
Chesapeake affair, 11, 15
Chesapeake Bay: raided by British, 75–80, 153–6; American weakness, 195–6
Cheves, Langdon, 17
Chicago, 41
Childers, 232
Chippawa, Can., 46, 48, 175
Chippawa, battle of, 176–7
Chippewa, 105
Chittenden, Gov. Martin, 167, 187
Choctaw Indians, 222, 234, 244
Chubb, 189, 191
Claiborne, Brig.-Gen. Ferdinand L., 222
Clay, Brig.-Gen. Green Clay, 100
Clay, Henry, 15, 16–17,19, 252, 253
Cleveland, Ohio, 99, 102
Cochrane, Vice-Adm. Sir Alexander: commander of the North American station, 141, 149; blockades, 144–5, 153; and reinforcements, 144, 155, 168, 194, 229; and slaves, 153–4, 227, 228; retaliation against Americans, 156, 157, 159, 202; pays American traitor, 158; and Nantucket, 160–1; attack on Washington, 194; attack on Baltimore, 205, 206, 207, 208; and Indians, 226, 227, 236; attack on New Orleans, 226, 227, 228, 230, 233, 238, 247, 265; attack on Fort Bowyer, 260; news of peace, 260
Coan River, raided into, 156
Cockburn, Rear-Adm. Sir George: raids in Chesapeake, 75–6, 155–6; raids North Carolina, 80; attack on Washington, 194, 195, 196, 197, 200, 201; burning of Washington, 201, 202; attack on Baltimore, 204, 205; takes St Mary's, 260
Cocke, Maj.-Gen. John, 219, 220, 221, 222
Codrington, Edward, Captain of the Fleet, 149

INDEX

Coffee, Maj.-Gen. John: Creek war, 219, 224, 225; reinforces Jackson, 234; at New Orleans, 239, 240, 241, 244
Columbia River, 146
Confiance, 185, 186, 189, 190, 191
Congress, 56, 63, 71
Congress, U.S.: war preparations, 18–21; declaration of war, 24; special session (1814), 210–11
Congreve's Rockets, 77, 138
Connecticut River, raided into, 158
Constellation, 78
Constitution: armament, 53; escapes British, 57; fights *Guerrière*, 60–2, 63, 64; fights *Java*, 65–6; into Boston, 71; cruises, 142, 261–2
Coote, Capt. Richard, 158
Cornwall, Can., 120, 121, 129–30, 184
Cornwallis, 262
Craney Island, 78–9
Creek Indians: war against, 218–25; Fort Jackson treaty, 225; contacted by British navy, 226
Croghan, Lieut.-Col. George, 102, 171
Croker, John Wilson, 67, 68, 141
Crysler's Farm, battle of, 128–9, 130
Cyrene, 261, 262

Dacres, Capt. James R., 60
Dallas, Alexander J., 210
Dartmoor Prison, 54, 162, 176, 248–9, 263–4
Dearborn, Henry: commander-in-chief, 31, 117, 118, 248; suspends offensive operations, 42–3; and Niagara frontier, 43–4, 47, 94, 95; Lake Champlain front (1812), 49–50; plans for 1813 campaign, 89–90, 91, 99; resigns, 96, 97
Decatur, Capt. Stephen, 64, 80, 261
De Rottenburg, Maj.-Gen. Baron Francis, 49–50, 120, 134, 187
De Salaberry, Lt.-Col. Charles, 126
Desertion, British, 26, 51, 54, 80, 121, 131–2
Desha, Joseph, 17
Detroit: in 1812, 29, 34, 39–41, 43, 49, 62, 81, 82, 83, 102, 268; in 1813, 84, 107 110, 111, 117; in 1814, 169, 171, 172, 175
Detroit, 45, 104, 105, 106, 108
Dickson, Brevet Lieut.-Col. Alexander, 242, 243, 248
Dispatch, 159, 160

Dover, Can., 156
Downie, Capt. George, 189–90, 191
Dragon, 162
Drummond, Lieut.-Gen. Sir Gordon: commands Upper Canada, 120, 134; and disloyal Canadians, 122; attacks across Niagara River, 134, 135; concern re Indians, 136; plans to attack Sackett's Harbor, 173; battle of Lundy's Lane, 178–9; siege of Fort Erie, 180–3; weaknesses, 184
Drummond, Lt. Col. William, 182
Dudley, Lt.-Col. William, 100
Dyson, Capt. Samuel T., 203

Eagle (brig), 186, 189, 191
Eagle (schooner), 116
Econochaca, Creek village, 222
Elliott, Master Commandant Jesse D., 44–5, 106, 107
Elliott, Matthew, 40, 44, 109, 110, 112, 135–6
Embargo: Dec. 1807, 12, 13–14; 1812, 21; 1813–14, 143, 168
Emuckfaw Creek, 223
Endymion, 162, 261
English Town, La., 237
Enterprise, 74, 151
Epervier, 148, 149
Erie, Pa. *See* Presque Isle
Erskine, David, 13
Essex, 57, 66, 70, 145–7
Essex decision, 7, 9, 10
Euryalus, 203
Eustis, William, 31, 32, 37, 216
Examiner (London), 24
Exports: American, 143; British, 12, 58

Fallen Timbers, battle of, 5
Federal Republican (Baltimore), 31
Finances, Canadian, 42, 119, 169
Finances, U.S., 20–21, 165–7, 210–11
Finch, 189, 191
Fischer, Lt.-Col. Victor, 181
Floridas, 8–9, 216–17, 231, 234–5
Floyd, Brig.-Gen. John, 221, 222, 223, 224
Forsyth, Capt. Benjamin, 90
Forts: Armstrong, 221; Barrancas, 235; Bowyer, 232–3, 234, 235, 236, 260; Charlotte, 217; Chippawa, 29, 45, 95, 97; Claiborne, 222; Covington, 207; Dearborn, 41; Defiance, 82, 83;

INDEX

Forts: (cont)
Detroit, 38, 39, 40; Erie, 29, 45, 89, 95, 97, 122, 175, 176, 179, 180–3; George, (in 1812), 29, 35, 43, 45, 46, (in 1813), 89, 94, 95, 96, 97, 98, 99, 104, 116, 117, 122, 133, 135, (in 1814), 176, 177, 179, 181, 183; Harrison, 82; Jackson, treaty of, 231; McHenry, 204, 205, 206, 207; Madison, 82; Malden, 11, 28, 29, 34, 35, 36, 37–8, 39, 41, 43, 83, 84, 85, 99, 102, 103, 106–7, 108, 172; Meigs, 85, 99, 100, 102; Miami, 101; Mims, 218, 219, 224; Mitchell, 223, 224; Niagara, 134–5, 169, 254, 256, 258; Schlosser, 178; St Charles, 237; St John, 237; St Joseph, 28, 36; St Philip, 237, 248; Stephenson, 102–3; Stoddert, 222; Strother, 219, 220, 221, 222; Sullivan, 159; Washington, 195, 198, 203–4; Wayne, 81, 83; Wellington, 127; Winchester, 83
Forty Mile Creek, 96
Foster, Augustus J., 31, 56 n
Fox, Charles James, 1
Fox's blockade, 8
France, ix, 1, 4, 5, 14, 21, 252. *See also* Napoleon
Fredericktown, Md., 77
French-Canadians, 27, 33, 37, 119, 121
French Mills, N.Y., 130, 131
Frenchtown, Md., 75
Frenchtown (Mich.), battle of, 84–5, 99
Frolic, British, 62–3, 66
Frolic, U.S., 148
Fulton, Robert, 145, 159

Gaines, Brig.-Gen. Edmund P., 180–1, 182, 248
Gallatin, Albert, 9, 20, 165, 166, 212, 251, 252
Gambier, Admiral Lord, 252–3
Garland, Lieut. James, 158
General Pike, 86, 97, 124
Georgetown, Md., 77
Georgia, 221, 222, 223, 226, 235
Ghent, Treaty of, 241, 252–9
Gibbs, Maj.-Gen. Sir Samuel, 242, 245, 246–7
Givins, Major James, 92, 93
Gloucester, 92
Gordon, Capt. James A., 202, 203, 204
Gore, Francis, 26 n
Gothenburg, 252

Goulburn, Henry, 253, 254, 255–6, 260
Great Lakes, 29–30, 208, 258, 264. *See also* individual lakes
Green Bay, Wis., 171
Greenbush, N.Y., 50
Greenville, Treaty of, 254, 255
Griffith, Rear-Adm. Edward, 162, 163
Growler, 116
Grundy, Felix, 17
Guerrière, 56, 60–2, 63, 64, 66

Halifax, N.S., 28, 56, 59, 80, 138, 141, 145, 162, 263
Hall, Maj.-Gen. Amos, 136
Hamilton, Paul, 16
Hampden, Me., 162, 163
Hampton, Maj.-Gen. Wade, 117, 124, 125–6, 127, 130
Hampton, Va., 79
Hampton Roads, 78
Hardy, Capt. Sir Thomas, 80, 159
Harmony, 163
Harper, John A., 17
Harrison, Maj.-Gen. William Henry: battle of Tippecanoe, 17; western commander, 81, 82; plans, 83–4, 85, 99; at Fort Meigs, 100–1; difficulties in 1813, 101–2; control of Detroit frontier, 108, 110, 111, 117, 118, 137, 156; battle of the Thames, 113–14; to Niagara frontier, 115, 132–3; to Sackett's Harbor, 133; Indian land cessions, 255
Hartford Convention, 211–12, 214
Havre de Grace, Md., 75
Hayes, Capt. John, 261
Henry, John, 21
Hermes, 228, 232, 233
Hill, Lord Rowland, 226
Hillibee Town, 221
Hillyar, Capt. James, 146, 147
Hopkins, Brig.-Gen. Samuel, 83
Hornet, 56, 70–1, 73, 262
Horseshoe Bend, battle of, 224–5, 236
Hotham, Rear-Adm. Henry, 161, 162
Hull, Capt. Isaac, 60–2, 65
Hull, Brig.-Gen. William: invasion of Canada, 34–8, 122; despairs, 38–9; loss of Detroit, 39–41, 62, 81; and Dearborn, 42–3
Hunter, 105

Illinois Territory, 3, 83, 255

INDEX

Impressment, x, 7, 10, 11, 16, 24, 54–5, 250
Indiana Territory, 3, 17, 255
Indians: British support for, 3, 4, 11, 15; on Detroit front, 37, 38, 39–41, 81, 100, 102, 108–12, 112–14; from west of Lake Michigan, 37, 41, 82, 170, 171; Niagara front, 45, 46, 96, 135–6, 178; defence of Montreal, 49; American attacks on, 83, 172; and American prisoners, 85, 101; at York, 92; supply problem, 102; at Crysler's Farm, 128; as barrier state, 169, 255; pro-American, 174, 175, 176, 244; problem at Ghent, 254, 255, 256, 257–8; and New Orleans attack, 226, 227, 229, 230–1
Isle aux Noix, 49, 116, 139, 186
Isle aux Poix, 239, 241
Izard, Maj.-Gen. George, 183, 185, 186–7

Jackson, Francis James, 13
Jackson, Maj.-Gen. Andrew: takes force to Natchez, 216–17; war against Creeks, 219–25, 233; battle of Horseshoe Bend, 224–5; treaty of Fort Jackson, 225; defends Mobile, 231, 232, 234, 235; attacks Pensacola, 234, 235; to New Orleans, 235–6; New Orleans defences, 237, 238, 239, 241, 244–5; attacks British, 240–1; battle of New Orleans, 244–8; fame, 248–9; effect of victory, 268
Jamaica, 16, 56–7, 141, 208, 228, 230, 236
Java, 65–6, 71
Jay, John, 5
Jefferson, Thomas, 8–9, 10, 11–12, 13, 20, 212, 266
Johnson, Richard M., 110, 113
Jones, Capt. Jacob, 62
Jones, Lieut. Thomas Ap Catesby, 238
Jones, William, 165

Keane, Maj.-Gen. John, 229, 230, 238, 239, 242, 245, 247
Kentucky: population, 3, 215; and coming of war, 15, 16, 17, 19, 24; troops from, 28, 83, 84–5, 100, 110, 113, 114, 115, 239, 245
Key, Francis Scott, 207
Kingston, Can.: importance, 29; American plans for, 89, 90, 91, 117–18; British troops at, 91, 94, 173; Wolfe launched, 97; supply problems, 119;
Wilkinson avoids, 123–4; fleet at, 87, 88, 97, 98, 127, 173, 180

Lachine, Can., 33
Lady Prevost, 104, 105
Lafitte brothers, 233
Lake Borgne, 237, 238, 239, 240, 244
Lake Champlain: American troops, 89, 90; Hampton's advance, 125–6; navies on, 116, 139, 185–6, 189, 193; Wilkinson advances, 185; British plans for, 169, 184; British attack along, 185–93; battle of Plattsburg Bay, 190–2
Lake Erie, navies on, 29, 82, 86–7, 88–9, 94, 99, 103–7, 169, 172
Lake Michigan, war west of, 36–7, 41, 82, 170–2
Lake Ontario: British naval forces, 29, 86, 139, 173, 177, 184–5; American naval forces, 86, 140; naval operations, 97–9, 124, 173–4, 179–80
Lake Ontario, head of, 95, 114, 116, 170. *See also* Burlington
Lake Pontchartrain, 227, 237
Lambert, Maj.-Gen. John: orders, 229, 230; reinforces Pakenham, 243–4; in reserve, 245, 246, 247; abandons attack, 247, 248; attacks Fort Bowyer, 260
Lancashire, 22
Laprairie, Can., 49
Lawrence, 105, 106
Lawrence, Capt. James, 70, 73
Lawrence, Major William, 232
Leeward Islands, 56, 141, 142
Leicester, 22
Legislative Assembly, Lower Canada, 27, 119
Legislative Assembly, Upper Canada, 27, 38, 119, 122, 156
Leonard, Capt. Nathaniel, 135
Leonardtown, Md., 155
Leopard, 11
Levant, 261, 262
Lewis, Brevet Major George, 154
Lewis, Maj.-Gen. Morgan, 96
Lewiston, N.Y., 45, 135, 136, 178
Linnet, 189, 191, 192
Little Belt, Atlantic, 16
Little Belt, Lake Erie, 105
Liverpool, 59
Liverpool, Robert Banks Jenkinson, 2nd Earl, 22, 256–7

INDEX

Lockyer, Capt. Nicholas, 233
Loire, 142
Long Island, 143, 145, 261
Long Point, on Lake Erie, 105, 156, 157, 172
Louisiana, 226, 227, 231, 239, 240, 244, 245
Louisiana, 242
Louisiana Purchase, 215
Luddites, 22
Lundy's Lane, battle of, 177-9
McArthur, Brig.-Gen. Duncan, 111
McClure, Brig.-Gen. George, 132, 133, 135, 136
McDouall, Lt.-Col. Robert, 170, 171
Macdonell, Lt.-Col. George, 90
MacDonell, Lt.-Col. John, 46
Macdonough, Capt. Thomas, 189, 191, 192
Macedonian, 64-5, 66, 71-2
Machias, Me., 163
McKay, William, 171
Macomb, Brig.-Gen. Alexander, 186-7, 188, 190, 193
Macon's Bill No. 2, 14, 15
McQueen, Peter, 218
Madison, 86
Madison, Dolley, 200
Madison, James: economic coercion, 9, 14; annual message (1811), 17; move for war, 20, 21, 24, 30; as leader, 31; reprieves Hull, 41; orders to Dearborn, 43; and Treasury, 166, 251; and abortive armistice, 173; and Armstrong, 196, 202; attack on Washington, 197, 198, 199, 200, 268; dislike of, 212, 227; and Floridas, 216, 217; and peace negotiations, 252
Maine, 158, 159, 162-4, 254, 258, 259
Majestic, 261
Malcolm, Rear-Adm. Charles, 194
Manners, Capt. William, 150
Maples, Capt. John, 74
Mariner, 77
Marines, British, 75-6, 77-9, 138, 139, 154, 155, 197, 205, 227, 229, 232, 238
Maryland, 47, 75, 195, 196
Marryat, Joseph, 152
Menelaus, 204
Michigan Territory, 3, 34, 169, 172
Michilimackinac, 28, 29, 30, 36-7, 115, 170, 171, 175, 256, 258
Milan Decree, 8, 14

Militia, Canadian: at start of war, 27; disaffection, 33; and Hull's invasion, 35-6, 41; hardships, 42, 47, 101, 119; better than expected, 51; lauded, 267
Militia, U.S.: war preparations, 19-20; New England attitude, 30, 31, 167-8, 187; refuse to enter Canada, 50
Miller, Lt.-Col. James, 39
Milne, Capt. David, 55-6, 144
Minerva, 56
Mississippi River, 69, 215, 237, 244-5, 247, 259
Mississippi Territory, 219, 222, 234, 239, 240
Mobile, 217, 226, 227, 230, 231, 232-3, 234, 235, 260
Mohawk, 140
Monguagon, battle of, 39
Monroe, James, 10, 157, 196, 197, 198, 199, 202, 234, 250, 253, 254
Monroe-Pinkney Treaty, 10
Montreal, 28, 32, 49-50, 89, 117-18, 124
Mooers, Maj.-Gen. Benjamin, 188
Moose Island, 159
Moravian Town, 111, 112, 113
Morgan, Brig.-Gen. David, 245
Morris, Capt. Charles, 163
Morrison, Lt.-Col. Joseph W., 127, 128
Moscow, 251
Muir, Maj. Adam, 39, 110
Mulcaster, Commander William Howe, 127-8
Murray, Lt.-Col. John, 134-5

Nantucket, 160-2
Napier, Lt.-Col. Charles, 59, 79
Napoleon, ix, xi, 6, 8, 10, 14, 25, 137, 165, 251, 268
National Intelligencer (Washington, D.C.), 201
Nautilus, 57, 66
Navigation Laws, British, 2
Navy, British: strength, 52, 56, 67-8, 74-5, 141-2, 144, 145; seamen, 54, 64, 86, 87, 104, 105, 149, 265; blockade, 6-7, 7-8, 24, 57-8, 60, 68-9, 71, 74, 142-3, 144-5, 151-2, 153, 160, 167, 209, 228, 261, 266; gunnery, 64, 72; criticism of, 149-50. *See also* Admiralty
Navy, U.S.: reduced by Jefferson, 9-10; war preparations, 18-19; strength, 52, 53-4; seamen, 55-6, 105, 265-6,

INDEX

gunnery, 62, 64, 74, 151; success (1812), 66
Negro: soldiers, 154, 155, 205, 206, 227, 240, 245; sailors, 263, 264. *See also* Slaves, Negro
Newark, Can., 133, 135, 156, 157
New Brunswick, 25, 28, 58, 59, 162
New England: ties to Great Britain, 2; commercial interests, 13; opposition to war, 17, 20, 30-1, 264; and militia, 30, 31, 167-8, 187; supplies to British, 58, 143, 158; blockade, 143, 144-5; coasts attacked, 157-64; and war finances, 166-7; troops from, 175; fear of disunion, 211, 268; Hartford Convention, 211-12, 214
Newfoundland, 56, 58, 59
New Hampshire, 17
New London, Conn., 80, 158, 159
New Orleans: defences, 30, 237-8, 240, 241, 243; British at New Orleans, 153, 236-44; importance of, 215, 225, 226; plans for attack, 226-8, 229, 236; difficulties of attacking, 237; martial law, 239; battle of New Orleans, 244-8, 260, 265, 267, 268
Newton, Capt. Vincent, 161
New York, city, 44, 56, 57, 69, 148, 209-210, 262
New York, state, 17, 44, 47, 143, 167, 184, 190, 193, 194, 209, 257
Niagara, at Isle aux Noix, 139. *See Linnet*
Niagara, on Lake Erie, 105, 106
Niagara frontier: danger to (1812), 43; American attack (1812), 43-9; American plans for, 89; in 1813, 94-7, 131-6; in 1814, 175-84
Nicholls, Brevet Major Edward, 227, 228, 230, 231, 232, 235
Nimrod, 161
Niemen River, ix, 251
Nomini Ferry, Va., 155
Non-Importation Act, 10, 11
Non-Intercourse Act, 14
Norfolk, Va., 78, 79
Nottingham, Eng., 22
Nottingham, Md., 194, 196, 197, 201
Nova Scotia, 25, 26, 28, 58, 162

Ocracoke Island, 80
Ogdensburg, N.Y., 90
Ohio, ix, 3, 24, 28, 34
Oneida, 86

Orders in Council, xi, 8, 12, 13, 14, 21-3; 42, 57, 250
Orpheus, 148, 226
Oswego, N.Y., 173-4

Pactolus, 159, 160
Pakenham, Maj.-Gen. Sir Edward, 230, 241-2, 243, 246, 247, 265
Pamone, 261
Parker, Capt. Hyde, 163
Parker, Sir Peter, 204
Passamaquoddy Bay, 159, 164, 259
Patuxent River, 155, 194, 195
Pearl River, 239
Peacock, British, 70-1
Peacock, U.S., 148-9, 151, 262, 263
Peake, Capt. William, 70
Pearson, Lt.-Col. Thomas, 177
Pechell, Capt. Samuel John, 72
Pelican, 74
Penguin, 262
Pennsylvania, 47, 175, 196
Pensacola, 217, 218, 226, 231, 234-5, 236
Perceval, Spencer, xi, 22
Percy, Capt. William H., 228, 232, 233
Perry, Capt. Oliver H.: Lake Erie commander, 86-7; builds fleet, 103, 104; escapes from Presque Isle, 105; battle of Lake Erie, 106-7, 110, 114, 137, 138, 156; on land, 203
Peruvian, 162, 163
Philadelphia, 209
Phoebe, 146-7, 148
Picton, 162
Pigot, Capt. Hugh, 226, 227, 230, 234
Pike, Brig.-Gen. Zebulon, 92
Pilkington, Lt.-Col. Andrew, 159
Pinkney, William, 10
Pitt, William, 2, 10
Pittsburgh, 103
Plattsburg, N.Y.: American army at (1812), 50; British raid, 116; Wilkinson brings troops, 131; British advance on, 184, 185 9, 193, 208; defence of, 187-192, 211
Plattsburg Bay, battle of, 189-92, 267
Poictiers, 63
Popham, Capt. Stephen, 174
Porter, Capt. David, 70, 146-7, 203
Porter, Brig.-Gen. Peter B., 17, 48, 175, 176-7
Port Royal, 69
Portsmouth, N.C., 80

Portsmouth, N.H., 150
Portugal, 12
Power, Maj.-Gen. Manley, 187, 188, 192
Prairie du Chien, 170, 171, 172
Preble, 189, 191
Prescott, Ca., 90, 119, 120, 127
President, 16, 53, 56, 63, 71, 72, 142, 261
Presque Isle, Pa., 86-7, 103
Prevost, Lt.-Gen. Sit George: sketch, 25; defence of Canada, 28-9, 42-3, 50, 123, 131, 177; issues army bills, 42, 119; and lake navy, 87, 95, 104, 116, 140; visits Upper Canada, 90-1; attacks Sackett's Harbor, 94, 97; defence of Montreal, 125-6; suggests retaliation, 156, 157; reinforcements for, 168-9, 172, 173; orders for (1814), 169, 253; and Michilimackinac, 170; Plattsburg expedition, 184, 185, 187-93, 208, 209, 257, 258, 268; weakness of, 193, 265
Prince Regent, 139, 173
Prince Regent, 139, 173
Princess Charlotte, 139, 173
Pring, Capt. Daniel, 186
Privateers, 53, 55, 59-60, 67, 141, 152-3, 263
Procter, Maj.-Gen. Henry: at Fort Malden, 36; and Fort Meigs, 82; battle of Frenchtown, 84-5; attacks Fort Meigs, 100, 101, 102; Fort Stephenson, 102; shortage of supplies, 102, 105; provides soldiers for lake navy, 105, 108; retreat from Fort Malden, 108-12, 135, 170; battle of the Thames, 112-14; at head of Lake Ontario, 132
Prophet, the (Shawnee), 16
Prophet's Town, 83
Pungoteague, Va., 154
Put-in-Bay, Lake Erie, 106
Purdy, Col. Robert, 126
Putnam, Maj. Perley, 159

Quebec, 28, 57, 59, 116
Queen Charlotte, 104, 105, 106
Queenston, Can., 45, 46, 177, 178
Queenston Heights, battle of, 45-6, 49

Raisin River, 84
Ramillies, 159
Rattlesnake, 151
Reindeer, 150
Riall, Maj.-Gen. Phineas, 134, 135-6, 176-7, 177-8

Richelieu River, 49
Ridout, Thomas, 120, 121
Rifleman, 162
Rio de Janeiro, 146
Ripley, Brig.-Gen. Eleazar, 175, 176-7, 179, 181, 182, 248
Roberts, Capt. Charles, 36
Robinson, Maj.-Gen. Frederick P., 187, 189, 192, 193
Rodgers, Capt. John, 56-7, 63, 71, 142, 203, 205
Rose, George Henry, 13
Ross, Colonel George, 244
Ross, Maj.-Gen. Robert: arrives Bermuda, 194; attack on Washington, 197, 200, 201, 204; attacks Baltimore, 206, 209; death of, 206, 230, 258; plans for New Orleans, 228, 229, 241
Rule of 1756, 4
Russell, Jonathan, 252, 256
Russia, ix, 251, 251-2, 253, 258

Saco River, 158
Sackett's Harbor: in 1812, 86; in 1813, 89, 90, 91, 117, 133; attacked, 94, 95, 97; in 1814, 140, 169, 173, 174, 177, 180, 184, 185, 186; discussed at Ghent, 254, 256, 257
St Lawrence, 184
St Lawrence River, 28, 29, 49, 89, 90, 117-31 *passim*, 264
St Louis, Mo., 171
St Mary's, Geo., 260
St Petersburg, 251
St Regis, 130
Salamanca, battle of, 242
San Domingo, 59, 72
Sandwich, Can., 35, 110, 111
Sandy Creek, engagement at, 174
Saratoga, 189, 190, 191
Savannah, Geo., 69
Sawyer, Vice-Adm. Sir Herbert, 56, 57-8
Scorpion, 106, 171
Scott, Col. Hercules, 178, 179, 182
Scott, Brig.-Gen. Winfield, 95, 132, 175, 176-7, 178-9, 248
Seahorse, 203
Shannon, 56, 72-3
Sheaffe, Maj.-Gen. Roger, 46, 47, 92-3, 126
Shelburne, 148, 226
Shelburne, Sir William Petty, 2nd Earl, 2

INDEX

Sherbrooke, Lt.-Gen. Sir John, 26, 162-3, 169
Shipping interest, British, 6, 12, 22
Ships, classification, 52 n
Shortland, Capt. Thomas G., 264
Slaves, Negro: as British troops, 78, 154-5, 156, 205, 206, 226, 227; construct defences, 237, 244
Smith, Margaret Bayard, 202
Smith, Maj.-Gen. Samuel, 205
Smyth, Brig.-Gen. Alexander, 44, 45, 46, 47, 48
South America, 12
Sophie, 232, 233
Southampton, 56, 66
Spain, 8, 9, 12, 216-17, 234-5
Stansbury, Brig.-Gen. Tobias, 197, 199
Stewart, Capt. Charles, 142, 261-2
Stonington, Conn., 159-60
Stoney Creek, battle of, 96
Stricker, Brig.-Gen. John, 205, 206
Strong, Gov. Caleb, 211, 214
Superior, 140
Susquehanna River, 75
Sylph, 162, 163
Syren, 151

Talladega, 220
Tallassahatche, 219
Taylor, Major Zachary, 82, 172
Tecumseh, 16, 37, 39, 109, 111, 112, 114, 218, 255
Tenedos, 162, 163, 261
Tennessee, 17, 24, 215, 216, 217, 219, 222, 223, 239, 240, 245
Terror, 159
Thames, battle of the, 112-14, 170, 258
Thornton, Col. William, 200, 239-40, 247
Ticonderoga, 189, 191
Tigress, 171
Times (London), 55, 56, 62, 66, 71
Tippecanoe, battle of, 17, 109
Tompkins, Gov. Daniel, 136
Tonnant, 236
Toronto. *See* York, Can
Trafalgar, battle of, 159
Tripoli, U.S. war with, 9, 60, 64, 86
Tristan da Cunha, 262
Tuckaubatchee, 223
Tucker, Lt.-Col. J., 180

United States, 53, 56, 63-5
Upper Marlborough, Md., 194, 196, 197, 198, 201
Upper Sandusky, Ohio, 102
Urbana, Ohio, 34

Valparaiso, 70, 146
Van Horne, Maj. Thomas, 37, 38
Van Rensselaer, Col. Solomon, 44, 46
Van Rensselaer, Maj.-Gen. Stephen, 44, 45, 47
Vergennes, Vt., 186
Vermont, 184, 187, 190
Victory, 80
Vienna, 252, 257, 258
Villeré, Maj.-Gen. Jacques, 240
Villeré Plantation, 240, 241, 244, 245, 246
Vincent, Maj.-Gen. John, 95, 96, 132, 134
Virginia, 75, 143, 155, 195, 196, 203
Vittoria, battle of, 137
Vixen, 66
Vixen, new schooner, 142

Wales, Capt. Richard W., 148, 149
Warburton, Lt.-Col. Augustus, 111, 112
Wareham, Mass., 158
War Hawks, 16-17, 17-18, 19, 20-1
Warren, Admiral Sir John B.: given unified command, 58; requests reinforcements, 59, 67-8, 104, 142; blockades, 69, 71; criticized, 72, 140-1; raids in Chesapeake region, 77-8, 79, 80; sends seamen to lakes, 88, 138; removed, 141; hands over command, 144; orders re peace (1812), 250
Warrington, Capt. Lewis, 148, 263
Washington, George, 5
Washington, D.C.: burning of, 93, 200-2, 204; attack on, 153, 194-200; impact of capture, 209-10, 229, 257
Wasp, British, 116
Wasp, U.S., 66
Wasp, new U.S. sloop, 148, 150, 151
Waterloo, battle of, 267
Weatherford, William, 218, 222
Wellington, Arthur Wellesley, 1st Duke, 25, 26, 187, 192, 230, 194, 241, 242, 258
West Indies, 4, 53, 58, 62, 67, 78, 141, 142, 154, 239, 245
Whinyates, Capt. Thomas, 62
White, Brig.-Gen. James White, 220
Wicomico River, raided into, 156
Wilkinson, Brig.-Gen. James, 117-18, 123-4, 124-5, 127-30, 131, 185, 217
Willcocks, Joseph, 122

Williams, David R., 17
Winchester, Brig.-Gen. James, 81, 82, 83, 84–5, 99
Winder, Brig.-Gen. William H., 96, 195–196, 197, 198–9, 200, 203
Wolfe, 97, 124, 139

Yeo, Capt. Sir James Lucas, 88, 96, 97, 98, 104, 124, 138, 139, 174, 185, 190, 193
York, Can., 89, 91–4, 97, 104, 122, 175, 182, 183
York Gazette (Can.), 202
Yorkshire, 22